Getting the Books Out

Papers of the Chicago Conference on the Book in 19th-Century America

Edited by Michael Hackenberg

The Center for the Book
Library of Congress
Washington   1987

Library of Congress Cataloging-in-Publication Data

Chicago Conference on the Book in 19th-century America
(1985)
Getting the books out.

Includes bibliographies.
Supt. of Docs. no.: LC 1.2:B64/10
1. Book industries and trade—United States—History—
19th century—Congresses. 2. Booksellers and book-
selling—United States—History—19th century—
Congresses. 3. Publishers and publishing—United
States—History—19th century—Congresses. 4. Books
and reading—United States—History—19th century—
Congresses. I. Hackenberg, Michael R. II. Center
for the Book.
Z473.C48   1985   070.5'0973   87-600241
ISBN 0-8444-0569-8

Book design by William Chenoweth

(∞) The paper used in this publication meets the requirements for permanence established
by the American National Standard for Information Sciences "Permanence of Paper for
Printed Library Materials" (ANSI Z39.48-1984).

For sale by the Superintendent of Documents,
U.S. Government Printing Office, Washington, D.C. 20402

Contents

Contributors   v

Foreword   vii
   John Y. Cole

Introduction   1
   Michael Hackenberg

1. Getting the Books Out: Trade Sales, Parcel Sales, and   4
   Book Fairs in the Nineteenth-Century United States
   Michael Winship

2. From Printer to Publisher: Mathew Carey and the Origins of   26
   Nineteenth-Century Book Publishing
   James N. Green

3. The Subscription Publishing Network in Nineteenth-Century   45
   America
   Michael Hackenberg

4. Dissemination of Popular Books in the Midwest and Far West   76
   during the Nineteenth Century
   Madeleine B. Stern

5. "Spiritual Cakes Upon the Waters": The Church as a   98
   Disseminator of the Printed Word on the Ohio Valley
   Frontier to 1850
   Michael H. Harris

6. Copyright and Books in Nineteenth-Century America   121
    Alice D. Schreyer

7. Printing for the Instant City: San Francisco at Mid-Century   137
    Robert D. Harlan

8. California on Stone, 1880–1906: A Proposed Sequel to   165
    Harry Peters's Pioneering Study
    Bruce L. Johnson

9. Institutional Book Collecting in the Old Northwest,   175
    1876–1900
    Terry Belanger

Contributors

Michael Hackenberg, the editor of this volume, was the director of the Chicago Conference on the Book in 19th-Century America. He is Assistant Professor at the Graduate Library School at the University of Chicago.

Terry Belanger is Associate Professor at the School of Library Service at Columbia University.

James N. Green is Curator of Printed Books at the Library Company of Philadelphia.

Robert D. Harlan is Professor at the School of Library and Information Studies at the University of California, Berkeley.

Michael H. Harris is Professor at the College of Library and Information Science at the University of Kentucky.

Bruce L. Johnson is Library Director at the California Historical Society.

Alice D. Schreyer is Head of Special Collections at the University of Delaware Library.

Madeleine B. Stern is a Partner in Leona Rostenberg and Madeleine Stern Rare Books in New York.

Michael Winship is the Editor of the *Bibliography of American Literature.* He may be contacted at the Houghton Library at Harvard University.

Foreword

The historical role of books in shaping society is a topic of concern to an increasing number of scholars. The Chicago Conference on the Book in 19th-Century America brought together more than 130 scholars, librarians, book dealers, and students to consider how books, publishing, and the book trade influenced the growth of nineteenth-century America. The conference was sponsored by the Graduate Library School of the University of Chicago, the Center for the Book in the Library of Congress, and one of the center's statewide affiliates, the Illinois Center for the Book. The conference was held on October 18 and 19, 1985, at the University of Chicago.

Encouraging the interdisciplinary study of books is one of the principal aims of the Center for the Book in the Library of Congress. Created by an Act of Congress in 1977 to stimulate public interest in books, reading, and the printed word, the center sponsors a varied program of interest to both scholars and the general public. Its projects and publications are supported primarily by private contributions from individuals and corporations.

Michael Hackenberg, Assistant Professor at the Graduate Library School, organized the Chicago conference and edited this volume. Special thanks go to him; to W. Boyd Rayward, then Dean of the Graduate Library School, for his strong support; and to Jim Edgar, Illinois Secretary of State, State Librarian, and Chairman of the Illinois Center for the Book, who opened the meeting. It is a pleasure to present these papers to a wider audience.

JOHN Y. COLE
Director
The Center for the Book

Introduction

Michael Hackenberg

Like the more-than-threefold population increase in the United States between 1800 and 1900 or the over-fourteenfold increase in geographical area during the same era, the development and expansion experienced by the American publishing industry in the nineteenth century was also profound. Whereas only about 50 colonial printing shops had functioned in the entire country around the middle of the eighteenth century, their numbers had increased by 1859 to some 4,000, and there was a total of at least 400 publishers in the nation in that same year. The simple numerical increments of the industry's practitioners, however, are less revealing than are several major changes in the production, marketing, distribution, and use of its products, which took place throughout the nineteenth century. Several of those changes are subjects treated in the following papers from the Chicago Conference on the Book in 19th-Century America, which are presented here in the order of their delivery at the University of Chicago on Friday and Saturday, October 18 and 19, 1985.* Their authors have been undertaking innovative work in nineteenth-century American book history and draw upon much previously unexplored or poorly understood source material for their presentations.

Five of the papers focus upon aspects of book dissemination—that Achilles' heel for nineteenth-century American publishers and booksellers. James Green discusses the methods employed by the great Philadelphia publisher Mathew Carey to stabilize his southern and western book distribution system at the turn of the century. Michael Harris explores an

---

*James Meriwether's conference presentation "The Books of William Gilmore Simms," which treated that Southern writer's difficulties in securing books and getting his own work published both before and during the Civil War, could not, unfortunately, be included among these published papers.

equally fascinating network of proselytizing circuit riders and ministers who combed the Ohio Valley frontier during the first half of the century in order to spread great amounts of tract and Bible literature to settlers. Within the established book trade itself, the internal movement of books, plates, and other printing equipment was facilitated through the mechanism of the trade sale, which is the subject of Michael Winship's paper surveying the activities of a ten-day trade sale organized by the New York firm of Leavitt, Delisser & Company in 1856. Madeleine Stern looks at the midwestern and far western examples of the varied distribution techniques for popular and cheap publications during the century. The eastern origins and subsequent westward spread and operation of the vast subscription publishing network, that great counterbalance for rural areas to the retail book trade of the century, are outlined in my own contribution.

Spreading geographical frontiers not only brought East Coast books into southern and western regions, but also stimulated newer book and literary activity in those newly populated areas. The lure of the West in general and of California in particular brought the book trade to the West Coast in the wake of the establishment of the gold rush settlements. Robert Harlan notes the nearly instantaneous rise of the San Francisco printing industry during the years 1850 through 1869 and its necessarily heavy reliance upon job printing—a factor that is often elusive for the printing historian. The later packaging of the image of California as well as of its agricultural products occupies Bruce Johnson, who points out the importance of California chromolithography during the final quarter of the century.

American authors and institutional libraries were also influenced by the accelerated activity of nineteenth-century American publishing. Indeed, a considerable number of American writers spent much of their time negotiating with their publishers over questions of copyright provisions and infringement claims. Alice Schreyer, analyzing copyright records in the Library of Congress, traces some of those attempts at standardizing author-publisher contracts and at protecting serial publication rights for nineteenth-century literary works.

Institutional book collections, especially during the second half of the century, were spurred on by the rise of the land-grant college system and the public library movement. But in the states of the Old Northwest, Terry Belanger discerns trends in the developing institutional libraries which differed from those of comparable institutions along the eastern seaboard. He probes the motivations behind collection development (and occasional collection weeding) at several libraries of the Old Northwest and suggests that the results of those collection management policies from the final quarter of the century can still be observed today in libraries of the region.

The Chicago Conference on the Book in 19th-Century America was greatly enriched by both the contributors and the approximately 135 participants from across the country, whose ideas and comments generated much fruitful discussion. The editor is grateful to all for their contributions. Special thanks should be extended to the joint sponsors of the conference, which were the Graduate Library School of the University of Chicago, the recently formed Illinois Center for the Book, and the Center for the Book in the Library of Congress. My personal acknowledgment for their sustained and ever-heartening support goes most of all to W. Boyd Rayward, then Dean of the Graduate Library School, and John Y. Cole, Executive Director of the Center for the Book.

1. Getting the Books Out: Trade Sales, Parcel Sales, and Book Fairs in the Nineteenth-Century United States

Michael Winship

We have soothing news in store for the fluttering book trade. The "Trade Sale" is back! It sounds as familiar and cheery as to say Santa Claus is back, Barnum is back, Spring is back. Booksellers will smile all sorts of smiles at the tidings; and the fancy and drygoods stores, the street-corner, sidewalk, and basement bibliopoles, the auction, gift, lottery, butcher, great combination, dollar and fifteen-cents-to-the-dollar concerns will chuckle, chuckle. Also the binders, paper-mills, and notaries. How much per pound, yard, dozen, gross, and "what off" to ministers, lawyers, doctors, school-teachers, students, soldiers, sailors, farmers, cobblers, tinkers, tailors, and other "friends in the trade"? "After the wants of the bidder have been supplied, the lots will be doubled," "quadrupled," and so on, and so on. "Going, going, going!" The committees are dead, the "Ring" is dead, the Book Fair is dead, but the Trade Sale is back! *Le roi est mort;* long live the king![1]

I am afraid that the author of this note, which appeared in *Publishers' Weekly* in January 1877, is guilty of the sin of irony. And yet many of his allusions are not immediately clear. What exactly were trade sales and how could they cause such an outburst?

As I began work on this paper, I quickly found myself confused by a rainbow-like array: trade sales, parcel sales, lot sales, clearance sales, remainder sales, assignee's sales, sheriff's sales, peremptory sales, private sales, and book fairs. Only gradually was I able to discover some sort of order among them. Trade sales are indeed distinct and played an important, but forgotten, role in the nineteenth-century American book trade. I found six features that characterize American trade sales.[2]

First, trade sales were auctions. This means that goods were offered for sale in lots and that the price was determined by bids from the buyers, not by the seller. The minimum price and size for each lot were set in advance, but the actual price was the result of competition amongst the purchasers.

Second, trade sales were restricted to members of the book trade. Just how this restriction was enforced is not entirely clear, but—in the early years, at least—it seems likely that admission to the actual sale was by catalog, which had been issued only to members of the book trade and had to be shown at the door.[3] There is no evidence, however, that admission was limited to a select group of the trade. Instead it seems that any bona fide member of the book trade had the right to participate at the sale.

Third, the stock offered at trade sales included only material which was of interest to the trade. This is not to suggest that the variety was limited. In fact, all sorts of items were offered: new books, either bound or in sheets, remainders, English imports, printing paper, binding cloth and other bindery material and tools, stereotype and electrotype plates with accompanying copyrights, stationery and fancy goods, and many other things that made up the stock-in-trade of nineteenth-century publishers, jobbers, and booksellers.

Fourth, each trade sale contained invoices contributed from many members of the book trade. When a sale was announced, both local and out-of-town firms were invited to participate. There was never a suggestion that the number of consignors would be limited; rather, the success of a trade sale was often gauged by the number of contributors. Many sales even included a number of invoices listed anonymously.

Fifth, trade sales were regulated by a committee made up of members of the book trade. As a result, any participant at a trade sale had recourse to fellow members of the trade for redress in case of a real or supposed wrong or misadventure at the hands of the auction house. Just how effective the committee's control was is by no means clear, but it existed in theory. The membership of the committee tended to remain constant from year to year and must certainly have established close ties with the auction houses that held the trade sales.

Sixth and finally, trade sales were regularly scheduled from year to year. If semiannual, they were held in the spring and fall; if annual, in the summer or fall. But in either case, the date was predictable and fixed in advance, often as beginning on a specified day of a particular week in the month. The sales were also numbered, and a particular sale was advertised, described, and recognized as, say, the thirty-second of a series.

Having listed the distinguishing features of a typical trade sale, I will now attempt to explain how one worked. Books, both new and remaindered, made up by far the greatest part of the stock offered at the sales, and special rules were devised for their disposal. I assume that other material, such as stationery and stereotype plates, were sold by regular bidding. Books, however, were listed in the catalog in lines of multiple copies: the total of each line had to exceed a specified minimum number or retail value. At the sale, each line was offered in smaller lots, often as small as three or five copies, and the price per copy was set by competitive bidding. The buyer who bid the highest would begin the sale by stating the number of lots that he wanted. At this time, other purchasers also had the option of buying lots at this price. If the line was not exhausted, the remaining copies were then put up for auction again with the lot size doubled. Generally, but not always, the greater quantities involved meant that the second price was lower than the first. Eventually the remaining copies would be offered as a single lot, and occasionally this resulted in direct bargaining between the consignor, who was often present and active during the sale, and the purchaser.[4]

This raises a peculiar feature of the trade sales. General practice gave the consignor the option to decide during the sale if he wished to multiply the number of books offered in a line. In some cases, he was also allowed to withdraw the remaining copies of a line from the sale. Clearly if he felt that his books were going at too low a price, it would be to his advantage to withdraw the remaining copies, but if they were going at a high price, he might wish to offer additional copies. Although the original bidder was always guaranteed the right to purchase his lots at the auction price, withdrawal caused a tremendous amount of discussion and dissension in the trade, and, at various times throughout the century, attempts were made to reform the sales so that withdrawing, and often multiplying as well, were forbidden. Under the reform, all books listed in the catalog were to be sold unless withdrawn or added to before the beginning of the sale, which seems to me at least to be by far the fairest and most sensible arrangement.

A close look at one trade sale should give a fuller picture. In March 1856 the new firm Leavitt, Delisser & Company held one of two spring trade sales in New York. This was the first of what would be the firm's many trade sales, and it was the second trade sale held under the direction of the New York Book-Publishers' Association. Trade sales flourished during the 1850s, but New York's two spring sales that year reflect more than good times in the book trade. The Publishers' Association, formed the preceding year, was attempting to establish its right to manage the trade sales. One point at issue was the very one just discussed, the practice of allowing consignors to withdraw or multiply their contributions. It is perhaps also relevant that the three partners in the new auction house—

George A. Leavitt, Richard L. Delisser, and Jonathan K. Allen—had close ties with the book trade. Leavitt & Allen had been publishing books under that imprint since 1852. Leavitt had begun his career as a clerk for the New York publisher C. M. Saxton. Leavitt's cousin, William H. Appleton, was a member of the executive committee of the Publishers' Association, which was directing the trade sale, and the president of the important publishing and jobbing firm of D. Appleton & Co. Delisser had served that firm as confidential clerk for many years.[5]

The sale was announced in an advertisement in the January 12 issue of the *American Publishers' Circular,* the organ of the Publishers' Association. This announcement gives the schedule and terms of the sale. Credit was offered on the basis of the total amount of purchases at the sale: approved endorsed notes, dated the first day of the sale, payable in New York City, and due in four and six months, were allowed for purchases over $1,000; four-month notes for purchases over $100; but cash was required for smaller purchases. Procedures were also outlined to redress cases of imperfections in the stock sold at the sale and cases of delay or default by those owing money to the auction house. The catalog was scheduled to go to press on January 20, and invoices of consignments received by that date were to appear at the beginning of the catalog, whereas invoices received later would be added at the end. Finally, Charles B. Norton offered his services as an agent for those members of the trade unable to attend the sale in person.

On January 22 the *American Publishers' Circular* published a more detailed set of regulations for the upcoming trade sale, signed by the executive committee of the Publishers' Association. The first regulation—set entirely in upper case letters to indicate its importance—was the requirement that all contributors agree not to participate in any trade sale in New York not authorized by the association. Next, the arrangement of the invoices in the catalog was specified: the order was to be determined by chance. Third, all withdrawals during the sale were forbidden and multiplication only allowed with certain limits. The fourth and fifth rules set the minimum amounts to be offered in each line in the catalog and to be sold in one lot. The sixth rule regulated the delivery of books to the auctioneer. The seventh rule established the process of bidding, and the eighth limited participation to booksellers, presumably a general term meant to include publishers, wholesalers, and jobbers as well as the retail trade. Rules nine through fourteen set forth the responsibilities of the auctioneers and established the amounts they might charge both consignors and purchasers for their services. In rule fifteen the auction house agreed to limit itself to trade sales sanctioned by the Publishers' Association, and the final rule affirmed the right of the executive committee of the association to regulate all aspects of the sale.

During February, both Leavitt's advertisement and the Publishers'

Association's regulations were published repeatedly in the *American Publishers' Circular*. The catalog must also have been sent to the printers sometime that month and was available for distribution early in March, for a copy was received at Harvard University Library on March 7. It is a thick octavo of over 384 pages, bound in paper wrappers. The sale terms and regulations are again printed, on the inner front wrapper, followed by a brief introductory statement setting forth the advantages of these regulations for both contributors and purchasers. Next comes the index, dividing the invoices into three sections: books, plates, and stationery. The bulk of the catalog proper, a total of 325 pages, contains the invoices of books from 112 publishers. The 24 invoices of stationery cover 48 pages, a third of which list sheet music consigned by Horace Waters. The three invoices of stereotype plates fill only 9 pages. A second catalog, containing corrections and additions, would certainly have been prepared for distribution on the first day of the sale, but I have not located a copy.

Crates of books from the consignors must have arrived throughout March at Leavitt's rooms at 377 and 379 Broadway. By the end of the third week of March a large company was assembled, including publishers and other contributors, as well as over three hundred buyers, many of whom came from a considerable distance. Of course, many of the out-of-towners must have come planning also to attend the rival trade sale held by Bangs & Co. beginning March 18.

A contemporary account describes Leavitt's rooms as follows:

> Their packing and delivery rooms are situated in the basement and sub-cellar, in length 150 feet by 50, with a large number of vaults for storing paper and stereotypes. Their sales room on the second floor, a large and most perfectly lighted room, 75 feet by 50, is unequalled for convenience and comfort, either in this country or Europe. Being particularly adapted for the purposes of trade sales, every arrangement has been made for the facilitating of all the various details connected with so arduous an undertaking. Large and spacious room is afforded behind the auctioneer's desk for the arrangement of samples and classifying of goods. In connection with their sales room, a reception and smoking room, 22 feet by 25, has been tastefully fitted up for the comfort of buyers. Immediately adjoining the sales room is the counting room, arranged for the purpose of making out all the accounts and sales. During the trade sale, this department is in the charge of ten writers who are occupied day and night. On the third floor of this building is the dining room, arranged with seats for three hundred persons, and with every convenience for the comfort of the inner man. The cooking is carried on by gas in a kitchen adjoining, well supplied with stores, ranges, pantry, etc. The business

of this immense establishment occupies the services of some fifty hands, the different departments being under the charge of experienced parties, who attend solely to their special duties. Mr. Delisser's well-known experience as an accountant has given additional facilities to this department, by which all bills can be delivered within ten minutes after the purchases are made.[6]

The sale began Thursday morning, March 20, with the sale of books and ended ten days later, Saturday, March 29, with the sale of stereotype plates. The heavy schedule required to work through the many lines in the 384-page catalog meant that sales began each morning at eight o'clock and often lasted as late into the night as ten o'clock. Throughout the course of the sale, the auction house provided meals for the assembled company in their attached rooms, but a special event was held at the beginning of the sale:

On the first day of the sale, quite a pleasant re-union of buyers, contributors, and members of the press took place, by invitation of the auctioneers, in the spacious dining-hall attached to their establishment. The table was bountifully covered with those things which rejoice the inner man, such as meats, poultry, game, salads, pastry, and fluids to match. After proper attention had been bestowed upon these, the health of the hosts, Messrs. Leavitt, Delisser & Co., was proposed.[7]

This report continues by giving a full account of the speeches and toasts that followed.

I have already described how bidding proceeded, but the following account gives a nice sense of the atmosphere during the sale:

No one can attend these book-sales without being highly impressed with the good understanding that seems to exist among all parties concerned. It is very common for publishers to act as volunteer auctioneers of their own books, and intersperse their labors with speeches that are fine specimens of wit and good feeling; altogether the sales are colloquial and sociable, and it is astonishing that so much business can be done with so little seeming restraint and apparent want of discipline; the close observer, however, will notice that there presides over all, the quick eye and attentive ear of the clerks, and at nightfall, when the labors of the day are closed, everything is correctly down in black and white.[8]

The clerks must have been busy indeed! Before the sale they had to receive and unpack the crates of books shipped by the consignors and check the contents against the invoices. During the sale they had to record carefully the price per lot and the number sold to each buyer. Afterwards they had to sort and pack the purchases. An 1859 account estimated that the ordinary quantities bought in single bids at trade sales varied in value from five to fifty dollars, and that a single buyer's purchases for the whole sale hardly averaged more than $1,500, made up on average of at least 100 lots. If these averages hold true for the March 1856 sale, imagine how long it must have taken for Leavitt to work through the 384-page catalog. The gross amount of this sale was predicted to fall not far short of $300,000, and this for only one of two sales held simultaneously. The total for fall sales was generally claimed to be much higher than that for the spring sales, perhaps twice as high.[9]

The records of Ticknor & Fields of Boston, now on deposit in the Houghton Library at Harvard University, allow a closer analysis of that firm's participation in this sale. I can find no record of the first invoice the firm sent to the auctioneers, but probably it accompanied a crate including one sample copy of each book on the list. This was probably sent in January or early in February, since the Ticknor & Fields list is printed near the beginning of the catalog. Their records do, however, give a full list of the books shipped subsequently to the auctioneers. The first five crates were sent in the middle of March before the beginning of the sale, but twelve further crates were shipped between March 26 and April 15. These crates completed the quantities given in the catalog and also included additional copies sold at the auction according to the rules for multiplying lots. A crate shipped on April 21 contained odd quantities needed to make up for shortfalls and errors in the previous crates, as did the final shipment of April 24.[10]

If we analyze Ticknor & Fields's consignment, we find that it contains a good representation of their titles then in print. There is little indication that any of the titles were being sold as remainders. In fact, eight titles are offered under the category "if ready," but none of these was shipped. Comparison of the trade sale list with the firm's catalog printed in March 1856 shows that all but one of the trade sale titles are also listed there.[11] One line in the trade sale catalog, that for Longfellow's *Evangeline,* was never filled, probably because the book had gone out of print. However, one line seems to have been added to the trade sale, since 26 copies of De Quincey's *Confessions of an English Opium-Eater* were shipped on March 28. Other lines were multiplied, most notably Longfellow's *Song of Hiawatha,* of which only 140 copies were listed, but about 1,900 copies were shipped.[12] These brought 67, 62, or 60 cents per copy depending on the size of the lot: the retail price was $1.00. Unfortunately, we have no record of the purchasers' names, except for 200 copies of *Hiawatha,* which were delivered directly to Whittemore, Niles & Hall in Boston, and another 600 copies, shipped directly to E. P. Rudd of New York. The total retail value of the books shipped was $6,862.32, which brought in a total of $4,288.68 or an average of 62.5 percent of the retail price, very close to standard trade discount. From that total, the auctioneers subtracted 9.5 percent, or $407, for their commission, another $8 for cataloging, and $23.13 for freight. An advance of $100 was also subtracted. The remaining $3,750.55 was paid in cash on April 22. These charges reduced the net trade sale total to 56.1 percent of retail.[13]

A brief report in the *American Publishers' Circular* allows us to analyze the auction of plates at this sale.[14] Curiously, none of the plates listed in the catalog are offered with copyright. Although most of the texts are by foreign authors and thus not eligible for protection, it is a little surprising that copyright is not mentioned for those by American authors. The first invoice from Smith & Jones of New York was a set of thirteen *English Miniature Classics,* almost certainly used plates imported from England, which brought $30 each, or just under 10 percent of cost. They were later used by Derby & Jackson of New York and show considerable wear. The long list of plates offered by James B. Smith & Co. of Philadelphia is quite various. Since the cost of manufacture is not generally given, I divided the price realized at the sale by the number of pages in order to form a rough estimate of the comparative value of the plates. The majority of sets brought between 20 and 50 cents per page, though a few did considerably better. Others fell below 10 cents per page and must have been bought mainly for their value as metal. The price of five of the sets offered by D. Appleton & Co. is known and varied from about 20 to 50 percent of cost, roughly reflecting the length of time since the date of original publication (table 1).

The sale of stationery may have preceded the sale of books, but more likely it followed the sale of plates. The catalog clearly states that the plates were to be sold directly after the books and that no two separate portions of the sale would be carried on at the same time. No account of the sale of stationery survives. One third of the section of the trade sale catalog devoted to stationery was made up of sheet music, and the remainder is devoted to paper and envelopes, as well as pens, ink, cards, fancy goods, blank books, and a single line of 12 pieces of binder's cloth.

Let me now summarize the major features of the trade sales. Most importantly, they served as a means of distribution. Although all articles of interest to the book trade were offered at these sales—including stationery, binding material, and stereotype and electrotype plates with their accompanying copyrights—it is evident that their main function was the transfer of books from publishers to jobbers and booksellers. The contribution from Ticknor and Fields further suggests that the bulk of books offered at the sales was from the current lists of publishers. All in

Table 1
Stereotype Plates Sold by
D. Appleton & Co. at the March 1856 Trade Sale at New York

Title and Size	Publi- cation Date	Pro- duction Cost	1856 Sale Price	Price as a % of Cost	Price per Page
Life of Luther, by Jules Michelet, 12mo., 314pp.	1846	$234	$65	27.8	21¢
History of the Roman Republic, by Jules Michelet, 12mo., 404pp.	1847	360	70	19.4	17
Grantley Manor, by Lady Georgiana C. Fullerton, 12mo. 329pp.	1848	237	80	33.8	24
Ellen Middleton, by Lady Georgiana C. Fullerton, 12mo. 328pp.	1849	245	60	24.5	18
Lady Bird, by Lady Georgiana C. Fullerton, 12mo. 328pp.	1853	262	130	49.6	40

all, the catalog for Leavitt's spring sale in 1856 seems very much to serve the function of our modern *Books in Print,* and the prices realized on different lines must have helped publishers gauge current demand for their books. These sales also provided a means of disposing of remainders and dead stock—a practice that became more typical as the century proceeded, according to frequent editorials published in book trade journals.

A second important function of trade sales was financial: they provided an excellent means for transforming stock, whether new or dead, into cash. Harper and Brothers is reported to have disposed of $75,000 of stock at a single sale probably sometime in the early 1850s. The case of Ticknor & Fields is probably more typical: their sales in 1856 were larger than ordinary, due to the popularity of Longfellow's *Hiawatha,* but their average net sales from 1853 through 1859 were $2,896.96 at the New York spring sales and $2,735.67 at the fall sales.[15] The important financial role played by the auction houses must also be considered. They were responsible not only for the physical arrangements of the sales, but also for handling credit. They rendered accounts to the consignors, usually within a month of the close of the trade sale, and settled them either in cash or by short-term notes. In some cases, advances were made to the consignors upon receipt of their invoices, well before books had been shipped or the sale had taken place.[16] Purchasers at the sales whose total exceeded a small minimum were granted credit of four or six months by the auction house. The auctioneers must have served as bankers to the trade, establishing and granting credit and handling notes and bills, for which services they took a commission.

A third function of the trade sales was to provide a forum for communication within the trade. The regular nature of the sales and their importance must have attracted a large gathering of the trade, which provided a perfect opportunity for different parties to get together to conduct business and to socialize. To take advantage of this, special bankruptcy and closing-out sales, as well as special announcement issues of the trade journals, were scheduled to coincide with the trade sales. The auction houses also hosted special celebratory dinners for the trade as part of the sales and provided regular meals during the course of the sale. The trade sales must also have played an important role in the beginnings of book trade organization in the nineteenth century. In their own way, the trade committees that were formed to oversee the management of the trade sales were themselves rudimentary trade organizations. As we have seen, one of the major concerns of the New York Book-Publishers' Association was the regulation of the trade sales. It is not surprising that this trade association and later ones often held meetings in the halls of the auction houses.

Before turning to a brief overview of the history of American trade sales, two closely related types of events must be mentioned: parcel sales and book fairs. Parcel sales were auctions of exactly the same material that was sold at the trade sales, and parcel sale catalogs look very much like trade sale catalogs. Parcel sales included new books and remainders, imports, stationery, binding material, and stereotype and electrotype plates. Parcel sales were held regularly, once or twice a year, usually about a month after the trade sales. Two features, however, distinguish them from trade sales: they were not restricted to members of the trade, and they were organized and regulated by the auction houses themselves, and not by a committee of members of the trade. I suspect that at parcel sales the lots were smaller and contained a greater proportion of remainders and English imports, but only further analysis of the catalogs will confirm this impression.[17]

Book fairs, modeled on those that had been regularly held at Frankfurt and Leipzig since the late Middle Ages, were gatherings of the book trade where a participant's publications were displayed and offered to the trade at a standard discount. Although never an important or regular phenomenon in nineteenth-century America, fairs represented an alternative to trade sales that was proposed and attempted several times.[18]

In fact, the earliest attempt to establish a formal system for distribution of stock within the book trade was a series of book fairs held during the first decade of the nineteenth century. On December 19, 1801, Mathew

Carey published a broadside addressed to printers and booksellers throughout the United States. In this fascinating document, Carey called for the establishment of a literary fair modelled on those of Frankfurt and Leipzig in order to facilitate the exchange of stock. Carey suggested that the decentralized nature of the book trade in America—quite different from that in Britain, where London predominated—made the book fair necessary. Summarizing the beneficial results to be expected of such an event, Carey claimed that printers' "past industry will be requited, future exertions stimulated, and their means of supporting their families and of benefiting the community be vastly increased."[19]

As a result of this call, the first literary fair was held in New York City beginning June 1, 1802. At this fair, a trade organization, the American Company of Booksellers, was formed. Hugh Gaine, the oldest printer and bookseller in the United States, was named president, and Mathew Carey secretary. On June 7 resolutions were passed recommending the establishment of regular fairs, cooperation among American printers and booksellers, and the formation of local book trade associations in the principal cities in the United States. Fairs followed in Philadelphia in December 1802, in New York again in June 1803 and June 1804, and in Newark, New Jersey, in June 1805. Carey became president of the association at the June 1804 fair. Many features of these literary fairs are familiar from the discussion of trade sales. They were regular, limited to the trade, served for the exchange and distribution of stock, fostered the formation of trade organizations, and included a dinner where the trade could socialize. One added feature was the encouragement of the American book trade by the establishment of medals to reward excellence in American printing and binding, and the manufacture of American paper and ink.[20]

In his *Autobiography,* published in 1836, Carey explains the failure of these fairs to survive:

> The plan appeared to work well in the commencement. It produced a good understanding and harmony among the booksellers, and valuable interchanges of books. This state of things continued for a year or two. But at length it produced an evil that had not been foreseen, and that outweighed all its advantages. Country booksellers published large editions of popular books with half-worn types and on inferior paper, with which, by means of exchanges, they deluged the country—and in many cases the city booksellers had on their hands good editions of the books thus republished. This unexpected result rendered the city booksellers dissatisfied, and they by degrees withdrew. The fair, however "dragged its slow length along" for four or five years, and then sank into oblivion.[21]

Further reasons for the demise of the literary fairs can be surmised. The Napoleonic wars in Europe and the subsequent American embargo and war with Britain caused a severe depression which was certainly felt by the American book trade and may have dampened enthusiasm for these fairs. Also I suspect that the lack of an English model for book fairs may be significant. During the first fifty years of the American republic, our book trade changed from being a minor provincial part of the English trade to an important and independent business in its own right. However, the ties to the London trade remained strong throughout the century, and almost every feature of the American book trade can be traced back to some English model. The book fair, based on a German system, must have been unfamiliar to many American printers and booksellers and perhaps suffered from the prejudice of ignorance.

Trade sales, on the other hand, which dominated the American book trade during the nineteenth century, had clear English precedents that dated back into the seventeenth century. Trade sales seem to have become an important feature of the London trade early in the eighteenth century: the earliest printed English trade sale catalog that survives dates from 1718. These early trade sales differed from the American ones that we are examining in many ways. Generally restricted to the property of a single bookseller, they were held when the proprietor died or was leaving the trade and were chiefly concerned with passing along his "shares"—copyrights or fractions of copyrights—in texts that were proven steady sellers. The distribution of books does not seem to have been an important feature at these sales and was generally restricted to the remaining stock of sheets of those titles whose shares were being sold. By the nineteenth century the nature of the English trade sales had changed. They had become dinners hosted by an important member of the London trade at which his new publications, and occasionally remainders, were offered to the invited members of the trade at a one-time-only prepublication price. They seem in fact to have become subscription sales, and there is no evidence that any sort of auction was held. They were also an important social event for the London book trade, and many accounts emphasize the variety and quality of the food and wine served by the host.[22]

The connections between these English sales and the American practice already described is not immediately evident, but certain common features can be found. These are especially clear in William Gowans's account of the earliest American trade sale of which any record survives, held in New York by Robert M'Mennomy, probably in 1812. Gowans writes:

> Robert Mc.Menomy[!], for a long time the principle auctioneer in the city of New York, a gentleman of remarkable urbanity of manners,

general intelligence and strict honorable business habits, informed
the writer that about the year 1812 . . . he made a sale of books to
the trade. The sale took place in the large hall of the Tontine coffee
house, situated on the N.E. cor[ner] of Wall and Pearl. On this occasion
all the buyers were specially invited by the auctioneer by means of
a circular to that effect. This invitation as I understood him, indicated
that the notes of the invited parties would be taken for purchases,
made at the sale, without indorcers, of course non[e] but the invited
attended. The modus operandi of conducting the sale was as follows.
It was quite aristocratic, much more so than at any similar sale
subsequent. The buyers and auctioneer assembled in the great hall
and ranged themselves round a large table covered with a fancy
cloth, the auctioneer being placed at the head upon an elevated
armed chair. The samples were brought into the room as required
by a colored gentleman; (perhaps a slave dressed in white) upon a
waiter or server, and when sold taken off by the same. The sale took
up about two thirds of the day and the remainder in making out
each buyers bill, when they respectfully gave their notes as per
previous agreement payable in three, six and nine months to the
auctioneer.

After the business was all completed the whole company were
invited into the dining room, where was ready prepared for them a
most inviting repast, named a dinner, which it was believed that all
present did ample justice. The worthy auctioneer told me that the
sale amounted to between thirty and forty thousand dollars, and that
he never realized more than forty per cent of these notes taken for
the proceeds of that sale.[23]

If this is true, it is small wonder that the experiment was not
immediately repeated. Most nineteenth-century chroniclers agree that the
first regular trade sale was that held in Philadelphia on August 20, 1824,
organized by Henry C. Carey. Carey's firm, Carey & Lea, was the sole
contributor to the sale, and stock was offered in sheets at a special, but
set, trade sale price. The firm's records suggest that Moses Thomas, the
auctioneer, served only as crier, and that the purchasers, limited to the
trade, settled directly with Carey & Lea. Again the similarities with English
practice are obvious. The success of this sale led to the establishment of
similar sales in New York in June 1825 and in Boston in August 1827.[24]

By the 1820s auction sales had become a well-established means of
distribution of all sorts of American products, including books. The
unregulated sale of books at auction was felt to hurt the trade, as we learn
from this letter of February 6, 1820, from John Babcock, New Haven
bookseller and publisher, to Mathew Carey:

For several years past I have stood trembling near the brink of ruin, not for the want of property, but for the want of a market.—Our market for books has been totally destroyed by *Auction Sales*.— Yesterday I attended the sales but for a few minutes, having no money to spend—and saw your Olive Branch knocked off at 40 cts.—This is a pretty fair specimen of the prices at public sales here for several years past.[25]

Henry C. Carey made a similar complaint in a letter of June 5, 1823, to the London bookseller John Miller,[26] and his experiment must have been intended to remedy this situation. Although the history of American trade sales during their first years remains obscure, it seems clear that auctions very quickly became a feature of trade sales. By the 1830s a struggle was going on between the book trade and auction houses to determine who would control and regulate the trade sales. By the end of that decade compromise had been reached, and the trade sales had settled down in the form described earlier with the auctioneers under the supervision of a committee made up of members of the book trade.[27]

During the following two decades trade sales were an important and regular feature of the American book trade. March and September sales were held annually in Philadelphia and New York. In Boston a single sale was held each summer, either in June or August, though none was held from 1853 through 1858. In October 1838 Cincinnati, which had become an important center for trade throughout the west and south, became the fourth and final American city to hold trade sales.[28] Spring and fall sales were held there until the Civil War. Spring and fall parcel sales were held regularly in New York beginning in the 1840s but seem to have been held only occasionally elsewhere. The practice of allowing withdrawals of stock was introduced at the trade sales in the 1840s and during the 1850s caused a split within the trade, as has been illustrated by the spring 1856 sales discussed earlier. With this single exception, trade sales seem to have been accepted by the trade during this period as a proper and normal system of book distribution, only rarely subject to question or criticism.

The disastrous effect of the Civil War on established systems of book distribution, especially in the south and west, is reflected in the trade sales. Philadelphia, which had always had close ties with the south, continued to hold semiannual sales through the war years, but not much beyond. The last Philadelphia trade sale of which I find any record was the 66th, held in March 1865. Similarly, in Boston trade sales barely survived the war. The Boston sales were revived with much ballyhoo in 1859 and were held irregularly until the final one held in March 1865. However, regular late fall parcel sales had also been instituted in Boston with the revival of the trade sales, and these continued until the late 1870s. In Cincinnati, closer to the war, the situation was different. No trade sales were held after April 1861 until the fall of 1865, when a regular October trade sale was instituted. These were held annually, with the exception of 1870, until 1879, when the sales were opened to the public and thus became parcel sales. The Cincinnati parcel sales continued through the 1880s.

Only in New York did regular semiannual trade and parcel sales continue with the same importance as in the prewar years. The predominance of these sales certainly reflects the predominance that New York had gained as the center of the American book trade. However, the nature of the New York trade sales during these years had changed. More of the lots that were offered were made up of remainders and dead stock. Trade sales were used less to introduce a publisher's new list, and new publications were often only offered when a publisher needed to raise ready capital to pay off debts and notes. The discounts on the retail price realized at the sales became larger, and jobbers and wholesalers were able to swamp the book market with cheap books at "trade sale" prices. These features did not reflect an absolute change in the nature of the trade sales, but the trend was clear.

The problems of price-cutting and underselling in the book trade, which came to be blamed on the New York trade sales, led to a second serious attempt to establish regular book fairs in the United States.[29] The American Book Trade Convention held at Put-in-Bay, Ohio, in July 1874 passed a resolution calling for the replacement of trade sales by a semiannual book fair. According to a notice in *Publishers' Weekly:*

> The details of this scheme were unofficially explained to contemplate a large salesroom, in which each publisher should have a desk, where, for the specified time, he should offer by samples at special rates, but that only principals should be allowed to buy and sell; that a general gathering of the trade should be assured. It is generally agreed that it would be wiser to ship goods directly, but to give Messrs. Leavitt charge of the fair, and use them as a clearing house to settle bills, permitting also auction sales of remainders, stereotype plates and other acknowledged dead stock for a day or two at close of the fair.[30]

It is interesting to note that Leavitt & Co., whose first trade sale in March 1856 we have already discussed and who had been the sole firm to hold trade sales in New York since 1858, was named to oversee the fair. The book fair committee named at this convention was chaired by Leavitt's cousin, William H. Appleton, who for many years had served as chair of the trade committee formed to supervise the New York trade sales. The report of this committee is printed in *Publishers' Weekly* of February 6, 1875, and sets forth the rules and regulations under which the first "Booksellers' Exchange and Clearing House" would be held. These were very much along the lines just explained, and Leavitt was responsible for providing rooms and credit arrangements for the fair. No arrangement was made for an auction sale in conjunction with the fair, and Leavitt and the other participants were to pledge that they would not take part in trade sales in the future. The relevance of the German book fairs as a model is made explicit in a detailed account of "The German Book Exchange System" published in *Publishers' Weekly* on April 3, 1875.

There was insufficient time to organize the first fair for the spring of 1875, so Leavitt advertised and held his so-called "last" trade sale beginning April 5, 1875. The first fair was scheduled for July. *Publishers' Weekly* issued a special "Book Fair Supplement" on July 3. In their issue of July 31 they gave the following account of the fair:

> The first Book Fair of the American book trade opened at Clinton Hall, New-York, Monday, 19th July, at nine, and closed at noon of Saturday, 24th July. There were represented at it 97 publishing houses, of whom 58 were of New-York, 17 of Boston, and 15 of Philadelphia, and 52 manufacturing stationers, art publishers, or paper makers. There are recorded 94 buyers, from 17 different States, who were present in person; this list may be incomplete, and there were some present who did not buy. Our figures, which are nearly complete and approximately correct, record 32,694 samples as exhibited, of which 22,598 were from New-York, 3982 from Boston, and 5886 from Philadelphia houses. Some houses exhibited their full stock, with duplicates in extra bindings; others only those books to which they wished to call especial attention. The former was the general rule, and Harper & Bros. led the list with 4400 volumes. The sales for the week can not yet be given with any accuracy, but they are estimated at something above a quarter of a million dollars—more than was ever sold at a trade sale. These sales were made chiefly by the large houses, and four leading firms sold nearly $150,000 of this total, or about half. These were Harpers, Appleton, Osgood, and either one of two or three other firms. Those houses which did not make large sales were nevertheless greatly pleased with the opportunity of showing their stock and making new personal acquaintances through the trade, and hope for definite results from the Fair in the ensuing fall trade.[31]

Not surprisingly, a trade dinner was held in conjunction with the fair. At seven on the Friday evening preceding the closing of the fair, some two hundred members of the American Book Trade Association gathered at the dining hall of the St. James Hotel to enjoy an excellent dinner, sociability, and a round of speeches and toasts.

All in all, the first fair seems to have been a reasonable success. Leavitt held a supplementary book fair beginning October 21, 1875, but apparently it followed too closely on the first fair to attract much business. Additional fairs were held in March and September of 1876, but at these Leavitt also held auction sales of remainders and plates. These auctions attracted much more attention than the fairs, in fact, since James R. Osgood of Boston, successor to Ticknor & Fields, was in financial trouble. In an attempt to keep his firm solvent, he was forced to sacrifice much of his stock, as well as the plates and copyrights of one of the most important backlists of literary books in America. But these sales also suggested that the fairs were not fulfilling the needs of the trade, and regular trade sales resumed in the spring of 1877. Leavitt's announcement of this resumption provoked the editorial outburst from *Publishers' Weekly* quoted at the beginning of this article. But not all reaction was so negative, as we learn from this letter of January 16, 1877, written by J. Blair Scribner to his London agent Charles Welford:

> The Trade Sale is going to be revived this spring and much to our satisfaction, certainly, for the Book Fair was surely a great humbug at least as far as selling was concerned and that is the all essential thing. We had expected to welcome the old Trade Sale next Fall but not before. It seems however that Osgood started the ball rolling by contributing for the opening sale this spring a $50,000 (at retail prices) invoice of his own books and at once Leavitt issued his circular and it is now all arranged.[32]

The total sales at the September 1877 trade sale were over $240,000,[33] which probably equaled the sales at the first and largest book fair. This is roughly the same total realized at Leavitt's spring 1856 trade sale discussed earlier.

The trade sales were back, but their days were numbered. George A. Leavitt, who had been responsible for the New York sales for almost thirty years, died in December 1885. His firm continued under the same name until May 1892, and held the final trade sale the preceding September. Trade sales were not revived, at least not under that name. In February 1895, however, Bangs & Co. held the first of a regular series of annual clearance and remainder sales, which, as an editorial in *Publishers' Weekly* pointed out, were little more than trade sales under a different name.[34] Bangs was even more venerable than Leavitt: they had held their first trade sale in March 1839 and, since 1858, had held regular parcel sales. The latter-day trade sales were but shadows of their former selves, and the final one was held in February 1903. Bangs & Co. was sold to John

Anderson of the Anderson Auction Company on April Fool's Day of the same year.

A number of factors combined to bring about the decline and end of the trade sales. They had become predominantly a means of disposing of remainders and dead stock and were seen by the trade as a principal cause of the evils of price-cutting and underselling. National trade organizations had been formed, which advocated standard pricing and discounts. Improved communication had reduced the need for the periodic meetings of the trade which had been such an important feature of the trade sales. After the Civil War, commercial travellers became common, and publishers generally sent salesmen to call on their retailers. *Publishers' Weekly* had become the organ of the trade and regularly announced and listed new publications. The *American Catalog* and the *Uniform Trade List Annual* also replaced trade sale catalogs as sources of information on current publications. And yet trade sales had been an important feature of the American book trade for most of the nineteenth century. I am convinced that they served an important role in the distribution of books across the continent, in establishing the paths of credit, and in fostering better communication and cooperation within the trade.

Trade sales did not survive long in the twentieth century. Or did they? *Publishers' Weekly* prints the following tantalizing note in the issue of November 8, 1902:

> Miss McDevitt has opened rooms at 113 Nassau Street, New York, where she will conduct the business on the lines established by her father, which consists in selling at auction "returns," "remainders" and "plugs" in general for which publishers and booksellers can find no other outlet.[35]

I have found no further mention of the enterprising Miss McDevitt, but clearly the need for a means of disposing of such stock remained. Neither do I know how remainders are handled today. How exactly do Publisher's Clearing House and Barnes & Noble acquire the books that fill the catalogs that litter our mails? Could it be by auction? I do know that copyright, in the guise of subsidiary film and paperback rights, is still sold by auction. In the fall of 1977 Sotheby Parke Bernet & Co., of London, announced a plan to hold a series of three or four trade sales of publishers' remainders during the coming season: the first and only sale was held on October 20, 1977. Perhaps there will be more. As J. Blair Scribner stated, selling is, after all, "the all essential thing."[36]

Notes

1. *Publishers' Weekly,* vol. 11, 20 Jan. 1877, 60.

2. Much of this paper based on close scrutiny of trade sale catalogs themselves and of nineteenth-century American book trade periodicals. The best guide to the former is George L. McKay, *American Book Auction Catalogues, 1723–1934, a Union List* (New York: New York Public Library, 1937), and to the latter Adolph Growoll, *Book Trade Bibliography in the United States in the Nineteenth Century* (New York: Dibdin Club, 1898). I am compiling a list of American trade sales and would welcome information on surviving accounts and catalogs.

3. Two of the very earliest catalogs that I have examined—one, at the New York Historical Society, is for a New York sale in December 1825, and the other, at the American Antiquarian Society, is for a Boston sale in June 1832—have an admission ticket printed in them. Other early trade sale catalogs generally have the name of a book trade firm written on the front cover, and I suppose that they were issued thus by the auction house. This practice seems to have become less common by the 1850s, and participation may have been regulated by some other means.

4. I believe that this account is in general correct, though actual practice may have varied slightly from time to time. Frequently some lines in trade sale catalogs do not meet the minimum size or value established by the regulations for the sale. It is also possible that at some sales only the highest bidder could purchase at the established price; other purchasers would have to compete for the remaining copies, which were put up to auction again after the wants of the original bidder were filled.

5. See the records of Dun & Company in the Baker Library, Harvard University Graduate School of Business Administration, passim.

6. *American Publishers' Circular,* vol. 2, 29 Mar. 1856, 190.

7. Ibid., 189.

8. "New York Book Trade Sales," *Frank Leslie's Illustrated Newspaper,* vol. 1, 5 Apr. 1856, 264. This account includes two large wood engravings depicting the trade sales in progress at Leavitt, Delisser & Co. and Bangs & Co.

9. "The Booksellers' Trade Sale," *New York Tribune,* copied in *American Publishers' Circular,* vol. 5, 16 Apr. 1859, 186; *American Publishers' Circular,* vol. 2, 29 Mar. 1856, 190. For a full account of the clerks' activities, see an article from the *Boston Traveller,* reprinted in *American Publishers' Circular,* vol. 5, 9 July 1859, 329–30.

10. Records of Ticknor & Fields, Letter-books, domestic: fMS Am 1185 (5), 40–41, 49–50, 52, 74–75, 81, 97, 107, Houghton Library, Harvard University.

11. Ticknor & Fields issued two 12-page catalogs dated March 1856, which vary slightly in arrangement and detail but list the same titles. They do not list George Combe's *The Constitution of Man,* of which 57 copies were sent to the New York trade sale. I thank John William Pye for providing me with photocopies of both catalogs from his collection.

12. *American Publishers' Circular,* vol. 2, 29 Mar. 1856, 190. According to this account, 2,400 copies of *Hiawatha* were sold, though the records of Ticknor & Fields only account for 1,911 copies. I cannot account for this discrepancy.

13. These figures are reckoned on the basis of the invoices of Ticknor & Fields (see note 10) and from their Journal: fMS Am 1185.11 (2), 529, Houghton Library. They do not take account of the extra copies listed in the invoices, which were clearly meant to fill shortfalls in previous shipments, nor the 489 additional copies of *Hiawatha* called for by *American Publishers' Circular.* If the latter are reckoned into the account, the percentages become 58.3 percent of the gross and 52.4 percent of the net realized at the sale. If Ticknor & Fields had taken their payment by note due in four months from the final day of the sale, the commission of the auction house would have been reduced to 7.5 percent or $322, making the net realized at the sale 57.3 percent (or 53.6 percent if the extra copies of *Hiawatha* are reckoned in).

14. *American Publishers' Circular,* vol. 2, 5 Apr. 1856, 205–6.

15. "New York Book Trade Sales," *Frank Leslie's Illustrated Newspaper,* vol. 1, 5 Apr. 1856, 263. The averages are based on figures posted in Ticknor & Fields, Ledgers C & D: fMS Am 1185.14 (3), 351, 395, 466; and (4), 300–301, Houghton Library. These figures vary slightly from those given in Warren S. Tyron, "Book Distribution in Mid-Nineteenth Century America," *Papers of the Bibliographical Society of America* 41 (1947): 224.

16. Many advertisements by the auction houses in book trade journals indicate their willingness to grant advances for invoices offered for auction other than at the trade sales. The same option was probably available at the trade sales, as suggested in a communication published in *American Publishers' Circular,* vol. 5, 17 Sept. 1859, 461.

17. A brief account of parcel sales is given by Donald Sheehan, *This Was Publishing: A Chronicle of the Book Trade in the Gilded Age* (Bloomington, Ind.: Indiana University Press, 1952), 157–58.

18. Accounts of the German book fairs are found in Henri Estienne, *The Frankfort Book Fair . . .,* ed. James Westfall Thompson (Chicago: Caxton Club, 1911), and Helma Schaefer, "Zur Geschichte der Leipziger Buchmessen," *Marginalien: Blätter der Pirckheimer Gesellschaft* 21 (Dec. 1965): 33–34. The modern American book fair, quite a different affair, was first held in 1919 according to Hellmut Lehmann-Haupt et al., *The Book in America,* 2d ed. (New York: Bowker, 1951), 375–76.

19. Mathew Carey, *Address to the Printers and Booksellers throughout the United States* (Philadelphia: Carey, 1801), item 275a in Ralph R. Shaw and Richard H. Shoemaker, *American Bibliography, a Preliminary Checklist for 1801–1819,* 23 vols. (New York: Scarecrow Press, 1958–83).

20. This account is chiefly based on Charles L. Nichols, "The Literary Fair in the United States," in *Bibliographical Essays: a Tribute to Wilberforce Eames* (Cambridge, Mass.: Harvard University Press, 1924; reprint New York: B. Franklin, 1968), 83–92. See also Mathew Carey, *Autobiography* (New York: Research Classics, 1942), 49–50; Joel Munsell, "American Company of Booksellers," *American Publishers' Circular,* vol. 1, 22 Sept. 1855, 49–50; and Joel Munsell, *Typographical Miscellany* (Albany: Munsell, 1850), 99–101. Warner & Hanna of Baltimore printed an exchange list for a June 1806 fair (item 11795 in Shaw and Shoemaker, *American Bibliography*), but I have found no further evidence that this fair was held.

21. Carey, *Autobiography,* 50.

22. The following are scholarly accounts of English trade sales: Cyprian Blagden, "Booksellers' Trade Sales, 1718–1768," *The Library,* 5th ser., 5 (1950–51): 243–57; Stephen Parks, "Booksellers' Trade Sales," *The Library,* 5th ser., 24 (1969): 241–43; and Terry Belanger, "Booksellers' Trade Sales, 1718–1768," *The Library,* 5th ser., 30 (1975): 281–302. Contemporary accounts of nineteenth-century British trade sales are found in an article from the London *Athenaeum* reprinted in *Literary World,* vol. 6, 9 Feb. 1850, 136–37; an article from the *Philadelphia Press* reprinted in *American Publishers' Circular,* vol. 3, 5 Sept. 1857, 562; an excerpt from the article on the "Book Trade" from Chambers's *Encyclopedia* printed in *American Publishers' Circular,* vol. 7, 26 Jan. 1861, 37–38; and Joseph Shaylor, "Booksellers' Trade-Dinner Sales," *Fortnightly Review* 88 (1907): 1031–39. Hugh Amory suggests that the transformation in the English trade sales resulted in part from the landmark decision of *Becket* v. *Donaldson* in the House of Lords (1774), which effectively ended the London booksellers' legal claim to perpetual copyright (personal communication).

23. William Gowans, "History of the Trade Sales in America" (unpublished manuscript, mid-nineteenth century, the Grolier Club, New York). Gowans's manuscript is an incomplete draft, but he clearly indicates that an earlier trade sale had been held, probably at the end of the eighteenth century. I have not been able to discover any further record of this earlier sale, nor is it known to Robert B. Winans, bibliographer of American book catalogs to 1800. I thank Robert Nikirk, librarian of the Grolier Club, for permission to quote from Gowans's account.

24. David Kaser, "The Origin of the Book Trade Sales," *Papers of the Bibliographical Society of America* 50 (1956): 296–302. For New York, see *American Publishers' Circular,* vol. 3, 19 Sept. 1857, 594–95. An article in the *New York Daily Tribune* of 9 Sept. 1857, quoted in *American Publishers' Circular,* vol. 3, 19 Sept. 1857, 594–95, states that a trade sale took place in New York in January 1822. Gowans, in "History of the Trade Sales in America," ignores Carey's sales and describes instead a sale at which he was present sponsored by P. W. Johnson in New York in 1825 as the successor to M'Mennomy's 1812 event. For Boston, see *American Publishers' Circular,* vol. 5, 18 June 1859, 294.

25. Quoted by Walter Sutton, *The Western Book Trade: Cincinnati as a Nineteenth-Century Publishing and Book-Trade Center* (Columbus: Ohio State University Press for the Ohio Historical Society, 1961), 263. The original is at the Historical Society of Pennsylvania, Philadelphia.

26. Quoted by Kaser, "The Origin of the Book Trade Sale," 297. The original is at the Historical Society of Pennsylvania.

27. For a general discussion of auction sales during the nineteenth century in the United States, see Fred Mitchell Jones, *Middlemen in Domestic Trade of the United States* (Urbana: University of Illinois, 1937), 33–43. Evidence of the struggle between the auction houses and the book trade is provided by *Booksellers' Advertiser,* vol. 1, Apr. 1834, 25; a letter from Henry C. Carey to Hilliard, Gray & Co. of 12 Sept. 1834, quoted in Kaser, "The Origin of the Book Trade Sale," 301 (the original is at the Historical Society of Pennsylvania); and a broadside printed by the publishers and booksellers of Boston entitled *Trade Sales,* dated 12 Jan. 1835 (for a copy see bMS Am 1925.4 [40], folder 44, Houghton Library).

28. A nearly complete run of the Cincinnati trade sale catalogs has survived and is now at the Public Library of Cincinnati and Hamilton County, Cincinnati. These were used by Walter Sutton for his excellent "Cincinnati Trade Sales, 1838–77," in his *Western Book Trade,* 262–76. In addition to the four cities in the United States, regular trade sales were apparently also held in Toronto; see the notice in *American Literary Gazette,* vol. 14, 1 Oct. 1870, 315.

29. A single book fair had been held in Boston under the direction of Harrison Gray in June 1842; see *American Literary Gazette,* vol. 8, 15 Mar. 1867, 293–94. A letter published in *American Publishers' Circular,* vol. 5, 24 Sept. 1859, 473–74, explains that this fair was "a failure, the contributors being few, the expenses large, and the attendance of purchasers extremely limited." This letter was a response to a call for the substitution of book fairs for trade sales published in *American Publishers' Circular,* vol. 5, 17 Sept. 1859, 461.

30. *Publishers' Weekly,* vol. 6, 1 Aug. 1874, 140.

31. *Publishers' Weekly,* vol. 8, 31 July 1875, 249.

32. Quoted by Sheehan, *This Was Publishing,* 154–55. The original is presumably in the Scribner archives at Princeton University.

33. *Publishers' Weekly,* vol. 12, 6 Oct. 1877, 401.

34. *Publishers' Weekly,* vol. 47, 19 Jan. 1895, 58.

35. *Publishers' Weekly,* vol. 62, 8 Nov. 1902, 969.

36. See note 32. I would like to acknowledge the help and encouragement of friends and colleagues in preparing this paper, especially Hugh Amory, Terry Belanger, James N. Green, Marcus A. McCorison, Rollo G. Silver, Roger E. Stoddard, and Michael Turner.

2. From Printer to Publisher: Mathew Carey and the Origins of Nineteenth-Century Book Publishing

James N. Green

The eighteenth-century American printer was essentially like the provincial printer in England, subsisting in the interstices of a book market dominated by London, producing works of local interest for local consumption or reprinting standard works in abridged form or smaller formats. By about 1830 the leading American publishers were practically the equals of their London colleagues and were capable of producing almost all the books Americans read. We do not know very much about how and why this change happened, but I believe that Mathew Carey played a major role. In this paper I will show how Carey actually made this transition from printer to publisher in his own business in the 1790s, becoming one of the first American publishers to secure a national market for his books and one of the first whose books competed successfully with English imports.

When Mathew Carey began his printing business in Philadelphia two hundred years ago, America had won its independence from England, but its book trade was still dominated by London. Why was American printing so provincial? Why were our books almost always smaller, cheaper, and cruder than the English?

We were technically capable of producing books as large, expensive, and fine as the English, but we did so very rarely for two reasons which had nothing to do with technology or skill. First, the American market for such books was small and fragmented into a number of isolated regions, none of which was large or sophisticated enough to absorb an entire edition of an expensive book. Second, large amounts of capital were hard to raise and had to be paid back quickly, making success contingent not on just a large sale, but a rapid one. Until the 1790s American printers rarely even considered printing an equivalent to an expensive book available by import from England, because they knew that a competing bookseller could always import a few copies and satisfy the immediate demand for a small fraction of the capital needed to print a whole edition. Like every other American craftsman or tradesman, the colonial printer had to confine himself to products that required a modest capital outlay and were pretty sure to sell out locally. Anyone who exceeded these limits risked bankruptcy.

There were a few large, expensive books printed in colonial America, but in each case their publishers raised capital by means that reduced their risk: selling enough copies by subscription before printing to cover the costs, forming shared-risk partnerships with other printers, or printing partially or entirely at the expense of some civil or religious body.[1]

After the Revolution, however, the desire to be independent of England and to make larger profits stimulated printers to attempt direct competition with English imports. Until about 1790 our economy was in a shambles, and the English were dumping their goods in America. Then the establishment of a national bank and the disruption of British shipping during the war with France improved matters.[2] The first three years of the 1790s saw a sudden leap in the number of large books printed, but most of them were financed by advance subscription. Only a very wealthy and established publisher like Isaiah Thomas could do without this sort of protection against risk, and even Thomas's few large ventures were cautious and prudent.[3]

What a surprise it is, then, to find that in 1794 and 1795 Mathew Carey, a poor young printer, published not just one, but two of the largest and most expensive general interest books ever published in America, without prepaid subscription, partnership, or subsidy. The books in question were lavish reprints of highly approved English works. The first was William Guthrie's *New System of Modern Geography* (1794–95), two hefty quarto volumes (1,332 pages) with an atlas of about fifty large engraved maps, in an edition of 2,500 selling for $12 (later $16) bound. A separate issue of the maps was the first American atlas. The second was Oliver Goldsmith's compendium of natural history *An History of the Earth and Animated Nature* (1795), 4 volumes octavo (1,854 pages) with fifty-five plates, in an edition of 3,000, selling for $6 (later $10) bound.[4] At first glance they do not seem so remarkable, and in the next few years American books this big became almost common,[5] but at the time they represented an almost unprecedented publishing risk.

To decide to publish a book is one thing, to sell it and make a profit is another. What makes the Guthrie and Goldsmith books even more interesting is that they were not successful at first and nearly bankrupted Carey. The difficulties he faced were exactly the ones that had discouraged colonial printers from producing large books—too small a market and not enough credit. As I will show, Carey attacked the first difficulty by creating the most intensive and extensive book distribution network the nation had ever seen. The second difficulty proved harder to overcome. Though he sold huge quantities of books, the expense of maintaining his network wiped out his profit, and remittances were so slow that every bill falling due threatened to ruin him. When he escaped from the burden of the Guthrie and Goldsmith books about 1800, he used this network and the financial sophistication he had gained to sell successfully his quarto family Bible, which finally generated enough profit to allow him to accumulate capital.

Before beginning this story, I will briefly sketch Carey's career up to 1794. In 1784, at the age of twenty-four, Carey fled to Philadelphia from his native Ireland to escape prosecution because of a seditious article in the radical newspaper he had edited there. He established a printing business and in 1787 began printing *The American Museum*. It was an American version of the English monthly magazines, consisting of reprinted newspaper articles and other fugitive pieces worthy of more than local attention, mixed with poems and essays by the best writers on political, economic, and social issues. His intention was to make the *Museum* America's first national magazine. It was immediately popular. Its support of the Federalist party program, especially the ratification of the Constitution and Hamiltonian economics, quickly earned commendations from several national public figures. But despite its high reputation, the *Museum* never became a money-maker. As Carey wrote in his 1834 *Autobiography,*

> Never was more labour bestowed on a work, with less reward. During the whole six years, I was in a state of intense penury. I never at any one time, possessed 400 dollars,—and rarely three or two hundred.[6]

The problem was that there was no preexisting mechanism for distributing any kind of publication throughout the country, and Carey did not begin the work of inventing one until after the first issue was printed. He wrote letters to literary friends and fellow printers all up and down the country begging them to solicit and forward subscriptions, receive shipments, and collect payment.[7] He made extensive journeys to establish contact with distributors. Subscriptions poured in; having sold out the first issues he had to reprint them to supply new subscribers.[8] He sent out box after box of the magazine, not infrequently poorly packed and labeled or entrusted to unreliable shippers. He was unprepared for the wretched American roads. Subscribers became disgruntled by delays and irregularity, and agents were often unable or unwilling to collect payments. He was forced to hire other agents to dun delinquent subscribers at a cost equal to his profit. Carey's dogged persistence kept the *Museum* going for six years; but when Congress raised postage rates on magazines to the same rate as letters in 1792, it ceased publication.

The *Museum's* lasting benefits to Carey were two: first, it gave him a national reputation, and second, it had driven him to establish contacts with dozens of booksellers all across the country, a network which already at this early stage in his career was as extensive as that of any of the established publishers. The *Museum* gave Carey a taste for doing business on a large, national scale. As soon as he was free of it in 1792 he struck out boldly in a new direction: wholesaling books imported from London, Edinburgh, and Dublin. Unlike most booksellers, he made most of his sales to booksellers in other regions. Here he put his *Museum* network to good use. Larger booksellers in his network exchanged books with him for the mutual diversification of their stock, while smaller booksellers without enough stock to exchange took books either by sale at a discount or occasionally on consignment for a 12½ percent commission, with unsold books being returnable. Credit for this expansion came from British publishers, with whom Carey ran up debts of thousands of pounds.[9]

Carey's love of America and his hatred of the English had made him an ardent advocate of domestic manufactures and economic independence. He must have chafed under the necessity of importing books which, technically at least, could just as well have been printed in America with American paper and type. By 1794 the business outlook was good for Carey. He had several years' experience dealing with the problems of reaching a national market and maintaining credit. His reputation was high with his colleagues, political leaders, and the public. Though deeply in debt, the volume of his bookselling business was large. As economic conditions improved and English imports slackened in the early 1790s, and as Philadelphia emerged as the political, banking, and printing center of the nation, Carey was tempted to gamble by commencing publication in the London style of producing large numbers of books, in order to replace British imports. In 1794 and 1795, he published not only the two large books of Guthrie and Goldsmith mentioned above, but also about sixty other books and pamphlets, a total equal to his entire output until then.[10] He was also in those two years a partner in ten joint publishing ventures, the largest of which was Isaiah Thomas's edition of Morse's *American Universal Geography,* a book sure to compete with Guthrie since it was similar in scope but much smaller and cheaper. He bought a full third of the edition from Thomas and Andrews at one-third discount.[11]

On October 28, 1795, Carey wrote a long letter to the president of the Bank of Pennsylvania, which gives an account of his business and finances at the time:

From the time in which I entered extensively into the Bookselling business 1792–3 I have given employment to a large proportion of the Journeymen printers in this City. At some periods I have had working for me in different printing offices a full fourth probably a third of the whole. The proceeds of one work Guthries Geography, executed in about twenty months, is exclusive of binding 30,000 dollars, i.e. 2,500 copies, at 12 dollars each. The binding will amount to 5000 dollars. And this book was not half of what I had done during the time within eight months of the year 1794, I had 30,000 volumes printed from 3/9 to 15/ in price exclusive of 3,000 Sp. Books 13,500 pamphlets & 13,000 Chapmans Books at 12/ per doz. . . .

The Paper I have purchased for printing from Wm Lewis, from the 22 of February 1794, to the present time amounts to about 4000 dollars. From Mark Wilcox, in one year beginning April 94 & ending April 95 I had 1900 dollars worth & from Cruckshank within the last 15 months I have 1500 dollars worth. . . .

The engravings of Guthrie cost me about 5000, the edition help 1000 dollars.[12]

Another important fact about his business which has been overlooked is that just after the first volme of Guthrie had been printed, Carey sold his printing shop and let go his eight printers. He wrote his father in Ireland in 1794, "I have lately quitted the printing business, finding it impossible to pay the necessary attention to it and the Bookselling."[13] For the next eight years all Carey's printing was done for him by a large number of independent printers.[14] This in itself was a considerable innovation. His principal rivals in the publishing business in America still operated their own printing shops, subcontracting printing only when their workers were fully occupied with other jobs. In order to concentrate on publishing, Carey was relegating printing to the status of a supporting trade like binding and papermaking. From 1794 on he was more nearly a publisher in the modern sense than any other American.

Without a doubt Carey was extended financially to the limit by these publishing ventures, coming as they did on top of a large wholesale bookselling business. He had no capital; all these undertakings were financed either by borrowing from banks or by making notes to printers, papermakers, and binders payable in short terms varying from thirty days to a year. He could have his notes extended, but only by finding wealthier businessmen with enough faith in the soundness of his business to act as cosigners. Just how large his debt was at any time cannot be determined, since the only financial records which survive from this period are bills and receipts. The total volume of his claimed sales ranged as high as $50,000 a year, yet he was never out of debt in the 1790s.[15] All his income went to pay off creditors. Even a momentary slowing of his huge cash flow could spell trouble. On August 23, 1794, he wrote to his brother James, "I sometimes fear I have ventured too far—& that by putting my all to the risque, I have done what I shall have reason to repent a long time."[16] In a typical letter to a country bookseller at the end of 1794 he wrote,

> The extreme want of money which I experience at present, imposes on me an unavoidable necessity of being more troublesome & more importunate with you than my inclination would otherwise prompt me to be. I assure you by the oath of a freemason, that my payments in the month of January are 7000 dollars and as our banks have nearly stopt discounting I shall find it hardly possible to raise that sum.[17]

Carey used every technique he knew to sell his huge stock and to reduce his debt. In 1796 he cut back his new publishing to a fraction of what it had been the previous two years. Through his network of book dealers he solicited subscriptions for books already published. He offered exchanges and made journeys to drum up business. He even hired a traveling salesman named David Clark to go from house to house in the back country in Virginia gathering subscriptions for Goldsmith in the fall of 1795.[18] The books sold, but not as fast as his notes were falling due.

Carey needed a new way of selling books if he were going to continue this compulsive expansion of stock. It was both genius and necessity that inspired him at this moment to hire the most spellbinding itinerant book salesman of his time and send him on the road to build a distribution network in Philadelphia's great uncharted commercial hinterland of the south and west. That salesman was the legendary Mason Locke Weems, better known as Parson Weems, author of the *Life of Washington* that perpetrated the cherry tree myth. Carey's and Weems's was one of the most dynamic partnerships in the history of publishing. Both men had an inexhaustible fund of brilliant ideas for selling books, and both pursued them with manic intensity. In prosperity their expressions of mutual esteem reached lyrical heights; in adversity they reviled one another and raked over the coals of old wrongs like quarreling lovers. They seem to have first met in the winter of 1795. Weems described the occasion in a reminiscent letter to Carey in 1817.

> On our first acquaintance you took me into yr back room on Market Street, where you told me of 3,000 copies of Goldsmith's A[nimated] Nature on hand—not a single sub[scribe]r save 100 by a young Hibernian [probably the above mentioned David Clark] who had gone off with his paper. People knew nothing of the A. Nature & had

done nothing to so simple a Subn. paper. At your own instance, I sketchd. out a prospectus that gave the People to expect that "Worlds on Worlds inclosd were to burst upon their senses," if they wd but seize the precious moment to subscribe for this marvellous book.[19]

Their correspondence shows that early in 1796 Weems was acting as Carey's agent, soliciting subscriptions for Goldsmith in Lancaster County, Pennsylvania. Then on April 1, 1796, Weems entered into a contract to canvass subscriptions for and deliver bound copies of Goldsmith and the atlases accompanying Guthrie. His commission was to be 25 percent. The territory assigned was Virginia and Maryland; Weems was to remit through Carey's old agents in Georgetown, Maryland, and Dumfries and Petersburg, Virginia.[20] Weems did not let the grass grow under his feet; within four months he had almost one thousand subscriptions for Goldsmith.

Weems's success was not achieved by wandering about the country knocking on doors. He had a system.[21] He would travel to a town, distribute a prospectus or a subscription paper, perhaps show off a neatly bound sample volume, deliver his compelling sales pitch, collect subscriptions for a day or two, and leave town having appointed a local resident "adjutant," with himself as "general," just like his hero Washington. As people in the surrounding country came into town to visit a general store, church, or tavern, the adjutant would be on hand to talk up the wares and take orders. He was usually promised one copy in six or seven to sell on his own behalf.

Carey still maintained his contacts with booksellers all over the country, but in the south and west Weems supplemented Carey's old network and covered the countryside far more intensively. Carey had relations with booksellers in Lancaster, Carlisle, Baltimore, Richmond, Alexandria, and Wilmington, as well as contacts with postmasters in Dumfries, Georgetown, and Petersburg. These last three, it will be recalled, were the agents through whom Weems was to remit. These postmasters also had some of Carey's books to sell on consignment, but since they dealt exclusively with Carey they were considered different from the other booksellers and functioned more like branch stores. Weems's contacts extended further, to such places as Middletown and York, Pennsylvania; Snow Hill and Frederick, Maryland; Fredericksburg, Norfolk, Martinsburg, Winchester, Smithfield, Shepherdstown, and Richmond, Virginia—the list goes on and on. Before long Weems even had his own agents in Dumfries (where he made his home) and Petersburg, preferring them to Carey's postmasters there. The adjutants were, in military fashion, subordinate to Weems and did not deal directly with Carey at first. Weems forwarded their subscriptions, arranged for delivery not to them but to himself at some central depot, and forwarded money they had collected to Carey.

Weems was so convinced of the benefits of almost unlimited extension of Carey's network that he soon began authorizing adjutants not only to collect subscriptions but also to fit up stores in their houses and apply to Carey for an assortment of books on consignment. Here is a typical adjutant's letter:

> Falmouth 16 Nov. 1797
>
> Sir, The Revd M.L. Weems in passing thro' this place yesterday made me an offer of an assortment of Books to Sell on a Commission, which were to be furnished by you, and wrote a letter which will accompany this, requesting you to forward them—and requested me to make out a Bill of the Books I thought would be most Saleable & inclose it to you—I shall just annex a list of a few that I am pretty well satisfied will sell very readily, & leave it to yourself to add others you think proper, untill I see a Catalogue of yours, which will enable me to compleat a list suitable for our market, & to engage to procure any that may be called for at any time—Let the Books be sent by the first vessel for Fredericksburg, if you please as the business of the place is much brisker at *this,* than any other Season of the year. . . . No person keeping an assortment of Stationary near this place I think a *small* assortment of it would sell very well, as general as possible, but not extensive.[22]

Weems's optimism was incurable. As he wrote to Carey in the fall of 1796,

> This country [i.e. Virginia and Maryland] is large, and numerous are its inhabitants; to cultivate among these a taste for reading, and by the reflection of proper books to throw far and wide the rays of useful arts and sciences, were at once the work of a true Philanthropist and prudent speculator. For I am verily assured that under proper culture, every dollar that you shall scatter on the field of this experiment will yield you 30, 60, and 100 fold.[23]

Carey knew he did not have the capital to scatter dollars, but his need for cash tempted him to follow the Guthrie and Goldsmith editions with new ventures. He sent out perhaps a score of lots, each worth about five hundred dollars, of assorted consignment books.

Weems had clearly opened up a vast new market. The population in the rural areas of the south was indeed growing rapidly, and there were hardly any bookstores outside of the seaboard towns. Though legend has it that Weems was one of a horde of book salesmen traveling for many publishers, the Carey papers reveal no traveling agents at this time besides Weems and his adjutants. That there were hordes of pedlars selling almanacs with their pins and buttons is quite likely, but they were quite a different thing from Weems with his large assortment of fine books.

Weems's letters make almost no mention of competition from traveling agents for other publishers. At this period Philadelphia was the commercial center for a vast area south as far as Charleston and west to the Ohio Valley. Carey's chief bookselling rivals were not in Philadelphia but in New York and Boston, and there is abundant evidence that if they wanted to sell books in the south and west they did so through Philadelphia dealers.[24] So there is some reason to believe that not only did Weems open up a vast new market for Carey, he also had it virtually to himself, at least for a few years.

The question for Carey was whether this market as tapped and organized by Weems and himself could yield money quickly and steadily enough to pay off his debt as it fell due. The answer is, it could not. A network so dense and widespread, with many middlemen in remote places, by its nature returned money slowly, as Carey soon learned. Furthermore, it cost so much money in commissions, lost or damaged books, bad debts, and interest, that his profit was wiped out. By the first anniversary of Weems's employment, Carey still had not received much money, either from the books sent on consignment or from copies of Goldsmith and Guthrie, despite the fact that thousands of dollars worth of books had been "sold." As Carey wrote to Weems at the end of 1796,

> I have Sacrificed to you *nearly* THE WHOLE profits of the second work in point of importance that I ever printed [i.e. Goldsmith]. . . . Remittances should keep pace with shipments of Goldsmith at least. . . . Since the 10th of October I have received only 370 Dollars, this would not pay 25 per cent of the expence of binding for you since that time.[25]

Returns on Goldsmith and Guthrie copies were delayed for many reasons. The problems Carey encountered were reminiscent of those that had plagued the *Museum*. Carey had been caught with only a few copies bound; it took several months to have a supply bound, packed, and shipped to Weems's depots. Then the adjutant system introduced another delay: boxes lay unopened until Weems passed through and had a chance to unpack them and cart them upcountry in his wagon. Terrible roads, especially in the winter, caused further delays. After so much time had passed, the customers sometimes no longer wanted the books or did not have the cash to pay for them.

Returns from the consignment stores were slow simply because books had to sit on the shelves awaiting buyers, and even when they were sold the storekeepers usually kept the money until an opportunity presented itself to forward the cash or notes to Carey. Carey wrote to Weems,

The propriety of the Store Scheim is rendered very Questionable, by a circumstance which I am going to Communicate to you. From Bedinger, Lee, and Martin [adjutants to whom Carey had sent books on consignment], I have not yet recd a Single Dollar, not a Single line, and it is impossible for any man of Common Capital to carry on Business on the Extensive scale contemplated without the utmost regularity in remittance.[26]

Unable to get any account from Weems of some of the back country stores, Carey bypassed his general and demanded they report to him directly. For example, in March of 1798 Carey wrote to Henry Bedinger of Shepherdstown. He received this reply:

The books you mention were Delivd. me pr. the Revd. Mason L. Weems. . . . I knew not that I was accountable to any person but Mr. Weems for them. . . . The books are nearly one Half sold. . . . Sometime after they were Delivd. I paid Mr. Weems somewhere about fifty Dollars and expected to have paid him as fast as they sold. Mr. Weems has not Called for sometime past—am Ready and Willing to pay all the moneys in my hands . . . & think it would also be best to Remove the books now on Hand as I see no prospect of their selling speedily.[27]

By 1800 the weakest of these back country stores had returned their unsold books and rendered to Carey their final accounts. They tell a melancholy tale. Most of them sold less than one hundred dollars' worth a year, and the lists of books returned run page after page.[28] And the returned books, having been pulverized by deeply rutted wagon roads and dampened in the holds of boats twice, not to mention sitting on shelves for a year or more—or rather not sitting at all, but being frequently handled and consulted—were a dead loss.

Carey pruned the luxurious network Weems had set up by minimizing the number of middlemen he dealt with in the South and maximizing the volume of business per outlet. He kept his three branch stores and maintained close ties with one or, occasionally, two dealers in each of the medium-sized towns in Virginia, Maryland, and North Carolina. These were not branch stores, but they seem to have made practically all their wholesale purchases through him, in return for which favor he gave a good discount on cash sales and was liberal about the return of consigned books. It is not clear how profitable these stores were, but at least they did a far greater volume than any of the back country stores. By 1800 he had a lean and effective network, but he had paid a heavy price to achieve it.

In a further desperate effort to increase the sales Weems could make in his travels, Carey had at the end of 1796 begun buying—or, more likely, obtaining on exchange for copies of Guthrie and Goldsmith—large quantities of books printed by others, specifically for Weems to sell by subscription. As he wrote to Weems,

> I bought 400 Rambler 3 or 400 Life of Christ, and 150 Burket on the Testament, wholly & entirely for you. . . . On my last Journey to the Eastward, I made extremely large exchanges merely to a view to the new subscription plan I took 1000 copies of Cooks Voyages alone, of several other books I took 1, 2, & 300. . . . Of the Laws of the U. States, I engaged not only an exchange, but to be paid for in Cash no less than 1500.[29]

This strategy, too, was unsuccessful, and instead of increasing the flow of cash to Philadelphia it actually increased Carey's debt. Weems found many of the books unsalable. He insisted that his customers wanted light works in cheap editions; if it was necessary to send theology, let it at least be well "dulcified." The books Carey sent were like fiddles for a Methodist conventicle, Weems said more than once. Burkitt's *Expository Notes on the New Testament* (Philadelphia, 1796) was often cited by Weems as a prime offender; it is a hefty folio, densely printed and far longer than the Testament it discusses. Carey probably got 150 copies by exchange simply because it was one of the few American books as big as Guthrie's *New System* and exchanges could only be made with comparable books. Weems felt he was being buried under a load of Carey's dead stock of dull, unsalable, expensive old books. Carey was throwing good money after bad.

In his letters Weems tried to explain what his customers were like and what would please them. His exhortations are little masterpieces. Here is one on cheapness from a letter of 1809, worth quoting in full:

> Every new beginner behind the counter writes "Cheap Store" on his sign. He well knows that among our Christian Mammonites cheapness is everything. What made Lackington in Moorefields? Cheapness. What made Rob. Campbell Philada.? Cheapness. And here to'ther day in Fredericksbg a School Master wd not touch Murray's Grammar at 87½ cents, because he said Johnson at *Richmond* furnishd them at 75. Thus you see a Man, tho' wanting a book wd wait for some random opportunity to send 80 miles for it, rather than "THROW AWAY" as he said, 12 cents!! . . .
>
> "Here's a FAMOUS BOOK, Tom,"—says one of the throng at a Courthouse. "Begad you ought *to get one.*"
>
> "Indeed!" replies the other—"And do you think it will *divarte me?*"

"Yes I'll be d--d if it wont to the nicest," quoth the first, *"and besides, 'tis a quarter of a dollar cheaper than they ask'd me for it there in Richmond!"*

"The Devil you say!"

"Yes, I'll go to h--l if it isn't"

"Well now I'l be d--n-d if I wdn't buy one if I had but the money."

"Oh d--n my Soul if you shall miss it for want of that, while I have it you know Tom, So here's the Ryno."[30]

Carey knew his books had to be cheap in order to compete with imports. He had in fact priced the Guthrie and Goldsmith titles too low for this reason and only with great reluctance raised the price to cover the expense of distribution.[31] What Weems was advocating was not cheapness for its own sake but cheap editions of popular standard books or new books just like the old familiar ones. The profit per sale might only be a few pennies, but Weems knew from experience that tens of thousands of them could be sold in the rural South. His feel for popular taste was infallible. Carey attempted to follow his advice: beginning in 1797 the mix of books he published changed markedly in the direction of the cheap, the popular, and the standard, and he stepped up his purchases of such books from other booksellers. Here at last he met with success. The cheap books helped make up financially for Carey's earlier misjudgment in the books he sent to the South.

By 1799 the editions of Guthrie and Goldsmith were nearly exhausted, perhaps half of them sold by Weems. Carey had made little if anything from them, and in the process of selling them had incurred new debts. As if this were not discouraging enough, at the end of 1798 a new sort of pressure was brought to bear on Carey which, when combined with his chronic indebtedness, created a serious crisis. The source of this pressure was politics. Carey had broken with the Federalists over Jay's Treaty in 1795 and, over the next three years, had published a number of pamphlets in support of the new pro-French party of Jefferson.[32] In 1798 the Alien and Sedition Acts were passed as part of the Federalist backlash against the fear of a Jacobin influence in America. As a former Irish radical, Carey may have been involved with the revolutionary group called the United Irishmen. In December 1798 the Federalist newspaper editor and propagandist William Cobbett began to hint at such a connection. If a formal accusation had been made, it would have led to a prosecution under the Sedition Act and probably a curtailment of his credit by the banks. His debt made him too vulnerable; it had to be reduced immediately by any means possible. Carey paid a visit to Weems in Dumfries at a great expence of money time & trouble & exposed to a great inclemency of weather to [show] to you the difficulties I laboured under & to urge you to some adequate exertions. You were extremely liberal in your promises. I was to have from 1000 to 2000 Dollars from your Brother & four or five hundred dollars from your parishioners besides the collections of money due you. . . .[33]

But by the middle of January Weems had not sent "one single solitary dollar," treatment "shameful beyond expression." Bitterly Carey complained,

The disadvantage I experience from the confidence I placed in you, and from the very great preparations I made of various kinds of Books for you, is incalculable. But for you, I should at this hour be easy & independent in my circumstances; instead of which I am constantly harassed, & my credit is at stake, and in the utmost jeopardy.[34]

On January 22, 1799, an advertisement was placed with the *Pennsylvania Gazette* reading,

"Books Selling Very Cheap. MATTHEW CAREY, Proposing to quit the Book Selling business, offers his large and valuable Collection of Books for sale, by retail, at a discount of 12 and an 1-2 per cent. from the usual prices. Those who purchase considerable quantities, shall have a further discount."

For Mathew Carey the darkest hour was just before dawn. In March he wrote and distributed throughout the country a satirical poem against Cobbett so witty and devastating that the Porcupine was struck dumb. Popular opinion rallied to Carey's side. The Federalists began to feel Cobbett was a dubious asset, and no more was heard about Carey as a United Irishman. Shortly thereafter Cobbett was convicted of libeling Benjamin Rush and had to leave the country. Meanwhile the Republicans' star rose swiftly. Carey's continued support of Jefferson was rewarded after the election of 1800 by an appointment as a director of the Bank of Pennsylvania, which, as he disingenuously wrote in his autobiography, "afforded considerable facility for meeting my engagements. My debts rose extravagantly high, and . . . I was treated with great lenity by the Directors, who allowed my notes to run on, without curtailment. . . ."[35] That was the end of his credit troubles.

At this point, a word of summary is in order. Carey's problem was that, regardless of the huge volume of his business, he was not making a profit. The huge volume was the result of what he was doing right, for he had built up the largest network for distributing books the nation had ever seen. The lack of profit resulted from what he was doing wrong: his profit margin was too slender; he used too many middlemen; he published or sold wholesale too many titles that were not readily salable; too many sales were on consignment and not enough were for cash; and finally his debt was too large, causing cash flow problems. These points were also implicit in Carey's own account of his troubles, written many years later in his 1834 *Autobiography*. In that remarkable document he tells of

> the various difficulties and embarrassments that for so long a period oppressed and brought me to the verge of bankruptcy, and which nothing but the most untiring efforts, and indefatigable industry and economy could have enabled me to wade through. I must confess that they were brought on me by my own folly. . . . I printed and published above twice as many books as were necessary for the extent of my business; and, in consequence, incurred oppressive debts to banks—was laid under contribution for interest to them, and to usurers, which not only swallowed up my profits—but kept me in a constant state of penury. . . . I have owed for months together from 3 to $6000, borrowed from day to day, and sometimes in the morning to be paid at 1 o'clock the same day, to meet checks issued the preceding day. . . . I have walked, lame as I was, from 9 or 10 o'clock in the morning, till 2 or half past 2, trying to borrow money. . . . My fatuitous course of conduct, for which it is difficult to account but on the principle of monomania, produced the most destructive consequences. . . . But for this miserable infatuation . . . I might have retired from business ten years earlier than I did.[36]

In 1800, when Jefferson's election seemed assured, Carey embarked on a new publishing program designed to solve the problems mentioned in the summary above. The centerpiece in that new order was to be that perennially profitable large book, the family Bible. Weems has left us a dramatic account of the moment the inspiration struck:

> On entering into your service I importund you for a Family Bible. I spoke of it to you, (you cannot but recollect the *terms*) as of a *vein of* Potosi to your purse. Long I plead, but in vain, till one day, one lucky day, when the stimulus of an unlented dinner and a cheerfull glass had raisd your spirits to noble darings, you snatched the ready [pen] and after a few minutes of rapid calculation you turnd to me with a, by G-d I'll undertake it.[37]

In July 1800 he tested the water for a quarto Bible by sending Weems to a new territory—New Jersey and New York City—to gather subscriptions in a new way—prepaid and in advance of printing. He sold hundreds of subscriptions in a territory which "but a short time before that, had been coverd with Isaac Collins Bibles," and even a few in New York City, where of Bibles "no families [had] less than a *pair,* some good Quakers had *Seven!*"[38] Then he shifted to his old territory in the south and sold hundreds more. This success was encouraging, but Carey was growing cautious. He realized he was relying too heavily on Weems and resolved to exert himself to line up wholesale buyers for large parts of the edition among the big-city booksellers. He delayed going to press for almost a year. The delay might also be accounted for by the fact that the election of 1800 was surprisingly a dead heat, and Jefferson's ascension to the presidency suddenly looked less certain. The quarto Bible finally went to press in April 1801, a few weeks after the tie was broken in Jefferson's favor. It appeared in November of 1801 and was an immediate success. Weems had been allotted about half the edition of two thousand, and he sold it easily by filling his subscription orders and by incidental direct sales made in the course of his deliveries. Thomas and Andrews in Boston took four hundred copies on exchange immediately, and the other booksellers followed suit.[39] The finances were simple. It cost Carey about $4 to print; he sold it to Weems and other wholesale purchasers for $5; the cost to subscribers was $6; and the cost to non-subscribers was $7. Thus Carey made a clear $1–$2 per copy by sales through middlemen and $3 by sales in his retail shop. Subscribers had to make a down payment when they signed up, thus bringing in some cash in advance of printing and ensuring that they would accept the book when it was printed. In a year the edition was sold out; in 1802 he printed two more separate editions and yet another in 1803. When he printed the 1803 edition, he purchased the type before it was distributed and kept it standing for future editions. It was America's first standing quarto Bible. At about the same time he acquired standing type for a duodecimo school Bible from Hugh Gaine of New York for seven thousand dollars.[40] With the type for both Bibles standing, Carey never again had to incur the expense of typesetting and proofreading; from then on he could undersell any competitor, and the success of the Bibles was assured. He printed an edition of the quarto Bible each year until 1820, and he became a rich man at last.

The Bible venture generated a profit where the editions of Guthrie and Goldsmith had not because Carey had learned from his mistakes. First, the Bible was an eminently salable book. It was modeled on the quartos published with great success in 1791 by Isaiah Thomas and Isaac Collins, which were in turn modeled on the standard Edinburgh and Oxford quartos. Its price was about a third that of the sumptuously illustrated hot-pressed folio published in Philadelphia by Thompson and Small in 1798, yet its plates were as good and it had a generally luxurious appearance. Second, Carey was finally using his network efficiently, aggressively pursuing exchanges with reliable booksellers all over the country, cutting down on middlemen and consignments, and allowing Weems to concentrate his efforts on what he did best—selling prepaid subscriptions in the rural South. Third, the retail price was high enough to ensure a profit, yet low enough to be competitive. In short, Carey had finally solved the two problems that had bedeviled so many eighteenth-century printers, including himself: he now had efficient access to a market adequate for the book he was selling; and his venture was placed on a sound financial footing by the combination of easy bank credit and quick, profitable returns.

The success of the Bible lifted the weight of debt from Carey's shoulders, making every aspect of his business simpler and every new venture less risky. It gave him the financial security he needed to do what he had been trying to do since 1794—publish a wide variety of high-quality books to replace British imports in every sector of the American market. This he proceeded to do with gusto for the next twenty years, thereby creating the first great publishing house of the nineteenth century.[41]

Notes

1. The earliest large American books were folio compilations of laws. They were usually paid for by the colonial government, as in the case of the oldest extant Massachusetts compilation, a folio of ninety-eight pages printed in Cambridge in 1660, or else protected from competition, as in the case of a 199-page folio printed in 1672, for which the General Court of Massachusetts gave exclusive right to its publisher, John Usher of Boston, for seven years—the first American copyright granted by law. The first non-legal folio was Samuel Willard's *Compleat Body of Divinity* (Boston: Printed by B. Green and S. Kneeland for B. Eliot and D. Henchman, 1726), a monster of a thousand pages for the printing of which about five hundred subscribers paid as a posthumous tribute to the great divine. The even larger Ephrata Martyr Book (1748) was printed by the Brethren as an act of piety or penance. Christopher Saur's 1743 quarto German Bible seems to have been subsidized by pietist churchmen who supplied him paper so that the Bible could be sold for less than imported Lutheran ones. An edition of Abraham Swan's *British Architect,* with sixty folio plates engraved by Philadelphian John Norman, appeared in 1775 with a list of about one hundred eighty "encouragers," almost all of them carpenters—the Carpenters' Company was one of the wealthiest and best organized in America. Just before the Revolution, patriotic Americans subscribed for Robert Bell's editions of standard British works, such as Cullen's *Lectures on the Materia Medica* (in quarto, 1775) and Blackstone's *Commentaries on the Laws of England* (1st American edition, 1771–72, 4 vols. in octavo), both bearing imprints reading, "America: Printed for the Subscribers." In 1775 naturalist Bernard Romans in New York published at his own risk his *Concise Natural*

History of East and West Florida, with huge maps in three and six sheets. The author raised money himself by subscription from individuals and from booksellers in several cities; Henry Knox of Boston "subscribed" for fifty copies. Obviously the production of large books was technically possible for the colonial printer, but in every case some means of subsidy or prepublication subscription was used.

2. See the Philadelphia *Evening Star,* 30 Oct. 1810: "For many years after the peace of 1783, books could be imported into the United States and sold cheaper than they could be printed here and indeed until 1793 nothing like a competition with English printers and booksellers could be maintained. The war then raging in Europe and added duty on paper made some difference but it was not until the union of Ireland and England [in 1801] that a decided advantage was ascertained to exist." Quoted in Charles L. Nichols, "The Literary Fair in the United States," in *Bibliographical Essays, A Tribute to Wilberforce Eames* (Cambridge: Harvard University Press, 1924), 85. Nichols points out that this statement was made by striking printers of Philadelphia, but it could as easily have been written by Mathew Carey (a frequent ghost writer of public statements), since it neatly describes the evolution of his own business vis à vis English imports.

3. In 1790 Isaiah Thomas issued the second American edition of Blackstone's *Commentaries* (4 vols. in duodecimo), following in 1791 with the first American Bell's *System of Surgery* (4 octavo vols. with 99 plates), both apparently without subscription. These were large undertakings, but their risk was considerably reduced by the fact that they were targeted at wealthy and bookish professions, a market which had already been successfully reached by Robert Bell's Blackstone and Cullen in the 1770s (see note 1).

4. The edition sizes are given in Mathew Carey's *Autobiography* (Brooklyn: Research Classics, 1942), 43–44. The autobiography had first been published in *The New England Magazine* for 1833–34 and was reprinted without a title page about 1835. The prices are quoted from Carey's business papers and catalogs.

5. So Carey says himself in his *Autobiography,* 43.

6. Ibid., 22.

7. The Lea & Febiger Papers at the Historical Society of Pennsylvania include practically all the surviving correspondence of Carey's firm from 1785 to 1822. Outgoing letters are preserved in letterbooks containing abstracts or retained copies; incoming letters are filed alphabetically in one series from 1785 to 1796 and in annual alphabetical arrangements from 1797 until 1822. The correspondence is voluminous and seems rather complete, but the wealth of information it contains about Carey's business is completely undigested. The Lea & Febiger collection contains no digested financial records, such as ledgers, journals, day books, or cost books, for the time of Mathew Carey's ownership of the firm, which lasted until 1817, and few for the period after that. A complete series of financial records was made available by Lea & Febiger to Earl L. Bradsher for his *Mathew Carey, Editor, Author, and Publisher* (New York: Columbia University Press, 1912), as Bradsher describes in his note to p. viii. But most of the financial records had apparently been discarded before the correspondence came to the Historical Society of Pennsylvania in 1928. (See also note 9.)

8. See Carey's account of *The American Museum*'s vicissitudes in his *Autobiography,* 23.

9. See the bills from British booksellers in the Mathew Carey Papers, American Antiquarian Society (AAS). One example from among dozens is that of James and Andrew Duncan of Glasgow, amounting to £3,067, for books imported from 1793 to 1800 (vol. 15, no. 5955). The only financial records to survive from the Carey archive are bound volumes of bills and receipts at AAS. These are bills sent to Carey by people from whom he *purchased* books, paper, printing, binding, etc., not records of his *sales* of books, though bills often balance purchases against sales. They are bound in series parallel to those of the incoming correspondence, which they originally accompanied. The receipts at the AAS are difficult to use separately from their covering letters, which are at the Historical Society of Pennsylvania, and vice versa.

10. For a list of Carey's imprints year by year, see William Clarkin, *Mathew Carey: A Bibliography of his Publications, 1785–1824* (New York: Garland, 1984).

11. Thomas and Andrews to Carey, 8 Mar. 1795, Lea & Febiger Papers. Carey's account with Thomas and Andrews for 1795–99 shows he bought over two thousand dollars' worth of Morse's *Geography* (Mathew Carey Papers, vol. 14, no. 5388).

12. Carey to John Barclay, 28 Oct. 1795, Letterbook 1792–1796, 182–85, Lea & Febiger Papers.

13. Mathew Carey to Christopher Carey, 20 June 1794, Letterbook 1792–1796, 154, Lea & Febiger Papers.

14. In about 1802 Carey established his own "printing office" on separate premises, primarily to do the printing of his Bibles. It was a sort of branch business and even presented bills to Carey for the printing, which are preserved in the Mathew Carey Papers. He continued to use independent printers as well.

15. Bradsher, *Mathew Carey,* 14.

16. Mathew Carey to James Carey, 23 Aug. 1794, Letterbook 1792–1796, Lea & Febiger Papers.

17. Carey to Joseph Clarke, 26 Dec. 1794, Letterbook V, 65, Lea & Febiger Papers.

18. David Clark to Carey, correspondence running 21 Aug. to 25 Oct. 1795, Lea & Febiger Papers. It closes with Clark's claim of "little success"; his excuse was a painful swelling of his leg—caused by wading through too many creeks—which kept him confined to his bed for weeks.

19. Weems to Carey, 8 Aug. 1817, Lea & Febiger Papers. Weems's letters to Carey and some of Carey's replies are published in vols. 2 and 3 of *Mason Locke Weems: His Works and Ways,* 3 vols. (New York, 1929), vols. 2 and 3 containing letters, 1784–1825, ed. Emily Ellsworth Ford Skeel. This letter (3: 205–6) probably refers not literally to the first meeting of Weems and Carey, but to a slightly later visit by Weems to Carey's shop, when the printing of Goldsmith was still underway. The printing was not finished until June 1796 (see 2: 20).

20. Carey, autograph document, 1 Apr. 1796, in *Mason Locke Weems,* ed. Skeel, 2: 7–8.

21. For a fuller account of Weems's methods and his relationship with Carey, see James Gilreath, "Mason Weems, Mathew Carey and the Southern Booktrade, 1794–1810," *Publishing History* 10 (1981): 27–49.

22. Seth B. Wigginton to Carey, 16 Nov. 1797, Lea & Febiger Papers.

23. Weems to Carey, 15 Oct. 1796, in *Mason Locke Weems,* ed. Skeel, 2: 47–48.

24. William Charvat, *Literary Publishing in America, 1790–1850* (Philadelphia: University of Pennsylvania Press, 1959), 23ff.

25. Carey to Weems, 8 Dec. 1796, in *Mason Locke Weems,* ed. Skeel, 2: 62.

26. Carey to Weems, 28 Nov. 1796, ibid., 61.

27. Henry Bedinger to Carey, 16 Mar. 1798, Lea & Febiger Papers.

28. See the receipt books in the Mathew Carey Papers.

29. Carey to Weems, 5 Dec. 1796, in *Mason Locke Weems,* ed. Skeel, 2: 61.

30. Weems to Carey, 22 May 1809, ibid., 406.

31 See Carey to James Rice, bookseller in Baltimore, 31 Dec. 1794, Letterbook V, 70, Lea & Febiger Papers: "The expence of this work [i.e., Guthrie] is extremely high and the proceeds come in so slowly that I am harassed in the prosecution of it. I have lately raised the subscription price two dollars."

32. Edward C. Carter II, "The Political Activities of Mathew Carey, Nationalist, 1760–1814," (Ph.D. diss., Bryn Mawr College, 1962), chap. 7.

33. Carey to Weems, 25 Jan. 1799, in *Mason Locke Weems,* ed. Skeel, 2: 112.

34. Carey to Weems, 10 June 1799, ibid., 118.

35. Carey, *Autobiography,* 48.

36. Ibid., 41–42.

37. Weems to Carey, 2 Sept. 1805, in *Mason Locke Weems,* ed. Skeel, 2: 326.

38. Weems to Carey, 25 Aug. 1800, ibid., 141.

39. The correspondence begins with a letter from Isaiah Thomas to Carey, 2 June 1801, Lea & Febiger Papers. For the account of the large exchange between Carey and Thomas and Andrews of quarto Bibles for school Bibles from November 1800 to October 1802, see Mathew Carey Papers, vol. 17, no. 7701. The amount of business on this account rose from over $1,700 in 1801 to over $2,700 in 1802.

40. Carey, *Autobiography,* 48.

41. For a brief sketch of Carey's whole career, see James N. Green, *Mathew Carey, Publisher and Patriot* (Philadelphia: The Library Company, 1985).

3. The Subscription Publishing Network in Nineteenth-Century America

Michael Hackenberg

When the drenched Huck Finn found himself washed ashore at the Grangerfords' house along the Mississippi, he discovered among other things in their parlor

> ... some books, too, piled up perfectly exact, on each corner of the table. One was a big family Bible full of pictures. One was *Pilgrim's Progress,* about a man that left his family, it didn't say why. I read considerable in it now and then. The statements was interesting, but tough. Another was *Friendship's Offering,* full of beautiful stuff and poetry; but I didn't read the poetry. Another was Henry Clay's Speeches, and another was Dr. Gunn's *Family Medicine,* which told you all about what to do if a body was sick or dead. There was a hymn-book, and a lot of other books.[1]

This was not simply idle filler or descriptive narrative, but rather dry parody of a publishing phenomenon with which Mark Twain himself was intimately familiar. For, as the publication of *Huckleberry Finn* neared completion in late 1884, its author had already weathered nearly two decades of subscription selling of his own works, first via the Hartford-based American Publishing Company and then through his own partnership with Charles L. Webster in New York.[2]

The decade of the 1880s represents in many ways the culmination of the subscription bookselling phenomenon, whose historical roots can actually be explored far back into the early part of the nineteenth century. By 1890, however, this publishing event had lost much of its initial

"The Subscription Publishing Network in Nineteenth-Century America" copyright © 1987 by Michael Hackenberg.

brilliance because of the endlessly repetitive issuing of hackneyed titles, and abuses were being chronicled by such trade organs as *Publishers' Weekly,* by countless newspaper exposés about local agents, and in a few blistering attacks such as Bates Harrington's 1879 *How 'Tis Done: A Thorough Ventilation of the Numerous Schemes Conducted by Wandering Canvassers* (which, by the way, took on agents selling patent medicines, fruit trees, and lightning rods as well as books and country atlases).[3]

The publishing apparatus producing subscription books peaked during that decade. Caspar's 1889 directory of the American book trade listed no fewer than 439 American and 15 Canadian firms as subscription publishers. New York City headed that list with 74 firms, followed by Chicago with 61, Philadelphia with 45, Boston with 24, Cincinnati with 19, St. Louis with 17, and Detroit with 16. There were also sizable figures for Hartford, Indianapolis, Kansas City, Syracuse, San Francisco, and Denver.[4] Such figures, however, because they represent subscription *publishing* firms, are somewhat misleading, since the strength of subscription book-selling was dissemination and not just production. To understand the subscription book network, one needs, however, to look at the development of some of its components.

Book peddling or colportage had been around for centuries and certainly had a place in the early part of the nineteenth century. Most of this activity was relatively unsystematized, depending upon the occasional trips of wandering peddlers into cities to replenish their book stocks from the general bookstores. At least one earlier attempt at systematically exploiting the rural southern market had failed. The decade-and-a-half-long cooperation (if that is the word) between Mathew Carey and Mason Locke Weems, which lasted until 1810, had attempted to sell books directly to rural customers through intermediary "adjuncts," leading members of communities who would be sent bundles of a few titles in multiple copies and expected to distribute them in exchange for a percentage allowance—a system not unlike that of setting up general subscription agents a bit later. That plan faltered, however, because of poorly selected titles, transport problems, and personality clashes between Carey and Weems.[5]

City directories from the first third of the nineteenth century are replete with advertisements from booksellers urging visits from both country merchants and peddlers. Oliver Steele, an Albany bookseller and stationer, invited country merchants in June of 1831 to look over his stock of miscellaneous books which he would "sell as cheap as any auction house [could] afford to do."[6] Country merchants and traders were similarly enticed by an advertisement of the Boston wholesale and retail bookseller John Marsh in an 1837 Boston directory. Indeed, the 1836 edition of that same directory had mentioned what is, as far as I know, one of the earliest operations of a book agent in what can be understood as a subscription context: the previous year Michael Bruns had been listed as a sexton and undertaker, but by 1836 he had metamorphosed into an agent for the Jared Sparks edition of the works of Washington and Franklin then being published by Hilliard & Gray of Boston.[7] In 1838 in Philadelphia the firm of Grigg and Elliot, who were booksellers, publishers, and wholesale stationers, can be found pitching its directory advertisements at country merchants, as can half a dozen others.[8] The Worcester, Massachusetts, bookseller S. A. Howland crows in 1848 to merchants, traveling dealers, and peddlers that they can be "supplied with books and goods in their line, on better terms than at any other place in the state."[9]

Technological Developments

Newer book production technology in the period provided impetus to the development of subscription publishing. During the second and third decades of the nineteenth century, commercial printing from plates became a reality for books in high demand, including schoolbooks, Bibles, and what are often referred to in contemporary advertisements as "standard and miscellaneous works"—that is, popular literature and illustrated common biographies. Harper and Brothers were already producing 46 percent of their New York output by stereotyping in 1834.[10] The Boston Stereotype Foundry was established by 1822, and an even more impressive stereotyping industry developed in Hartford, Connecticut, with the 1836 creation of Case, Tiffany & Co. (to be known at mid-century as Case, Lockwood and Brainard). When that Hartford firm bought the plates and rights to the *Cottage Bible* in 1840, it opened the floodgates to issues of stereotype titles in large quantities. By 1857, 150,000 sets of the *Cottage Bible* had been issued. By the end of the Civil War, Case, Lockwood and Brainard were producing the majority of the titles issued by the many Hartford publishers as well as by many publishing houses in Boston, New York, Chicago, San Francisco, and elsewhere. The Hartford giant also operated its own bindery, which turned out in one year over 354,000 bound titles; the entire fourth floor of its 1867 building was occupied by women gathering, folding, and sewing sheets.[11]

Philadelphia directories of 1839 already refer to two wholesale stereotype foundries in that city, and an 1842 directory· first attests the presence of Samuel D. Burlock, a major binder there. The number of binders would swell to 28 by 1849; they were to be intimately connected with the subscription book production that dominated the city by mid-century.[12] Cincinnati, another subscription publishing center, had its first stereotyping facility by 1830. By 1837, J. A. James, a former Harpers' worker, was employing 20 to 30 people in his Cincinnati stereotype foundry and already advertising his own firm as a publisher of standard and miscellaneous works ideal for visiting country booksellers. Binding operations were also in abundance there, with 30 binderies and 380 workers employed by 1859.[13] Chicago's later rise as a subscription publishing center after the 1871 fire owed much to the concentration of all technical facilities under the roof of the rebuilt Lakeside Building of R. R. Donnelley. There the multitudinous subscription atlas, map, book, and magazine projects could be efficiently carried out under one roof. Editorial work was done on the third floor, engraving and lithography on the fourth, hand coloring on the third, composition on the sixth, gold tooling in the basement, and binding on the fifth—all by subcontracting firms, with the printing coordinated by the Lakeside Publishing and Printing Company.[14] Thus the technical stage was set in those cities for the vast production which subscription publishing would entail.

Transportation and Advertising Improvements for Subscription Books

Improved transportation was the next hurdle. By 1830 the New England railway system was under development, and the Boston and Worcester Railroad was operating by 1834. Out of that company came William Harnden, a former conductor and passenger-clerk, who in March of 1839 began accompanying the express car between Boston and New York, which was "important to merchants, brokers, booksellers, and others" (according to a Boston newspaper ad). Harnden's successful express business expanded via Hudson River packets to Albany and, later, Buffalo. Philadelphia soon was added to his network. But so was competition, as Alvin Adams launched his express service, which included a California express by 1849 and lines to Mobile and New Orleans. By the early 1850s Adams connected Philadelphia to St. Louis by way of Pittsburgh. Henry Wells, a former Harnden agent at Albany who had earlier succeeded in getting a daily Western Express operation to Buffalo while undercutting United States mail agencies by one-fourth their price, joined with W. G. Fargo in 1845 to extend the Western Express yet further to Cleveland, Cincinnati, Chicago, and St. Louis (by railroad and steamer). The Wells, Fargo and Company's California Express began in 1852. There were, in addition, many other local express carriers.[15]

Book publishers and book agents were quick to avail themselves of these services, which could transport bulky book parcels to inland distribution points. In 1842 the Buffalo booksellers William and Charles Peck not only advertised their school and miscellaneous books, but also identified themselves as agents for Pomeroy's Albany and Buffalo Package Express and its Canadian extensions, as well as for connections with the Harnden Express Line to Boston, New York, and Philadelphia and Hawley's

Western Express to Erie, Cleveland, Detroit, and Chicago.[16] New York City wholesale booksellers were also quick to stress express service for their country dealers. Judd and Taylor supplied country dealers via package express as early as 1845, as did William H. Graham.[17] Three years later, Graham's New York successor, DeWitt and Davenport's Book and Periodical Establishment, stressed,

> All orders from country agents and booksellers will be promptly attended to. We have on hand a large assortment of new books, magazines, and cheap publications to agents, pedlers, store keepers and others at publishers' prices.[18]

The railroads and their express services convenienced many traveling book agents and must certainly have been a factor in bringing in the many women who sold subscription books. Sarah Ann Mendell, a subscription agent in 1852 from the upstate New York hamlet of Ellisburgh, notes with pleasure "the introduction of the railroad which has been in operation but a few months in our vicinity." She was later delayed during the winter while distributing her books at Cape Vincent and Malone, New York, and was forced to come home "by the stage route, which is soon to be superseded in quickness and comfort by a railroad."[19] In the Far West, Mrs. James W. Likins, who, between 1869 and 1874 traveled for both H. H. Bancroft and Anton Roman as far afield as Sacramento and Gilroy, probably found her husband's connections helpful, since he served as baggagemaster and freight clerk at the San Francisco offices of both the Southern Pacific and the San Francisco and San Jose Railroads.[20] William Still, the black Philadelphia author and subscription publisher of his own *The Underground Rail Road,* was using Adams's COD express service in shipping ordered copies and even agents' outfits to Davenport, Iowa, and Monrovia, Indiana, in 1873 and 1874.[21]

New channels of advertising were also essential to the early subscription publishers, who simply had to extend awareness of their products into relatively uncharted economic areas. Already-tried techniques of the earlier book peddlers were, of course, continued. Broadside prospectuses similar to those used in 1801 by Mathew Carey for his second Philadelphia quarto Bible are one example.[22] Often billed as a proposal for publication by subscription, such broadsheets generally listed contents of and terms for the proposed work, with space left at the bottom of the sheet for subscribers' names and addresses. During the 1830s and 1840s, this broadside format was modified into what came to be regarded as the traditional bound agent's prospectus.

An interesting transitional prospectus illustrates this change. *The English Version of the Polyglott Bible,* with a major introduction by Joseph A. Warne and numerous illustrations, was, in fact, published in 1843 in

Franklin, New Hampshire, by the firm of Peabody & Daniell, and D. Kimball. A surviving prospectus contains forty-two leaves of sample text and illustrated engraved and typeset title pages, separate title pages for the various sections of commentaries, twelve blank ledger leaves, and one leaf entitled "Proposals for publishing by Subscription a Handsome Stereotype Edition of the English Version of the Polyglott Bible." The last-named leaf resembles the earlier single broadsides, with contents, terms, and, at the bottom, a bit of space for subscribers' names, which is then expanded with the bound blank ledger sheets. The manufactured full prospectus had already arrived, although it stated it was but a proposal.[23]

Even earlier, however, is a full prospectus for an octavo, stereotyped edition of John Fleetwood's *The Life of Our Lord and Saviour Jesus Christ* (which became one of the century's subscription war-horses), printed and published in 1833 at New Haven by Nathan Whiting. One leaf of the prospectus, which is extant, mentions that Whiting *"has* recently published" the work (in other words, this was not prepublication subscription), describes the proffered product and terms ($2.75 in plain binding or $3.00 in extra gilt), and adds a statement of what soon would become a major advertising ploy for most subscription publishers: "We could print a long list of recommendations, but they are so common, that the Subscriber will rely on the reputation he has established as a book publisher."[24] This extremely early example of a type of product which later armies of agents would carry throughout the country as an advertising inducement deserves further attention because it was indeed used in an early subscription network. James A. Butler of Huntsville, Alabama, is named as the agent, and over 150 subscribers are recorded from that southern region. One woman actually noted that Butler left a copy of Fleetwood with her on October 12, 1835. Despite Whiting's avowal that his reputation was already well entrenched, posterity has not so viewed it. A Nathan Whiting and a Nathan C. Whiting appear in the New Haven city directories between 1840 and 1847, but neither is described as being connected to any publishing activity (although others in those directories *are* so described during that period). In any case, the beginning of the subscription publishing network can be established as early as the 1830s and 1840s.

However, by mid-century, advertising techniques beyond that of the agent's prospectus or occasional broadside were expanding the subscription network. It is significant to note the first appearance of such a firm as Volney B. Palmer's Country Newspaper Advertising Agency, which promised merchants new access to rural markets, in *Doggett's New York City Directory* for 1846 and 1847. That same directory also lists among its 120 publishers and booksellers at least six that are confirmable subscription publishers by that time.[25] One of those publishers, Robert Sears, of 128

Nassau Street, was already running display advertisements in the following year's directory for his popular pictorial works. By 1855 his display ads appeared in Detroit directories, addressed "to persons out of employment," offering agents opportunities to convass for his *An Illustrated Description of the Russian Empire* (1849, 1855, and 1856 editions are known), *Pictorial History of China and India* (annual stereotyped editions between 1850 and 1855), Neff's *Thrilling Incidents of the Wars of the United States* (five Sears editions between 1851 and 1860), and a quarto *Pictorial Family Bible* with one thousand engravings.[26]

Palmer's renamed American Newspaper Advertising Agency, with additional offices in Boston and Philadelphia, is also advertised in an 1852 Philadelphia directory.[27] Publishers and booksellers in many other cities were soon advertising in newspapers and directories far afield. Hiram M. Rulison, the Cincinnati owner of the Queen City Publishing House between at least 1853 and 1860, advertised heavily throughout the United States and Canada, as attested by his 1853 full-page ad in Rochester, New York, which extolled his publishing, printing, stereotyping, and binding organization and which sought traveling agents with claims of over $1,200 annual profits.[28] By 1855, the Baltimore firm of M'Gregor & White was advertising its *The Traveller* as

> an efficient means of laying advertisements directly before the country trade. . . . It is now in full tide of success, and as a means of advertising, its peculiar mode of distribution [is] similar to that pursued in New York and Boston for several years past.[29]

That method involved agents distributing *The Traveller* gratis at Wheeling, Washington, Cumberland, Frederick, York, and Havre de Grace, as well as on board all passenger steamboats and trains into Baltimore. Such heavy advertising for canvassers in local newspapers must certainly have strongly influenced the number of agents being assembled by mid-century.

The method was also widespread. The Boston firm of L. P. Crown and Company ran several months of advertising in the 1854 St. John, New Brunswick, *Morning News,* seeking book agents for new pictorial, standard, historical, and religious works and looking for no fewer than a hundred canvassers to sell Timothy Shay Arthur's *The Good Time Coming,* which appeared by subscription the following year both in Boston and, twice, in Philadelphia.[30] Those newspaper advertisements were almost certainly seen at St. John by the young Sarah Emma Edmonds, a local farm girl who left in 1858 to begin a career as a traveling Bible canvasser and Nova Scotia agent, camouflaged as a man under the alias Frank Thompson, for Hurlburt and Company of Hartford. Her ruse worked so well that she later was able to enlist in a Michigan regiment in the Civil War, occasionally volunteered to spy behind Confederate lines "disguised" as a woman, and published in 1865 a fictional account of her army experience as *Nurse and Spy in the Union Army,* issued by subscription only through W. S. Williams, the successor to the Hartford company for whom she had earlier worked. The book was distributed in conjunction with Jones Brothers in Philadelphia and Cincinnati and J. A. Stoddard in Chicago. One of myriads of Civil War subscription tales, it is said to have sold 175,000 copies; a single agent's prospectus for it at the University of Chicago lists a full 118 subscribers from three very rural townships in Perry County, Pennsylvania.[31]

With the exceptions of H. H. Bancroft's marketing of his own *Works* during the 1880s, Henry Howe's publishing at Cincinnati, the American Publishing Company's extensive correspondence with Mark Twain, and the yet unexplored William Still scheme to market his *Underground Rail Road* from Philadelphia, there really exists little in the way of substantial archival sources on the numerous subscription publishers.[32] Finding information about the general agents for those publishers and the agents' own local canvassers presents even graver problems, as many of the local canvassers were moonlighting individuals who briefly flirted with the hope of quick money and more often than not bowed rapidly out of the enterprise. At the local level, it was an occupation hardly conducive to a sedentary life or economic stability. George F. Carter of New Haven provides a good example of that instability. In the 1854–55 city directory, his occupation is given as blacksmith, but in the next three annual directories he is identified as a book and magazine agent. The year 1858–59 saw him back as a carriage smith, and his wife, Mary, identified as a book agent. Thereafter, both disappear from the directories.[33] William H. Penn, who lived at 123 Chapel Street in Lowell, Massachusetts, apparently found the life of an agent short, if not brutish. On January 28, 1875, he signed and dated his new prospectus outfit for Charles Sutton's exposé of New York criminality, *The New York Tombs* (published in 1873 and reissued in 1874 by the New York subscription consortium United States Publishing Company, as well as in 1874 by Anton Roman in San Francisco). Penn then recorded one paid subscriber on his first day and two not marked as paid on the following day. The remainder of the ledger is blank; Penn apparently decided that either the title was not parlor-table-bound or he was not cut out for the job.[34]

Extant sources which are, however, useful in determining the network for nineteenth-century subscription publishing are the numerous city directories of the period and the surviving agents' prospectuses and other ephemera. Microformatted sets of many of the former are now available, and a few collections of prospectuses, namely, those at the Library of Congress, the American Antiquarian Society, and Northwestern University, and an important private collection of about 1,400 dummies contain relevant material. Using these resources, it is possible to trace briefly the spread of the subscription network across the country from its New England inception.

Early East Coast Subscription Activity

The rise of the school district library systems and the early use of agricultural magazine subscription in New England and upstate New York were probably instrumental in the early rise of the publisher's agent during the second quarter of the nineteenth century.[35] For example, in New Haven in 1840 the bookselling firm Barnett and Roberts served as a publisher's agent for the School District Library being offered by Harper & Brothers and for the Methodist Book Depot. Both William Hyde and the firm of Colmon, Holden & Co. in Portland, Maine, claimed to be authorized agents for most American publishing houses and periodicals by 1834. By August of 1845, Hyde, Lord & Duren, the Portland successor to William Hyde, were proposing

> to add to the stock on the shelves, all works of value that can be obtained, and by the facilities at our command, to provide for the increasing demands for the books in this State. . . . Constant addition will be made, both of the new books as they issue from the press, and of old standard works.[36]

The term "standard works" during this early period is often a signal for subscription titles, and a reference occurs to them even earlier in an 1837 ad of Weeks, Jordan & Co. in Boston, which offers standard and miscellaneous books and mentions their "agency for American and English publications, comprising subscription books and periodicals of every description."[37] An 1851 Hartford directory identifies as subscription publishers Silas Andrus, Lucius Stebbins, and Case, Tiffany & Co.; names two book agents; and notes that employment will be given to agents by the publisher-bookseller Aaron C. Goodman and Co.[38] Although Nathan Whiting had published in New Haven much earlier, and earlier periodical and schoolbook agents were active in that town, the 1859–60 New Haven directories first identify nine book agents, including Alfred Woodward, who (as an agent for New York's Virtue and Co.) advertised a series of pictorial lives, histories, and family Bibles. Alfred's relative, Marcus, lived with him and is simply styled a "book deliverer."[39] The number of book agents at Boston, after Michael Burns's 1836 appearance selling Hilliard & Gray subscription titles, increased to thirteen by 1851. The 1854 Boston directory also identifies another major growing component of subscription selling, engravings. The publisher and bookseller Frederick Parker offered subscription engravings of "A Glimpse of an English Homestead," "The Landing of the Pilgrim Fathers," "Shakespeare and His Contemporaries," and "A Portrait of Robert Burns."[40] The year 1857 witnessed the arrival in Boston of the firms of B. B. Russell and Sanborn, Carter & Bazin and an agency for the New York firm Virtue. A year later, the entire subscription line of D. Appleton of New York was also represented in Boston. By 1860 W. S. Weightman acted as New England general agent for Johnson, Fry & Co. of New York and was selling Schroeder's *Life and Times of Washington,* Spencer's *National History of the United States,* and (in installments of forty parts at twenty-five cents each) Henry Dawson's *The Battles of the United States.* Weightman also was advertising for "men of good address" to serve as agents.[41]

New England's post-Civil War subscription publishing mushroomed quickly. In the 1870–71 Hartford directory are sixteen identifiable subscription publishers, many of them spun off from previous firms. Noting those operating on their own that year, it is interesting to backtrack through earlier directories to ascertain where they had acquired their experience in subscription publishing. Six years earlier (1864–65) only the firms of O. D. Case and Lucius Stebbins were mentioned in the directory, although S. S. Scranton was also connected then as an agent for the firm of Hurlburt. By 1865–66, Scranton served as an agent for the newly created American Publishing Company (as did John B. Burr, who by 1870–71 began operating independently). Alfred D. Worthington (of Worthington, Dustin & Co. by 1870–71) had started in 1867 as a lowly clerk of the new Hartford Publishing Co., but had become its secretary one year later. Richard W. Bliss, an accountant in 1868–69, directed his own subscription firm by 1870–71.

Much of this illustrates the rather interlocking directorates of many of those companies. The well-known American Publishing Company at Hartford under Elisha Bliss was, in effect, publishing (via relatives and associates) by subscription under many imprints, including Belknap and Bliss, Richard W. Bliss, F. C. Bliss, the Mutual Publishing Company, and the Columbian Book Company—all at Hartford during the early 1870s. As Mark Twain advised William Dean Howells in 1887, "If you want to write the Mutual Publishing Company, address the American Publishing Company—the former is buried in the stomach of the latter."[42]

General subscription agencies sprang up throughout New England after the war. The 1869 Boston directory is the first in that city to include the heading "book agents," and the directories of the following decade are filled with references to such general agents as N. C. Goddard, representing *Zell's Encyclopedia,* and Henry Hale, who both managed the Boston agency of Hubbard Brothers of Philadelphia and also served as a general agent for Homeopathic Mutual Life Insurance. Benjamin R. Sturges appeared between 1870 and 1878 as an agent for the New York subscription house of Wells & Coffin, but also sold "Leffingwell's patent gas governors" on the side. The 1881 directory lists at least fifteen subscription publishers or agencies out of a group of 159 booksellers and publishers in the city, including the better-known firms of Estes & Lauriat and Benjamin B. Russell, as well as out-of-town agencies for A. S. Barnes, Scribners, P. F. Collier, Harpers, and Hubbard Brothers.[43] Ten years earlier in Boston, a broadside circular for the subscription house of I. N. Richardson explained the nature of that firm's business to prospective agents. It stated that subscription publishing in America, "though of comparatively recent origin, and yet in its infancy," was nevertheless extensive and would soon be superseding bookstores. Its regular canvassing agents were purportedly already making one to three thousand dollars annually, coming with high moral standards, and receiving 40 percent of the book's price. Surviving prospectuses identify only three Richardson titles: Warren Goss's *The Soldier's Story of His Captivity* (issued in 1870 jointly with S. C. Thompson in Chicago), David Ross Locke's satirical *The Struggles . . . of Petroleum V. Nasby* (issued in 1872 with a joint St. Louis address in the imprint), and W. H. H. Murray's *Among the Adirondacks*. Ivory N. Richardson last appeared as a publisher in 1875, but was described two years later as a lawyer at the same address.[44]

At Portland, Maine, Chase W. Atwell's advertising agency not only received ads for the major Maine newspapers by 1869 but also sought subscription book agents. O. D. Case of Hartford must have been the major supplier of books, as Atwell needed canvassers for Franklin Chamberlin's *American Commercial Law, Relating to Every Kind of Business* (Case editions of 1869 and 1870), David Camp's *Key and Questions to Camp's Physical and Political Outline Maps* (an 1870 Case edition), Samuel Baker's *Exploration of the Nile Tributaries of Abyssinia* (1868 and 1871 Case editions), Camp's *The American Yearbook and National Register for 1869*, and Alexander Cruden's *Concordance to the Holy Scriptures* (probably one of several editions by A. J. Johnson of New York).[45]

Subscription Publishing in the Middle Atlantic Region

Marjorie Stafford erroneously suggested in 1943 that such larger publishing centers as Boston, New York, and Philadelphia had but three or four subscription houses each in 1869—a figure which (as has been seen for Boston alone) is ridiculously low.[46] An 1847 New York directory lists a full thirty-two wholesale booksellers, among whom at least seven can be spotted selling subscription books; the even larger list of "publishers" includes many others. Subscription publishers were active in New York by the early 1840s. The previously mentioned Robert Sears arrived there in 1839 from St. John, New Brunswick, and published heavily illustrated books, including 25,000 sets of his three-volume *Pictorial Illustrations of the Bible.*[47]

There are hints that the earlier Connecticut developments were transferred to New York's burgeoning book production industry. David F. Robinson, who began as an employee of Silas Andrus in Hartford and developed subscription book and schoolbook production there, relocated to New York during the 1840s. Robinson's own former employee, Albert S. Barnes, also arrived there by 1845, where he focused upon voluminous schoolbook production.

However, in the late 1840s and early 1850s, Barnes's company also issued many biographical subscription works, mostly connected with the American hero of the Mexican War, General Winfield Scott. Edward Mansfield's illustrated biography of Scott was issued in New York several times from 1847 onward (it sold 100,000 copies), as was his history of the Mexican War.[48] Fascination over the opening of California also caught the attention of Barnes and other subscription publishers. Nehemiah Nafis and Charles Cornish, who appear in New York directories by 1841, were issuing T. F. Farnham's *Life, Adventures and Travel in California* by 1849 in conjunction with Van Dien and Macdonald in St. Louis and were floating a proposal for publishing by subscription a "pictorial edition" of the same by mid-January of 1850. Nafis and Cornish also targeted the Canadian market by 1849, bringing in H. S. Samuels, who was reported to have had great familiarity with the Canadian book trade.[49] By 1846, Leavitt, Trow & Co., H. M. Onderdonk, George Virtue, and Daniel Appleton had also joined the ranks of subscription publishers.[50] Right in the middle of an 1853–54 directory appears a four-page ad for the publisher Alexander Montgomery at 17 Spruce Street, who would receive subscriptions for and deliver travelogues and histories of the Swiss, English, or Magyar peoples; *The Ladies' Work-Book;* a history of the painters of all nations; and two serial publications. Montgomery's ad also solicited agents throughout the United States and British America.[51]

James Cephas Derby arrived in New York City late in 1853, after having successfully launched subscription publishing in the upstate town of Auburn, New York, with Samuel Goodrich's *History of All Nations,* William Seward's life of Zach Taylor (forty thousand copies), and *Fern Leaves from Fanny's Portfolio* (eighty thousand copies during the first year). He joined later with Edwin Jackson in New York and Norman Miller in Auburn to continue subscription selling. The Derby and Jackson partnership, which finally dissolved in 1861, published over three hundred volumes (a good number of them by subscription). The Derby connection in upstate New York, through James's brother George H. Derby at Buffalo, was also important, of course, for the rise of Hubert H. Bancroft in San Francisco, himself a noted subscription publisher after the Civil War.[52]

At Buffalo, George Derby was an avid promoter of subscription publishing, operating his wholesale bookstore at Buffalo under the motto "small profits on numerous transactions" and advertising for agents to sell "new and valuable publications."[53] George Derby's Buffalo competitor Phinney & Co. also sought agents for selling throughout the United States and Canada; by 1857 the Phinney firm seems to have become general agents for the books of at least eight New York and Boston publishers. Neighboring Rochester also witnessed early subscription agencies, as was noted earlier.[54] Rochester booksellers, such as Garret & Co., D. M. Dewey, Erastus Darrow, and Ransom Curran, were constantly advertising during the 1850s and 1860s for salesmen wanted to obtain and fill orders for subscription books and engravings. Curran's large directory ads between 1864 and 1866 cry for more agents to peddle John Gunn's *New Domestic Physician,* Bayard Taylor's *Cyclopedia of Modern Travel,* Fleetwood's *Life of Christ,* and several sentimental engravings by Samuel Sartain. Curran also claimed branch offices in 1866 at Albany, Boston, Pittsburgh, Cincinnati, Cleveland, and Chicago.[55] The New York City firm of Johnson, Fry & Co. arrived in Rochester that same year, represented by its agent George Groutage, who also was advertising for competent canvassers by 1870. Appleton soon had two agents in Rochester, one selling *Picturesque America* and the other selling its *American Cyclopedia.* The Boston firm of Estes & Lauriat set up its agency there by 1878. The subscription book department of the American News Company arrived in Rochester one year later. Its local manager, H. B. Graves, advertised for "first-class canvassers" for its thirty-six subscription books being offered in 1880. Note should also be made of the local bookseller James G. Ardrey, who represented *four* different New York subscription houses in 1877.[56]

Philadelphia's subscription publishing was already well entrenched by the Civil War, with all of its essential components in place. By 1860, the city's combined book manufacturing totaled about $5.6 million annually and included 4 type foundries, 7 stereotyping foundries (employing 180 people), 80 printing offices, 60 binderies and blank-book manufactories, 9 paper mills, and a large number of lithographers, engravers, and stationers.[57] Seven years later Edwin Freedley's guide to the city's manufacturing could report that J. B. Lippincott alone was annually setting up twenty thousand octavo pages of "new standard works," plus storing in its vaults the stereotyped plates for over two hundred volumes. Freedley also noted that, of the city's 120 booksellers, about fifty would "occasionally publish a book when assured of a sufficient sale to justify reasonable expectations of profit." Among the city's better known subscription firms were those of John E. Potter, J. W. Bradley, Getz & Co., P. Garrett & Co., the Quaker City Publishing House of Duane Rulison, and the Jones Brothers. Potter apparently sold his first stereotyped work in 1854 (it sold forty thousand copies), and his catalog of 1867 is said to have included over five hundred titles in expensive bindings; he had one-quarter of a million dollars in sales annually. He also was a major publisher of the temperance literature of T. S. Arthur and produced over one hundred different styles of Bibles. William Harding, publisher of the *Philadelphia Inquirer*, continued his father's huge Bible manufactory and also extensively produced photographic albums for subscription selling, as did the aforementioned Samuel Burlock.[58]

The important Philadelphia subscription genre of illustrated biographies owed much to the early activities of James Longacre in publishing by subscription his series of engravings for the *National Portrait Gallery* between 1834 and the mid-1840s. The panic of 1837, a bindery fire, and flagging subscriptions forced him gradually to peddle his remaining sets through local agencies. Longacre's letters of 1836 regarding two agents conflicting over selling subscriptions in Cincinnati indicate that he had attempted to extend his network broadly, and his May 8, 1837, letter to a prospective agent in Pulaski, Tennessee, stressed his highest agent discount to be 30 percent (or 25 percent for sales of fewer than one hundred copies).[59] Although Longacre's network did not save him from eventual ruin, it set a precedent for later subscription firms selling illustrated biographies, who soon assembled them by using cut-and-paste snippets of other collected biographies, produced with wood engravings on cheap paper. William H. Brown's *Portrait Gallery of Distinguished American Citizens* (a Hartford subscription product of the Kellogg Brothers) and Benson Lossing's 1855 *Our Countrymen* and 1857 *Eminent Americans* led directly to the post-Civil War mug books of the later subscription publishers, which immortalized any farmer or town blacksmith able to pay the hefty fees required for inclusion.[60]

Pictorial biographies and other works were already receiving full-page advertising in Philadelphia by 1848. Charles J. Gillis was by then seeking book canvassers and agents in every state of the Union to peddle John Frost's *Pictorial Life of Washington* and three-volume *Pictorial History of the World* (the latter having already been sold in nine thousand copies in seven states over the previous two years). H. Hastings Weld's *The Pictorial Life of General Lafayette* was also then listed as in press. Gillis's competitor, J. W. Bradley, first appears in a city directory of 1849 as a publisher of subscription books and schoolbooks; he too was advertising heavily for agents one year later, and by 1860 Bradley titles were being itemized in local directories.[61] Other Philadelphia publishers quickly followed.

Dr. Frost, a Philadelphia schoolmaster, soon became a subscription publisher himself, and was joined during the 1850s by the Gihon firm, H. Cowperthwaite, J. T. Altemus, Duane Rulison, John Potter, the bookseller T. Elwood Zell, T. B. Peterson, and a bevy of others.[62] By 1856, the firm of Leary & Getz could call itself city headquarters for publishers' canvassers, book agents, and peddlers.[63] Out-of-town agencies were also soon in abundance, with representatives arriving for Appleton, Virtue & Yorston, Johnson and Fry (all of New York), and the London (Ontario) Printing & Publishing Company. Local agents within the city also began their own advertising. George W. Hankinton alternated between careers as a brick-layer and a book agent during the early 1860s and, then, found his later calling as a commissioner of highways at the end of the Civil War.[64] By 1868 the firm of Zeigler, McCurdy & Co. (the name would later change to Ziegler & McCurdy, and the company would have an important Chicago branch) was seeking a thousand agents.[65]

The Baltimore directories first reflect the arrival of book agents towards the middle of the Civil War, with the local bookseller James Sheehy dominating the list, although the New York firms of Johnson, Fry & Co., and Virtue & Yorston also had representatives in the city. Sheehy may have had some type of monopoly, as he advertised himself alone as "agent for all subscription books" in 1868–69. One year later, however, the floodgates had been opened, and a full fourteen book and subscription agents were then identified at Baltimore.[66]

Subscription Books in the American Interior

Walter Sutton's exemplary study of the nineteenth-century Cincinnati book trade lists more than thirty firms or agents operating in a subscription context. Agents of other publishers predominated in this western market, a good example being C. W. James, who operated as a traveling collector and agent for eastern and western publishers between 1838 and 1856. H. C. Gillis was promoting John Frost's Philadelphia edition of the *Pictorial History of the World* in Cincinnati by 1845. At least ten firms between 1847 and 1875 advertised themselves as employers of agents, although a number of those may have been periodical subscription agents.[67] Among the major Cincinnati subscription publishing firms was that of Henry Howe, state historian and both author and publisher of what were exclusively subscription books, who began operations about 1847 and ended them in 1878. An 1855 prospectus for six of his works (*Ohio Historical Collections, Travels and Adventures, Life and Death on the Ocean, Historical Collections of the Great West, Emblems and Allegories,* and *Illustrated Proverbs*) offered agents generous terms of 40–50 percent of the subscription price. Sample dummy books were priced between $1.08 and $2.14, and a separate ledger prospectus for garnering subscribers' names would be mailed for $.78. Howe was adamant about avoiding high subscription prices and repudiated dumping subscription titles at a discount upon booksellers (he even occasionally printed the subscription price on the title page in order to discourage discounting to booksellers).[68] Hiram Rulison's Queen City Publishing House is suggested by Sutton to have been active from 1853 to 1860, although other evidence places his operations in Cincinnati by about 1848; as was noted earlier, he was already advertising subscription books in upstate New York by 1853.[69] Several eastern publishers were also represented by their subscription agents, including Appleton from New York (1854), Crosby & Nichols of Boston (1855), and the three Philadelphia firms of Cowperthwaite (1857), Jones Brothers (1865–67), and the National Publishing Company (1866–72). Indication of the rising Chicago influence occurs in 1872 with the appearance of a Cincinnati agency for J. W. Goodspeed.[70] Indeed, Cincinnati's domination of the country's interior book trade waned considerably with the loss of its southern markets during the 1860s. With the strengthening of the nation's railway hub about Chicago, that city loomed more significantly as a subscription publishing center during the 1870s and 1880s. William H. Moore, who had stressed subscription books at Cincinnati, reported by 1874 that that type of business was entirely flat in southern Ohio; he moved to Chicago, where he apparently continued to publish Gunn's *New Family Physician* and served as agent for other subscription firms at the end of the decade.[71]

Two surviving agents' autobiographies were, however, written by agents operating out of Cincinnati. Annie Nelles spent the period 1865–67 there, according to Sutton, although her 1867 autobiographical account *The Life of a Book Agent* also showed her on the road to Detroit and Chicago during that period.[72] Ebenezer Hannaford, listed at Cincinnati in 1871 as an employer of agents, and possibly a subscription publisher, apparently copyrighted in 1875 his manual *Success in Canvassing,* although the earliest extant edition was published in pamphlet form in 1878 in San Francisco by Anton Roman as a guide for the latter's agents in the Far West. A printed author's note on the verso mentions obligations to Henry Howe, "the veteran subscription publisher of America, whose observations have been drawn upon with especial freedom," and suggests Hannaford may have had considerable contact with Howe.[73]

Throughout the midwestern cities, a subscription bookselling pattern generally developed shortly before the Civil War. Most of the actual production seems to have been done in the East, with the later exceptions of St. Louis and Chicago. What really counted in those areas was the distribution network itself, which usually entailed the arrival of general agents in the major cities, who then advertised for local canvassers in newspapers or annual directories. Canvassers' outfits were obtainable either through the general agencies or directly from the subscription publishers in the case of areas at considerable distances from the important cities.

By 1853, James Crawford's bookstore in St. Louis was offering stock to agents, peddlers, and canvassers; by 1859 four subscription book agents were active in the city. A general agent for Johnson, Fry and Company's *History of the War* and other illustrated books was leasing space there by 1863. By 1869, agents for Zeigler, McCurdy & Co., Charles Scribner, the National Publishing Company, the United States Publishing Company, and the Southern Publishing Company (the last-named offering *Lee and His Generals* and claiming branches in Louisville, Memphis, and Mobile) were also present. As of 1881, the city could boast at least eighteen subscription publishers, agencies, or advertising canvassers.[74]

Although it lacks river access, Indianapolis had at least one bookstore by 1855, which was seeking "enterprising men" for such popular subscription works as Belcher's *History of the Religious Denominations of the United States,* Edward Beecher's *The Papal Conspiracy Exposed,* Fleetwood's *Life of Christ,* the *Domestic Bible,* and Cruden's *Concordance.* A few agents appeared during the Civil War, and J. S. Reeves was seeking agents by 1865. By 1872 Samuel C. Vance advertised himself in Indianapolis as a dealer in first-class subscription titles of several East Coast publishers, as did three others. Vance had been a bank employee the previous year. Seven publishers' agents appeared in the 1880 directory.[75]

Other midwestern cities were targeted by agents *after* the Civil War. R. W. Bliss & Company left Hartford and set up in Toledo by 1869. Warren E. Bliss was noted as an agent there the following year, sharing a house on Elm Street with Otis Browning, another agent who shortly thereafter became an independent subscription publisher in the town. By 1880 the Browning Publishing Company was competing in Toledo for available canvassers and sales with John Stone and P. T. Kavanaugh—the latter advertising "subscription books of all kinds completed and bound at lowest prices."[76]

At Peoria an agent for semimonthly parts of Zell's Philadelphia-based *Encyclopedia* was active by 1870. George W. Borland, a New York native, soon joined with an Indianapolis resident named A. Jordan in selling subscription books out of the Peoria Post Office Book Store in 1876. By 1879, Borland had left the Peoria operations in the hands of Marcellus Jewett and, apparently, left for Chicago, where he gained by 1883 the reputation of having "a live, wide-awake subscription-book house doing an unprecedented business ..." with alleged international operations extending to Europe and Australia.[77]

At Des Moines, agents surely must have been active by 1869, when a revised city ordinance required itinerant agents selling books or maps by subscription (newspapers and magazines excepted) to pay a license fee of ten dollars monthly or twenty-five dollars for three months. Such local licenses for subscription agents may have been rather common, as two young female agents had discovered in 1853 at Petersburg, Virginia, when they were hounded by that city's commissioner of revenue for lacking licenses. Local booksellers in many towns apparently feared such competition and often reported canvassing agents to authorities. The previously mentioned Mrs. Likins was also briefly arrested at Stockton, California, in 1869 but was then told she did not legally require a license there.[78] Des Moines's other agencies appeared rather late, with Appleton represented by 1877–78 and George W. Borland (by then of Chicago) and the Jones Brothers of Cincinnati established in the Iowa town by 1881–82.[79]

Further north, the first agents are attested in Minneapolis and St. Paul in 1874 and 1875, respectively. Estes & Lauriat of Boston had an agent in the former by 1878, and five agencies were in place there by 1881–82. Six different subscription agents operated out of St. Paul that same year, including agencies for P. F. Collier, George Virtue, and Chicago-based Borland.[80]

Costly subscription books were first advertised by the Chicago bookseller S. C. Griggs in an 1859 directory, which also first mentioned two book agents, Owen Griffiths and Myron Pierce, on Lake Street. The Chicago directories during the Civil War document a steady increase in the number of general agents for the eastern publishers. Griffiths represented Virtue & Co., but was then superseded as the Virtue agent by Walter Cottle (1862–63), who himself was replaced in 1864–65, when John Gibson became manager of the general western agency of Virtue, Yorston, & Co. By war's end, Griffiths had moved to serve the recently arrived subscription firm of Johnson, Fry & Co. of New York. The publishers' agency of Erastus B. and Royal C. Treat had already set up by 1863. Philadelphia-based Ziegler, McCurdy & Co. arrived at Chicago in 1866–67, while C. F. Vent of Cincinnati and O. D. Case & Co. of Hartford appeared two years later. During the early 1870s book agencies for A. S. Barnes, Scribners, the National Publishing Company, J. B. Ford, Jones Brothers, Sheldon & Co. of New York, Zell, Cowperthwaite, and Osgood & Co. appeared in Chicago.[81] Warren Moses represented Appleton in 1868 (and also briefly served J. M. Stoddart of Philadelphia); by 1873 Moses was independently publishing *Hill's Manual of Social and Business Forms*, which is said to have sold 355,000 copies by 1892. Thomas Hill, the *Manual*'s author, bought out rights about 1881 and issued only it and *The Album of Biography and Art* under his new imprint, the Hill Standard Book Company—with such success that it had 1,200 agents active in Canada and the United States by 1885.[82] With excellent railway connections into the midwestern hinterlands, Chicago and its subscription publishing continued to expand so that by 1893 that local industry employed about 22,000 people.[83] Indicative of Chicago's control is a certificate of agency, which L. K. McIntyre, general agent for the Chicago-based Western Publishing House, gave J. W. Neals of Cedar Rapids, Iowa, on July 7, 1875, for selling its 1873 Bible and Livingstone's *Travels* with a 40 percent agent's discount. Unfortunately for Neals, the territory assigned was located in Floyd, Cerro Gordo, and Butler counties, which meant for the agent over 100 miles of travel northeast of Cedar Rapids.[84]

The Western Subscription Market

As was noted earlier, the western expansion and California experience were popular subscription book subjects by the early 1850s. Subscription agents arrived in San Francisco upon the heels of the gold rush. By 1852 the Philadelphia firm of Gihon and Johnson appeared in a San Francisco directory. Two years later, Charles Kimball's Noisy Carriers Publishing Hall on the Long Wharf offered not only issues of *Gleason's* and other cheap publications, but also bound Bibles, imprints of DeWitt & Davenport and Stringer & Townsend, and a great variety of Peterson's Philadelphia subscription imprints.[85] Hubert H. Bancroft, upon his arrival from Buffalo, found twelve bookstores in San Francisco and eight in Sacramento, and financial and publishing support from George H. Derby allowed the formal opening of H. H. Bancroft and Company in December of 1856. His new building was completed by 1870 with its subscription department on the second floor. The story of Bancroft's subscription network for his *Native Races* and other *Works* has been told in great detail. As holder of the entire western agency, the Bancrofts sent agents as far afield as Bozeman, Montana.[86] Bancroft's major bookselling competitor, Anton Roman, had finally set up in San Francisco by 1857 with a stock of standard and miscellaneous eastern publications and began his own publishing in 1860. In an 1868 city directory, he joined seven other firms which were for the first time listed as subscription book agencies. In 1879 Roman's publishing business finally collapsed, but he did resume his earlier career as a general agent for subscription books until leaving the book business completely in 1888.[87]

With the rapid settlement of the rural areas along the Pacific coast, San Francisco served as an important locus for general subscription agents who represented the East Coast publishers. An 1864 San Francisco directory first mentions the early partnership of Francis Dewing and Jeremiah Laws as importers of subscription books; within two years each was operating independently in the same field. Others swiftly joined that group, including Henry Payot, the Pacific Publishing Company, the Traver brothers, and Robert J. Trumbull.[88] Trumbull's career can be traced through several local directories—he served first as a compositor for a local book and job printer (1864), then dealt in photographic albums (1865), and finally became a subscription agent. His general agency for such books disappeared from the directories by 1872. However, Trumbull had Oregon agents afield, as is attested by a September 22, 1868, shipping invoice for a case of books worth $156, which he shipped to his agent H. H. Woodward in Roseburg, Oregon, via Marks & Co. of that town, who were in turn instructed to let Woodward take out only a few books for canvassing at a time.[89] The Portland directories during the mid-1860s generally listed San Francisco firms for standard works, and Michael Flood, a San Francisco canvasser, was in Portland by 1865. In 1868 S. J. McCormick's Franklin Book Store in Portland stressed the availability of such standard works "at San Francisco wholesale prices." One local agent there named David Halpruner canvassed from 1871 to 1875, but became a gasfitter later. His local competitor, F. F. Heroy, likewise gave up books after one year in 1873–74 and became a sewing machine agent thereafter.[90]

Back in the Bay Area, 14 subscription agents were present by 1881.[91] An 1872 business guide specifically mentioned Henry Keller and Co., which was said to be the exclusive agent for the East's largest houses and to have between ten and twenty agents leaving San Francisco monthly for distant points in Utah, Nevada, Oregon, and California. Keller frequently sold subscription works in parts, then having them bound by his book-binding subsidiary, Daniel Hicks and Co. Twenty-six subscription titles (mostly issued in parts) by this paired enterprise are given in an 1873 city directory, with titles of standard, illustrated works ranging from Fleetwood to the *National Portrait Gallery of Eminent Americans* (fifty-two parts at fifty cents each), Dore's *Gallery* (fifty parts at one dollar each), and a forty-seven installment *History of the United States* (at fifty cents per part).[92]

Illustrative of a West Coast subscription agent's activities is the little-known career, between 1868 and 1874, of Mrs. James W. Likins, who worked for both the Bancroft and Roman firms, canvassing the books for which they served as western agents. During her first year, Likins was given San Francisco, Santa Clara, and San Joaquin counties by Bancroft for selling engravings of Grant (just before his election), Lincoln, Washington, and Washington Irving. Her first assigned book was Mark Twain's *Innocents Abroad,* for which she received one of the three San Francisco districts in August of 1869. She also hawked Laura Langford's *Ladies of the White House* and Albert Evans's *Our Sister Republic.* The year 1871 brought her the San Francisco territory for George McWalter's *Knots Untied; or, Ways and By-ways in the Hidden Life of American Detectives* (an 1871 Hartford edition of J. B. Burr & Hyde), William Cullen Bryant's *Poetry and Songs,* a *Life of Barnum, Woman's Pilgrimage in the Holy*

Land, and *Cuba with Pen and Pencil.* By March of the following year she had begun working for Roman's bookstore, where she received territory in Santa Clara County and part of San Francisco for Mark Twain's *Roughing It* and also met two other women canvassers in the shop. Later that year, Roman had her selling *The Great Industries of the United States,* and, upon her return to San Francisco, Bancroft gave her the central business district for Stanley's *How I Found Livingstone.* Roman offered her the same territory in 1873 for Seward's *His Voyage Around the World* (she completed the business district canvass in five weeks and then took it to Gilroy), but she also was hawking General McClellan's *The Golden States; or, West of the Rocky Mountains.* Bancroft sent her to Watsonville and Santa Cruz with Albert Evans's *A la California,* while Roman later assigned her Josh Billings's (i.e., Henry Wheeler Shaw's) *Everybody's Friend,* an 1874 American Publishing Company compilation of wit and humor with Thomas Nast illustrations. Likins finished her subscription career with an 1874 canvass of Mark Twain's *Gilded Age,* a life of Sumner, and Johnson's *Sketches of the War.*[93]

> It is one of the mysteries of publishers' craft, which only they can explain, that subscription books have a larger sale than those which see the light in an ordinary way.[94]

Such rueful remarks from a mid-1870 book trade journal reflect the early success subscription books enjoyed. This survey has attempted to outline the swiftness and extent of the spread of the network for selling those books. Its stereotyped products involved continuous reprintings from the same plates, modified only by minor changes in title pages or other preliminary material; and its agency system, using improved transportation links, brought books thousands of miles from their places of production. Thus, one ought not be too surprised by Hubbard Brothers editions of the 1870s, which bear imprints containing title page references to eight or even eleven "publishers" and their regional agencies. An 1875 Philadelphia edition of Chambliss's *The Life and Labor of David Livingstone* bears an imprint statement of the Hubbard Brothers at Philadelphia, Boston, and Cincinnati; A. L. Bancroft in San Francisco; F. A. Hutchinson at both St. Louis and Chicago; H. A. W. Blackburn at Detroit; Schuyler & Smith at London, Ontario; G. L. Benjamin at Fond du Lac, Wisconsin; and finally Moore & Oliver at Davenport, Iowa. A slightly later reprinting of the same book added the names of M. M. Burnham at Syracuse and John Killam at Yarmouth, Nova Scotia.[95] Three extant but variant agents' prospectuses for Thomas Knox's *Life and Work of Henry Ward Beecher* bear identical dates of 1887—two are placed in Hartford for S. S. Scranton and the Hartford Publishing Company, and the third in Philadelphia for the International Publishing Company.[96] A local agent could also simply rubber-stamp his own imprint over a previous one, as Royal Treat, the Chicago bookseller, did with an 1872 Philadelphia edition of T. S. Arthur's *Three Years in a Man-Trap*.[97]

The spread of subscription books was really not so mysterious as its detractors might pretend. By employing a distribution network which seems to have already been well in place before the Civil War, by advertising and canvassing locally throughout the country, and by distributing books directly to their buyers, this publishing phenomenon truly transformed book dissemination in the nineteenth century. The sales figures are rather astonishing (even if rather exaggerated claims have been made). Between 1861 and 1868, Hartford subscription firms are said to have made $5 million, with 16,000 agents having sold 1,426,000 books. Bliss's American Publishing Company sold almost 338,000 copies for Mark Twain between 1869 and 1879. Greeley's *American Conflict* is said by 1871 to have been bought by 225,000 subscribers.[98] William Still, with a one-title operation for his *The Underground Rail Road*, told prospective agents he anticipated 100,000 sales and often held up as an example his excellent Baltimore agent who could sell (after five earlier agents had failed in the same locale) 300 subscriptions in about six weeks.[99] Printed agents' claims for an 1870 Worthington, Dustin & Co. edition of William Fowler's *Ten Years in Wall Street* suggest that a Rutland, Vermont, agent may have had 218 orders in eighteen days and that another in Elyria, Ohio, may have gathered 44 in a bit more than a day.[100]

"Why not try a little peripatetic enterprise?" asked *Publishers' Weekly* plaintively in an 1879 column, recommending that regular booksellers might emulate the subscription agents' success by sending out their younger clerks to promote sales for new books.[101] That editorial says much about the success of the network, which did, in fact, bring millions of books into the American heartland.

Notes

1. Mark Twain, *The Adventures of Huckleberry Finn* (New York: Charles L. Webster, 1885), 137.

2. Hamlin Hill, *Mark Twain and Elisha Bliss* (Columbia: University of Missouri Press, 1964) and Samuel Charles Webster, ed., *Mark Twain, Business Man* (Boston: Little, Brown and Company, 1946), chap. 25.

3. Many of the *Publishers' Weekly* attacks on the abuses are summarized by John Tebbel, *A History of Book Publishing in the United States* (New York: R. R. Bowker, 1975), vol. 2, 511–20. Bates Harrington, *How 'Tis Done: A Thorough Ventilation of the Numerous Schemes Conducted by Wandering Canvassers Together With the Various Advertising Dodges for the Swindling of the Public* (Chicago: Fidelity Publishing Company, 1879).

4. C. N. Caspar, comp., *Caspar's Directory of the American Book, News and Stationery Trade, Wholesale and Retail* (Milwaukee: C. N. Caspar's Book Emporium, 1889), 1047–49.

5. James Gilreath, "Mason Weems, Mathew Carey and the Southern Booktrade, 1794–1810," *Publishing History* no. 10 (1981), 41–42.

6. E. B. Child and W. H. Schiffer, comps., *The Albany Directory and City Register for . . . 1831–32* (Albany: E. B. Child, 1831), unpaged advertisement.

7. *Stimpson's Boston Directory . . . 1833* (Boston: Charles Stimpson, Jr., 1833), p. 100 (as a sexton and undertaker); *1834,* p. 104 (as a book agent); and *1836,* p. 8 (as an agent for the Spark's editions at the Boston shop of Hilliard & Gray).

8. *The Philadelphia Circulating Business Directory for 1838* (Philadelphia: Morris's Xylographic Press, 1838), 11.

9. Henry J. Howland, *The Worcester Almanac, Directory and Business Advertiser for 1848* (Worcester: S. A. Howland, 1848), 124.

10. Michael Winship, "Printing with Plates in the Nineteenth Century United States," *Printing History,* no. 10 (vol. 5, no. 2, 1983): 23.

11. Stowe-Day Foundation, *Hartford As a Publishing Center in the Nineteenth Century* (Hartford: Stowe-Day Foundation, 1971); Charles Hopkins Clark, "The Press," in James Hammond Trumbull, ed., *The Memorial History of Hartford County, Connecticut, 1633–1884* (Boston: E. L. Osgood, 1886), vol. 1, 605–27; and *A Sketch Descriptive of the Printing-Office and Book-Bindery of the Case, Lockwood & Brainard Co.* (Hartford: Case, Lockwood & Brainard Co., 1877).

12. *M'Elroy's Philadelphia Directory for 1842* (Philadelphia: Orrin Rogers, 1842), 34. In *Bywater's Philadelphia Business Directory and City Guide for the Year 1849* (Philadelphia: Maurice Bywater, 1849), 61, the bindery of Miller and Burlock is listed among the city's twenty-eight binderies. Burlock may have been an active binder there even earlier, as an 1867 manufacturing guide for the city mentions that he had already been active in local bookbinding "for nearly forty years." See Edwin Freedley, *Philadelphia and Its Manufacturers; a Hand-Book of the Great Manufactories and Representative Mercantile Houses of Philadelphia in 1867* (Philadelphia: E. Young, 1867), 146, and Michael Hackenberg, "Hawking Subscription Books in 1870: A Salesman's Prospectus from Western Pennsylvania," *Papers of the Bibliographical Society of America* 78 (1984): 143.

13. Walter Sutton, *The Western Book Trade: Cincinnati As a Nineteenth-Century Publishing and Book-Trade Center* (Columbus: Ohio State University Press for the Ohio Historical Society, 1961), 70–74, 79–80.

14. That Chicago job specialization under one roof and an illustration of the new building housing it are treated in Michael Conzen's fascinating discussion, "Maps for the Masses: Alfred T. Andreas and the Midwestern County Atlas Trade," *Chicago History* vol. 13, no. 1 (1984), 46–63.

15. Early documentation on the rise of the railway express agencies can be found in Alexander Stimson, *History of the Express Companies and the Origins of the American Railroads,* 2d ed. (New York, 1858) and Henry Wells, *Sketch of the Rise, Progress, and Present Condition of the Express System* (Albany: Van Benthuysen's Steam Printing House, 1864).

16. The unpaged advertisement for the Pecks appears in *Walker's Buffalo City Directory . . . 1842,* comp. Horatio N. Walker (Buffalo: Steele's Press, 1842).

17. *Sheldon & Co.'s Business or Advertising Directory . . . 1845* (New York: John F. Trow & Company, 1845), 14–15.

18. T. Morehead, comp., *The New York Mercantile Register for 1848–49* (New York: John P. Prall, 1848), 24.

19. Sarah Ann Mendell and Margaret Hosmer, *Notes of Travel and Life, by Two Young Ladies* (New York: published for the authors, 1854), 24, 107.

20. Mrs. James W. Likins, *Six Years Experience as a Book Agent in California, Including My Trip from New York to San Francisco Via Nicaragua* (San Francisco: Women's Union Book & Job Printing Office, 1874). Her husband's occupations first appear in *The San Francisco Directory for the Year Commencing December, 1869* (San Francisco: Henry G. Langley, 1869) and continue through subsequent directories until 1874.

21. William Still Letterbook, AMS 47, pp. 574–75, 734–35, Historical Society of Pennsylvania.

22. A copy of the Carey broadside, dated December 22, 1801, is in the Rare Book and Special Collections Division, Broadside portfolio no. 151, no. 26, Library of Congress.

23. Subscription prospectus for *The English Version of the Polyglott Bible* (Franklin, N.H.: Published by Peabody & Daniell, and D. Kimball, 1843) in the private collection of Robert Seymour of Colebrook, Connecticut.

24. Subscription prospectus for *The Life of Our Lord and Saviour Jesus Christ,* by John Fleetwood (New Haven: Printed and published by Nathan Whiting, 1833), in the private collection of Robert Seymour of Colebrook, Connecticut.

25. The unpaged advertisement for Palmer's Country Newspaper Advertising Agency appears in *Doggett's New York Business Directory for 1846 & 1847* (New York: John Doggett, Jr., 1846), which also lists on pp. 200–201 the early New York subscription firms of Leavitt, Trow & Co.; Nafis & Cornish; H. M. Onderdonk; J. S. Redfield; Robert Sears; and George Virtue; among the 120 booksellers and publishers cited there were almost certainly additional firms who engaged in some early subscription activity. Palmer's agency, which began in 1841, promised booksellers and other merchants special access to southern and western markets via its advertising connections with nearly 1,000 different newspapers. See also its advertisements in the *New York Daily Tribune,* 9 Feb. 1846, 2–3.

26. James Dale Johnston, comp., *Detroit City Directory & Advertising Gazeteer of Michigan for 1855–6* (Detroit: R. F. Johnstone & Co., 1855), 70, 138, 339, for Sears's advertising. Brief biographical sketches of Robert Sears can be found in *The National Cyclopaedia of American Biography* and in the *Dictionary of American Biography.*

27. *McElroy's Philadelphia Directory for 1852* (Philadelphia: Edward C. & John Biddle, 1852), unpaged advertisement.

28. *Dewey's Rochester City Directory for 1853–54* (Rochester: D. M. Dewey, 1853), ix. On Hiram Rulison and his subscription publishing network, see Sutton, *Western Book Trade,* 219, 336; and Hackenberg, "Hawking Subscription Books in 1870," 141–42.

29. *Matchett's Baltimore Director, for 1855–56* (Baltimore: R. J. Matchett, 1855), advertisement opposite p. 331.

30. The advertisements appeared in the *Morning News,* 5 April 1854, as cited by Sylvia G. L. Dannett, *She Rode with Generals; the True and Incredible Story of Sarah Emma Seelye, Alias Franklin Thompson* (New York: Thomas Nelson and Sons, 1960), 29–30.

31. S. Emma E. Edmonds, *Nurse and Spy in the Union Army: Comprising the Adventures and Experiences of a Woman in Hospitals, Camps, and Battle-Fields* (Hartford: W. S. Williams & Co.; Philadelphia and Cincinnati: Jones Bros. & Co.; Chicago: J. A. Stoddard & Co., 1865). Further details on her fascinating career are given by Dannett, *She Rode with Generals,* passim, and by Bette L. Fladeland, s. v. "Edmonds, Sarah Emma Evelyn," in *Notable American Women 1607–1950: A Biographical Dictionary* (Cambridge, Mass.: Harvard University Press, 1971), vol. 1, 561–62. The *National Union Catalog, Pre-1956 Imprints,* vol. 155, 691, gives her surname as "Edmundson." The 1865 agent's prospectus for *Nurse and Spy in the Union Army* is housed in the Department of Special Collections, Joseph Regenstein Library at the University of Chicago. Among the subscribers named in its printed list are J. B. Russell, Lucius Stebbins, and S. S. Scranton—all early Boston or Hartford subscription publishers.

32. Harry Clark, *A Venture in History: The Production, Publication, and Sale of the Works of Hubert Howe Bancroft* (Berkeley and Los Angeles: University of California Press, 1973). For the work already done on Mark Twain's subscription activities, see the sources cited in note 2. A description of the available archival sources concerning William Still's subscription marketing of *The Underground Rail Road* (Philadelphia: Porter & Coates, 1872) can be found in *Afro-Americana, 1553–1906: Author Catalog of the Library Company of Philadelphia and the Historical Society of Pennsylvania* (Boston: G. K. Hall, 1973), 678–81. See also Larry Gara, "William Still and the Underground Railroad," *Pennsylvania History* 28 (1961): 33–44.

33. *Benham's City Directory and Annual Advertiser, 1854–55* (New Haven: J. H. Benham, 1854), 49; *1855–56,* 48; *1856–57,* 47; *1857–58,* 268; *1858–59,* 57; and *1859–60,* 295.

34. Prospectus for Charles Sutton, *The New York Tombs: Its Secrets and Its Mysteries* (New York: United States Publishing Co., 1874), in the American Antiquarian Society.

35. Sidney Ditzion, "The District-School Library, 1835–55," *Library Quarterly* 10 (1940): 564–69; and Ulysses P. Hedrick, "What Farmers Read in Western New York, 1800–1850," *New York History* 17 (1936): 281–89.

36. *Patten's New Haven Directory for the Year 1840* (New Haven: Patten, 1840), 122; *The Portland Directory* (Portland, Maine: Arthur Shirley, 1834), advertising section, 24; and *The Portland Reference Book and City Directory for 1846,* comp. S. B. Beckett (Portland, Maine: Thurston, Fenley & Co., 1846), 27.

37. *Stimpson's Boston Directory . . . 1837* (Boston: Charles Stimpson, Jr., 1837), advertising section, 8.

38. *Wells' City and Business Directory, 1851* (Hartford: J. Gaylord Wells, 1851), 158–59.

39. *Benham's New Haven Directory and Annual Advertiser . . . 1859–60, no. 20* (New Haven: J. H. Benham, 1859), 18, 289.

40. *Boston Directory for the Year 1854* (Boston: George Adams, 1854), advertising section, 49.

41. *Boston Directory for the Year 1857* (Boston: George Adams, 1857), 387; *1858,* 11; *1860,* 35.

42. *Geer's Hartford City Directory for 1870–71* (Hartford: Elihu Geer, 1870), 116, 307, 435. Mark Twain's comment is given by Hamlin Hill, *Mark Twain and Elisha Bliss,* 16.

43. *The Boston Directory . . . for the Year Commencing July 1, 1869* (Boston: Sampson, Davenport, 1869), 684; *1870,* 634, 742 (Sturges's first appearance); *1881,* 1089.

44. The 1871 I. N. Richardson broadside circular is in the Rare Book and Special Collections Division, Library of Congress, Broadside Portfolio 306, no. 40, bearing the heading "Subscription Publishing House of I. N. Richardson & Co." *The Boston Directory . . . for the Year Commencing July 1, 1875* (Boston: Sampson, Davenport, 1875), 984, lists Ivory N. Richardson as a publisher at 68 Cornhill, but *The Boston Directory . . . 1877,* 751, places him as a lawyer at the same address. Prospectuses for Warren Lee Goss's *The Soldier's Story of His Captivity at Andersonville, Belle Isle, and Other Rebel Prisons* (Boston: I. N. Richardson: Chicago: S. C. Thompson, 1870) and for David Locke's *The Struggles (Social, Financial and Political) of Petroleum V. Nasby* (Boston and St. Louis: I. N. Richardson & Co., 1872) are known. The prospectus for the latter also included an announcement for the forthcoming W. H. H. Murray's "Among the Adirondacks." But Murray's work, described as "soon ready" in the prospectus, may never have actually appeared as a Richardson imprint although it was issued by several other Boston publishers under the title *Adventures in the Wilderness; or Camp-life in the Adirondacks.* The Goss prospectus is owned by Robert Seymour of Colebrook, Connecticut, and the Locke prospectus is held by the Special Collections Department of Northwestern University Library.

45. S. B. Beckett, comp., *The Portland Directory and Reference Book with a Business Directory . . . 1869,* (Portland, Maine: B. Thurston, 1869), 37, 345.

46. Marjorie Stafford, "Subscription Book Publishing in the United States, 1865–1930" (Master's thesis, University of Illinois, 1943), 48.

47. See notes 25 and 26.

48. "Sketches of the Publishers: A. S. Barnes & Co.," *The Round Table,* 17 and 24 March 1866, 170–71, 186.

49. Coverage of the Canadian market was noted in a Nafis & Cornish advertisement in *Wilson's Business Directory of New York City, 1849* (New York: John F. Trow, 1849), xxxv. The American Antiquarian Society owns a bound prospectus (with subscription proposal dated 21 January 1850) for a pictorial edition of T. J. Farnham's *Life, Adventures and Travels in California* (New York: Nafis & Cornish; St. Louis: Nafis, Cornish & Co., 1850). When the actual book was issued that same year, the St. Louis firm of Van Dien & Macdonald also appeared in the imprint.

50. *Doggett's New York Business Directory for 1846 and 1847* (New York: John Doggett, Jr., 1846), 200–201.

51. H. Wilson, comp., *Trow's New York City Directory . . . for 1853–54* (New York: John F. Trow, 1853), four-page advertisement following p. 490.

52. James C. Derby, *Fifty Years Among Authors, Books and Publishers* (New

York: G. W. Carleton, etc., 1884). His Auburn career has been treated by Madeleine Stern, *Books and Book People in 19th-Century America* (New York: R. R. Bowker, 1978), 11–14.

53. *The Commercial Advertiser Directory for the City of Buffalo, 1848–1849* (Buffalo: Jewett, Thomas & Co., 1848), advertising section, 8; *1849–1850,* 163.

54. See above at note 28.

55. At Rochester, Curran was heavily advertising for specific subscription titles by the mid-1860s: see *Boyd's Rochester and Brockport Directory . . . 1864–5* (Rochester: D. M. Dewey; Darrow & Brother, 1864), 103, and *1866–7,* 105.

56. *The Rochester Directory . . . for the Year Commencing July 1, 1870* (Rochester: C. C. Drew, 1870), 94, 265; *1878,* 138, 181, 522, and 650 for the two Appleton agencies of Charles Glover and Charles K. Judson and 650 for the agency of Ferdinand Kaiser for the Boston firm of Estes & Lauriat. James Ardrey represented J. M. Stoddart, Johnson & Miles, Gebbie & Barrie, and J. B. Ford in 1877, *The Rochester Directory . . . for 1877,* 527. See also *The Rochester Directory . . . for 1880,* 561.

57. *Cowell's Philadelphia Business Directory, 1860* (Philadelphia: E. J. Cowell, 1860), 14.

58. Freedley, *Philadelphia and Its Manufacturers,* 146–47, 152–54 (including full-page advertisements for Harding, Burlock, and Potter).

59. Longacre to a Mr. Greenleaf in Cincinnati, 3 October 1836, and Longacre to Cyrus Hawley in Pulaski, Tennessee, 8 May 1837 (extract), James B. Longacre Letterbook, Historical Society of Pennsylvania. An excellent discussion of Longacre's *National Portrait Gallery* is given by Gordon Marshall, "The Golden Age of Illustrated Biographies: Three Case Studies," in *American Portrait Prints: Proceedings of the Tenth Annual American Print Conference,* ed. Wendy Wick Reaves (Charlottesville: University Press of Virginia, 1984), 29–82.

60. Marshall, "The Golden Age," 67–71. The post-Civil War mug book has been treated by Oscar Lewis, "Mug Books," *The Colophon,* pt. 17 (1934, unpaged); Gerald Carson, "Get the Prospect Seated . . . and Keep Talking," *American Heritage,* August 1958, 77–80; and Archibald Hanna, Jr., "Every Man His Own Biographer," *Proceedings of the American Antiquarian Society* vol. 80, no. 2 (1971), 291–98.

61. John Downes, ed., *The Philadelphia Almanac and General Business Directory for the Year 1848* (Philadelphia: Charles J. Gillis, 1848), 2, 41. Bradley first appears in *McElroy's Philadelphia Directory for 1849* (Philadelphia: Edward C. & John Biddle, 1849), 37, and *O'Brien's Philadelphia Wholesale Business Directory . . . 1849* (Philadelphia: King & Baird Printers, 1849), 63. His advertisement for agents appears in the O'Brien directory for the following year (on p. 58). A list of some of his available subscription titles is given in *Cowell's Philadelphia Business Directory, 1860* (Philadelphia: E. J. Cowell, 1860), 33.

62. *McElroy's Philadelphia Directory for 1857* (Philadelphia: Edward C. & John Biddle, 1857), 760–61; and *McElroy's Wholesale Business Directory . . . 1857* (Philadelphia: Henry B. Ashmead, 1857), 3–4, 56–57.

63. *The Philadelphia Merchants' and Manufacturers' Business Directory for 1856–57* (Philadelphia: Griswold & Co., 1856), 321.

64. Hankinton appears first in 1860 as both a bricklayer and book agent (see

McElroy's Philadelphia City Directory for 1860, 58, 400). During the Civil War his occupational title alternates in the annual directories; he appears as highway commissioner in *McElroy's Philadelphia City Directory for 1865,* 294.

65. *Gopsill's Philadelphia City and Business Directory for 1868–9* (Philadelphia: James Gopsill, 1868), 1854.

66. On Sheehy's first designation as a book agent and the presence of the New York firm in Baltimore, see *E. M. Cross & Co.'s Baltimore City Business Directory 1863–1864* (Baltimore: E. M. Cross, 1863), 37, 47–48. See also *Wood's Baltimore City Directory . . . 1868–69* (Baltimore: John W. Woods, 1868), 679; one year later, *Wood's Baltimore City Directory 1870,* 761, identifies the fourteen book and subscription agents.

67. Sutton, *Western Book Trade,* gives the full list of publishers and agents (311–44), including the early activities of James (326–27) and Gillis (323).

68. Ibid., 215–35.

69. Ibid., 219, 336; and Hackenberg, "Hawking Subscription Books," 141–42.

70. Sutton, *Western Book Trade,* 287–97, 323, 327, 331.

71. Ibid., 126–27, 285, 307–9.

72. Ibid., 331. Annie Nelles Dumond, *The Life of a Book Agent,* 5th ed. (St. Louis: Published by the author, 1892). That edition states that the work was originally entered for copyright in 1867, but earlier editions have not been located.

73. Sutton, *Western Book Trade,* 324 ("Hannaford, E. & Co."). Ebenezer Hannaford, *Success in Canvassing: A Manual of Practical Hints and Instructions Specially Adapted to the Use of Book Canvassers of the Better Class* (San Francisco: A. Roman, 1878).

74. William L. Montague, comp., *The St. Louis Business Directory for 1853–4* (St. Louis: E. A. Lewis, 1853), advertising section, no. 89; *St. Louis Directory, 1859* (St. Louis: R. V. Kennedy, 1859), 488, 533; *Campbell & Richardson's St. Louis Business Directory for 1863* (St. Louis: Campbell & Richardson, 1863), 66, 331 (the agent was J. H. Chambers); *Edwards' Eleventh Annual Directory . . . for 1869,* 1086; *Edwards' Twelfth Annual Directory . . . for 1870,* 1109 (for the Southern Publishing Company branches); and *Edwards' Thirteenth Annual Directory . . . for 1871,* 809 (for five identifiable subscription agencies). The dozen subscription agencies in St. Louis by 1881 are amid the list of publishers in *Gould's St. Louis Directory for 1881* (St. Louis: David B. Gould, 1881), 1382–83.

75. The bookselling firm of Stearns and Spicer was advertising for subscription agents in *Grooms & Smith's Indianapolis Directory, City Guide, and Business Mirror . . . in 1855* (Indianapolis: A. C. Grooms & W. T. Smith, 1855), 151. J. S. Reeves's solicitation for agents appeared in the advertising section of *The Indianapolis City Directory for 1865* (Indianapolis: Hall & Hutchinson, 1865), 37. See also *Bailey's Directory Series: Indianapolis Directory 1871–72* (Indianapolis: Bailey, 1871), 201, for Vance as a bank employee; and *Swartz & Tedrowe's Indianapolis Directory 1871–72* (Indianapolis: Indianapolis Sentinel Printers, 1871), 314, for Vance as a subscription book dealer. *R. L. Polk & Co's Indianapolis Directory for 1880* (Indianapolis: R. L. Polk & Co., 1880), 598, lists the seven subscription book publishers.

76. *Scott's Annual Toledo City Directory for 1868–69* (Toledo: Daily Commercial Steam Book and Job Printing House, 1868), 145, for R. W. Bliss; W. E. Bliss and Otis A. Browning both appear in the following year's directory (102, 107, 112, and 391). The later arrivals are identified in *R. L. Polk & Co.'s Toledo City Directory for 1880–81* (Toledo: R. L. Polk & Co., 1880), 25, 135, 561, 597, and 604. Browning also wrote an instructional booklet for agents, *O. A. Browning's Confidential Instructions, Rules and Helps for His Agents* (Toledo: O. A. Browning & Co., 1881).

77. *Root's Peoria City Directory for 1870–71* (Peoria: N. C. Nason, 1870), 115 (Zell's agent, J. W. Marsh); Richard Edward, comp., *Edward's Peoria Census Report ... Embracing a Complete Director of the City ... 1876* (Peoria: Adair & Utley, 1876), 193, 409 (for the Post Office operations). Jewett is first identified in *Root's Peoria City Directory, 1877* (Peoria: N. C. Nason, 1877), 66, 148. Borland's Chicago activities are described in the *Chicago Tribune,* 1 Jan. 1883, 20.

78. Section 10 of the Des Moines 1869 ordinance covers subscription agents; see *Des Moines City Directory and Business Guide for the Year 1869* (Des Moines: Mills & Co., 1869), 53. Licensing problems elsewhere were attested by Mendell and Hosmer, *Notes of Travel and Life,* chap. 30, and by Likins, *Six Years Experience,* 84.

79. On the later subscription agencies, see *Bushnell's Des Moines Business and Resident City Directory, 1877–78* (Des Moines: J. P. Bushnell & Co., 1877), 257, and the same directory for 1881–82, 313.

80. *Minneapolis City Directory for 1874* (Minneapolis: Tribune Printing Co., 1874), 183; and *St. Paul City Directory for 1875* (St. Paul: St. Paul Pioneer Press Co., 1875), 446, and that same directory for 1881–82, 172, 201, 403, 586, 696, 806, 845, 855.

81. Griggs advertisements first appear in the *Chicago Business Directory & Community Advertiser 1859* (Chicago: S. C. Griggs & Co., 1859), 1, and *Hellier & Co.'s Chicago Business Directory for 1859–60* (New York: Hellier, 1859), 1, 32. The agents for Virtue can be traced in the following directories: *D. B. Cooke & Co.'s Chicago City Directory for the Year 1860–61* (Chicago: D. B. Cooke & Co., 1860), 402; *Halpin & Bailey's Chicago City Directory for the Year 1861–62* (Chicago: Halpin & Bailey, 1861), 85, 391; and *John C. W. Bailey's Chicago City Directory for the Year 1864–5* (Chicago: John C. W. Bailey, 1864), front endpaper advertisement and p. 621.

82. On the activities of Moses and Hill, see George Eugene Sereiko, *Chicago and Its Book Trade 1871–1893* (Ann Arbor: University Microfilms International, 1977), 286–92.

83. Ibid., 286.

84. The certificate lies loosely inserted in a copy of *The Holy Bible* (Chicago: Western Publishing House, 1873?), which is in the Special Collections Department of Northwestern University Library.

85. Gihon & Johnson first appear in *A. W. Morgan & Co.'s San Francisco City Directory* (San Francisco: F. A. Bonnard, 1852), 97. An early advertisement for the publications available at the Noisy Carriers Publishing Hall appeared in *Le Count & Strong's San Francisco City Directory for the Year 1854* (San Francisco: San Francisco Herald Office, 1854), 13.

86. Clark, *A Venture in History,* gives all the details.

87. On Roman, see Madeleine B. Stern, *Imprints on History: Book Publishers and American Frontiers* (Bloomington: Indiana University Press, 1956), 136–54; and *San Francisco Directory for the Year Commencing October 1868* (San Francisco: Henry G. Langley, 1868), 612. A Roman advertisement first appeared in the *San Francisco Directory for the Year Commencing July, 1860* (San Francisco: Valentine & Co., 1860), 347.

88. *San Francisco Directory for the Year Commencing October, 1864* (San Francisco: Excelsior Steam Presses, 1864), 133 (on Dewing and Laws); and *San Francisco Directory for the Year Commencing December, 1869* (San Francisco: Henry G. Langley, 1869), 681 (for the others).

89. Trumbull's career is traceable in the previously mentioned directories (note 88) as a compositor (October 1864, 392), dealer in photographic albums (December 1865, 434), and subscription agent (September 1867, 475). The manuscript invoice and instructions regarding the Oregon agent, dated 1 August and September 1868, are in the Kemble collections of the library of the California Historical Society.

90. *The Portland Directory for the Year Commencing January, 1865* (Portland: Oregon Farmer Book and Job Printing Office, 1865), lists three San Francisco firms advertising in Oregon (14, 16, 56); the 1868 edition has the advertisement in which McCormick claims, "I can sell . . . at San Francisco wholesale prices" (iv). Daniel Halpruner first appeared as a book canvasser in the *Portland City Directory for 1871* (Portland: A. G. Walling's Book and Job Office, 1871), 59, 109 (his first name is apparently incorrectly given as "David" at that time; in the later 1876 directory he is identified only as a gas fitter. Heroy is first identified as a book agent in the *Portland City Directory for 1873* (Portland: A. G. Walling, 1873), 141, 243.

91. *Langley's San Francisco Directory for the Year Commencing April, 1881* (San Francisco: Francis, Valentine & Co., 1881), 1051, 1128.

92. J. Price and C. S. Haley, comps., *The Buyer's Manual and Business Guide: Being a Description of the Leading Business Houses, Manufactories, Inventions, etc. of the Pacific Coast* (San Francisco: Francis & Valentine, 1872), 66, 123.

93. Likins, *Six Years Experience,* passim.

94. New York *Tribune,* 21 January 1870, quoted in *The American Booksellers' Guide,* 1 March 1870, 113.

95. Prospectuses for both the 1875 edition and the later reprint of J. E. Chambliss's *The Life and Labors of David Livingstone* are in the private collection of Robert Seymour of Colebrook, Connecticut.

96. Prospectuses for the 1887 Hartford and Philadelphia variants, in the private collection of Robert Seymour.

97. Bearing an 1872 imprint of Arthur's Select Works Publishing House at Philadelphia, Cincinnati, Chicago, Saint Louis, and San Francisco, a copy of an agent's prospectus owned by Robert Seymour bears an overstamped imprint of Royal Treat in Chicago.

98. Total sales through 1879 for *Roughing It, The Gilded Age, Sketches New and Old, Adventures of Tom Sawyer,* and *Innocents Abroad,* given by Hill, *Mark*

Twain and Elisha Bliss, 39, 157. On the Greeley sales, see Gerald Carson, "Get the Prospect Seated," 39.

99. William Still Letterbook AMS 47, pp. 67–68, Historical Society of Pennsylvania; see also Gara, "William Still and the Underground Railroad," 42–43.

100. Prospectus for William Worthington Fowler, *Ten Years in Wall Street* (Hartford, etc.: Worthington, Dustin & Co., etc., 1870), in the American Antiquarian Society.

101. "Booksellers As Local Agents," *Publishers' Weekly,* 8 March 1879, 279.

4. Dissemination of Popular Books in the Midwest and Far West during the Nineteenth Century

Madeleine B. Stern

In the card and directory catalog of the New York Public Library, there is nothing that stands between the listings BOOKS—DISINFECTION and BOOKS—DUMMIES. The hoped-for entries, BOOKS—DISSEMINATION and BOOKS—DISTRIBUTION are conspicuous by their absence. The publisher and printer of books acquire some documentation in history through their imprints: at the foot of a title page their names live on. Such immortality fails the bookseller. He remains a more anonymous agent who leaves few records of his transactions. If the bookseller is a ghostly creature, how much more ghostly is the distributor who moves his wares from publisher to selling agent or consumer—an undocumented intermediary. To reanimate that shadowy distributor into a creature of flesh and blood is a difficult task; yet it may be productive to attempt the reconstruction of his varied and often colorful methods and operations. For it was through those methods that books crossed a continent and helped civilize it in the course of the nineteenth century.

The book distributor was a protean creature who changed with the changing needs and resources of the country. He had many names: peddler or salesman, colporteur or correspondent, commercial traveler, news agent, jobber. He had many devices: from book wagon to store boat, from exchanges to trade sales, from express agency to news agency. And he had many vehicles: from stagecoach to sidewheeler and canal boat, from horse to iron horse.

As early as 1683, Cotton Mather wrote in his diary: "There is an old *Hawker,* who will fill this Countrey with devout and useful Books, if I will direct him," but he later worried about the corruption of minds and manners from the songs and ballads carried by hawkers and peddlers "into all parts of the country."[1] Cotton Mather could not have anticipated how intensively all parts of the country would be penetrated by these itinerant book salesmen. By 1790, over fifty book agents operated between Halifax and Georgia for Mathew Carey alone.[2] By 1859 three million families were visited by book agents who distributed among them some eight million volumes.[3]

Who were these distributors? How did they travel? What was their modus operandi? Were they cultural influences or nuisances, or both? How do they fit into the perplexing jigsaw that is nineteenth-century American book distribution?

If our distributor was called a chapman or hawker, he made his rounds in the early nineteenth century offering, along with pincushions or shoelaces, such edifying literature as the penny paperback entitled *The Affecting History of Sally Williams; afterwards Tippling Sally*. The colporteur who scattered "books of Truth and Goodness in all Corners of the Land" was fortified in his tendency to specialize in pietistic literature when, around 1820, the English book trade sent hawkers to America to sell hundreds of thousands of Bibles. Two decades later, Russell B. Cook, in the employ of the American Tract Society, developed a large-scale colportage system through whose agency pioneers were regaled with *The Swearer's Prayer* and *Pike's Persuasives to Early Piety*.[4]

Meanwhile, the postrider or carrier was distributing all types of printed matter on the frontier. In his saddlebags or locked pouch he carried letters, newspapers, pamphlets, and books along post roads to post towns on his route. One observer recalled, "I well remember the post-rider . . . a portly, good-natured, obliging man. . . . He came regularly, astride his stout nag . . . travelling . . . three days north and three days south. . . . His arrival . . . [was] usually heralded by the sounding of a horn."[5]   .

More of an entrepreneur than postrider or colporteur, the book peddler visited the publisher for stock but peddled his wares from door to door in the manner of the early chapman or hawker. He operated principally in rural America, following in the wake of schoolmaster and circuit rider, and he offered not merely pietistic and educational works but the cheap popular yellow-covered paperback. Sometimes the nineteenth-century distributor was known as a "correspondent." He received sheets or folded gatherings from his publisher and had them bound up on his own, thus serving not only as distributor but as copublisher, as well as taking on the duties of banker, postmaster, and general agent for his principal.[6]

While Nathaniel Hawthorne had in mind a subscription book agent when he described an itinerant distributor in *American Notes,* his portrait would hold for any independent book agent: with an "eager, earnest stare through his spectacles," Hawthorne's agent was "accustomed to hurry through narrow alleys and dart across thronged streets."[7] In fact, the book agent was as likely to be female as male. As one commentator put it, the woman agent "went boldly forth in God's sunshine and the pure air, canvassed and sold, feeling she was in the proper sphere of woman, engaged in a calling which promoted the welfare and happiness of the widow and the orphan, and of all to whom she sold, giving them cheerful companions for the leisure hours of long winter evenings."[8] Despite such euphoria, one woman book agent recorded in her diary

> This morning I bought a satchel for $2.25 and invested $4.00 in the books suggested by Mr. Smart, of the Elite Publishing Company. Perhaps it might have been wiser to have taken the agency offered me by the Insect Powder and Corn Salve man, for, as he said, "There are more insects than book lovers, and more corns and bunions than book buyers."[9]

Nevertheless, book agents formed an army, some carrying "stretchers"— the backs of a set of books pasted onto a strip of leather or cloth—to show how they would look on a shelf, others flashing engraved certificates of authorization, and most of them pushing west, especially "after Harvest, . . . always a good time to sell books in the country."[10]

The large personnel of book distributors was joined by the newsboy who "rushed through the streets, selling to thousands 'the last new novel' of [a] great English novelist for 25 cents." Indeed, when Bulwer-Lytton's *Zanoni* emerged hot from the press at 5:00 P.M. on 9 April 1842, and two hours later another house issued a second cheap edition of that masterpiece, it was said that three policemen were required to keep order.[11]

The last individual member of the nineteenth-century book distributing cast of characters (barring the subscription book agent, who has been treated by Michael Hackenberg in chapter 3) was the commercial traveler. In 1864 this descendant of the individual canvasser was hailed as the only evidence of progress in distribution. Five years later the *American Literary Gazette* voiced doubts about the need for such traveling salesmen in urban areas but conceded that "there is still a wide field for their operations in the distant west, where many towns would be entirely without books were it not for their yearly visits."[12] As wholesale representatives of publishers, the commercial travelers might be hired by one or more houses and paid accordingly. Dodd, Mead, for example, paid $1,500 annually plus a commission on sales over $12,000. In 1884, the Brotherhood of Commercial Travelers was formed, a fraternal order described at its one-hundredth anniversary as "a hardy band of book salesmen with a shine on their scuffed shoes, a sincere smile and a ninety-second summary for each of the books that they hope will include some of next season's best-sellers." By the end of the nineteenth century it was considered by many that this type of salesman, the publisher's representative to the bookstore, who "sold books wholesale to retail outlets" rather than to individual buyers, was the most important element in book distribution.[13]

The names of these commercial travelers, and of their predecessors the canvassers, are not all unknown. Among the former were James R. Osgood, first traveling representative of Ticknor & Fields, who carried his firm's list to Detroit and Cincinnati; Robert Porter; and A. L. Burt, who "built up a coast-to-coast staff of trade salesmen." Among the independent canvassers several colorful characters can still be recalled: Joseph A. Coe, known as "Bible Leaf Joe" for his technique of tearing out a page or two of his Bibles to offer potential customers; and James Gray whose death in 1705 was noted thus by the Boston *News-Letter:* "On Thursday last Dyed at Boston, James Gray, That used to go up and down the country selling of Books, who left some considerable Estate behind him." And then there were Alfred S. Barnes, who early in life traveled by stagecoach with books in his trunk, canvassing school teachers, and R. C. Barnum of Cleveland, who trained, it was said, over 25,000 student book agents and earned the title of king of book agents. Finally, there was of course Frank Hardy, hero of the story attributed to Horatio Alger, Jr., entitled *The Young Book Agent; Or, Frank Hardy's Road to Success.*[14]

Whether these book distributors were individuals peddling from town to town or commercial travelers converting Chicago's Palmer House into a literary bazaar, their operations and the extent of their activity were determined in large measure by their means of transportation. Early in the century, a town's situation at the head of a wagon road might well give it trading superiority or monopoly over markets to the west. Poor roads of course made book distribution excessively difficult, and distance frequently meant isolation. As William Charvat put it succinctly, "The rise and decline of literary centers is to be explained not by theories of 'culture cities' but by the facts of transportation."[15]

The early distributors of books relied principally upon the horse for their means of transportation. They might drive a one-horse wagon with "a large square cabinet" of books fitted to the rear—a traveling library to be opened for customers' viewing upon arrival. An entire wagon might be designed as a mobile bookhouse. "Built with high boxlike bodies that opened on three sides exposing many feet of shelving," such wagons offered the prospective buyer the opportunity of walking around and appraising titles. Farm wagons or Conestoga wagons drawn by four or six horses rumbled along pike roads carrying as cargo books and booksellers.[16]

Some of these itinerant distributors naturally aroused antagonism on the part of reluctant readers who had heard tales of schemes, swindles, and advertising dodges associated with book agents. A sign occasionally encountered at certain houses read clearly, "No book agents allowed here."[17] On 6 June 1880, Louisa May Alcott wrote to a relative who served as her lawyer, "A neighbor of mine wants to get $40 owed her for board by a man employed by Appleton as a book-agent. She has waited *three years:* ... I think a lawyer's letter might stir him up."[18]

Nonetheless, it must be conceded that the book distributing personnel of the nineteenth century did help push back cultural barriers. As one commentator observed, "An agent with good books is a moral benefactor. He goes into the highways, byways and dark places of the land, and circulates knowledge where it otherwise would not penetrate."[19] Another became even more euphoric: "The book agent is an intellectual nobleman in direct line of descent from ... Aristotle, who founded the school of peripatetic philosophy. . . . Wherefore the book agent is much given to walking."[20]

As the century unfolded, the book distributor combined his walking with other, more sophisticated methods of transportation. Until about 1850 shipping was probably the most relevant to developments in the book trade. Its hazards and problems punctuate the literary correspondence of the time. Did not the Utica publisher William Williams write to his Albany consignee in 1825, "Your letter of inquiry respecting the Box of Books was duly received. . . . I have enquired of my Agent here [in Albany], and find the vessel containing two boxes from me for yourselves and Grigg ran aground near Hudson and was there frozen in. The weather is now so mild that there is reason to hope they will get afloat soon"?[21] And seven years later, the publisher Carey wrote to his author James Fenimore Cooper of his most recent book, "*The Bravo* has been much liked, but the unfortunate close of our navigation immediately after it was published has prevented it from reaching over half the interior towns and has affected its sale."[22] Water routes were circuitous—books might, for example, be shipped from New York to St. Louis via New Orleans and up the Mississippi River. Costs were high. In 1812 it cost 12½ cents a cubic foot to ship of box of books from Philadelphia to Baltimore. And chance reigned supreme. As late as the 1840s a book agent would visit the docks "looking for a boat or sloop, to whose captain or mate he could entrust" a packet of cheap novels destined for a "far-off country town." His success depended not only upon the vicissitudes of wind and tide but upon the courtesy of the skipper.[23]

It is clear, then, that the completion of the Erie Canal in 1825 had a direct bearing upon the westward distribution of literature. As William Charvat has pointed out, it was the Erie Canal system which in large measure gave New York publishers their "crucial head-start in the Ohio trade."[24] And so it might be suggested that, since the canal made it possible for the literary productions of the East to reach the western reader, it also played a role in shaping literary taste. The connections that exist everywhere were surely at work here between the completion of an artificial channel in the East and the reading matter favored in the West.

If this is so, then the activities and operations of those book distributors who availed themselves of the nation's waterways take on a special interest. The *Cincinnati Enquirer* of 4 February 1853 immortalized one of them, a "Mr. Phillips," whom it described as "the polite distributor of light literature upon the steamboats at the river." And a few years later, Herman Melville immortalized another in *The Confidence-Man*—the peddler aboard the steamboat *Fidele* who specialized in sensational titles.[25] "Bible Leaf Joe" often availed himself of canal boats, and some pietistic literature was offered on a colporteur boat that plied the western rivers. After the completion of the Erie Canal, the Phinney family of publishers in Cooperstown, New York, developed a floating canal boat bookstore which anchored in winter at large towns along the canal and spread their books throughout the interior. In the West, the store boat or boat store carried books to villages along the Ohio tributaries and, thanks to keelboat and steamboat, Cincinnati attained for a time not only the title of Queen City of the West but a reputation as "the great mart for the book trade west of the mountains."[26]

As for the Far West, it was at first in the cargoes of clipper ships that crates of books from New York or Boston, having rounded the Horn, arrived at San Francisco's bustling wharves. In 1851, the *Alta California* could rejoice: "The reading community of San Francisco are not obliged as formerly to spend their leisure hours in poring over the pages of some old book which has found its way around Cape Horn, or across the Isthmus of Panama. Now we receive by every steamer the latest publications ... solid bound books, and the yellow covered whilers away of careless hours." Those "whilers away" were purveyed, it was added, by "A live Yankee [who] has adopted the plan of traveling up and down Long Wharf, with a horse and wagon, the latter filled with literature for sale, of every description, from the horrifying yellow covered stories of robberies and murderers up to the classics and histories."[27]

Often such literature was carried not only along the nation's waterways, but along its miles of track in a combination that coupled steamer with rail. Before long the steamer would all but yield to the rail. The railway age was fast approaching, and the railway would not only distribute literature but influence it and give it a name.

By mid-century, the railroad had crossed the Alleghenies and the Berkshires, enabling Boston publishers to reach the western reader.

Interior markets for literature were opening up. By 1852, the first rail link was established between the East and Chicago; and by the end of the decade twenty thousand miles of track had been laid. They indicated the direction of the future, the shift northward to the lake plains that would result in the decline of Cincinnati and the rise of Chicago and St. Louis as book centers. As one Cincinnati reporter put it dramatically, "'The railroads came and passed and the mountains moved east.'"[28]

If the mountains moved east, the tracks moved west. By 1865 they reached Kansas City, and four years later, on that historic 10 May 1869, the Overland Railway was completed. Despite Ralph Waldo Emerson, who had commented early on, "They have begun the Pacific Rail Road; ... Such projects cannot consist with much literature," the transcontinental railroad did indeed prove consistent with "much literature."[29] Obviously, the railroad facilitated the distribution of books from the East at the same time that it stimulated a need for books among an expanding population in the West. Booksellers could now purchase directly from publishers, and, with an enlarged market, came the increased motivation for mass production. The struggle of distributors to keep pace with that production accelerated.

A considerable amount of book distribution took place both at the station kiosk and on the train itself. Indeed many railroad car interiors were conducive to reading. A local branch narrow gauge railway running from Colfax to Nevada City, for example, had a "cozily-built carriage" with a Brussels carpet, velvet seats, gilded mirrors, and, of course, cuspidors. A band of minstrels might be singing solo or in full chorus, but they could not drown out the shrill cries of newsboy, "butcher," or train boy offering his wares.[30] America's first train "butcher," it has been said, approached Commodore Vanderbilt, then president of the New York and Harlem Railroad, with the proposal that he be permitted to sell printed matter and other articles to the Commodore's passengers. Before granting permission, Vanderbilt stipulated that, prior to going through the coaches with his publications, the newsboy should pass through with a bucket of water and a dipper, offering each rider a drink.[31] If this is so, it may explain the watered-down quality of some of the reading matter purveyed aboard trains.

Literature was distributed not only from car to car by train boys, but inside packing cases on the freight train. In both areas could be found supplies of cheap reprints, dime novels and songbooks, Allan Pinkerton's "thrilling narratives of detection," and the popular romances of the day. Mary J. Holmes remembered being offered her own latest work by a newsboy on the cars, and Louisa May Alcott had a similar experience on the morning train from Boston to New York when the train boy, shouting his wares, placed *An Old-Fashioned Girl,* published that day, on the lap of its author. After she had murmured that she did not care for it, Miss Alcott was addressed with the delightful exclamation "Bully book, ma'am! Sell a lot; better have it." It was Miss Alcott, too, who summoned up as well as anyone the image of the train "butcher" when she wrote, " A shrill boy has pervaded the car ever since leaving Portland, shouting, 'Papers, Corn, Books, Water, Lozenges, Sandwiches, Oranges,' . . . he must be the ghost of some lad killed on the road, who haunts the cars, and so avenges himself on the Corporation for having made a corpse of him."[32]

The books purveyed by shrill train boys whose name was legion were frequently described as railroad literature. Ushered in by the railway age of the seventies on a continent now knit together by parallel bands of track, railroad literature consisted generally of cheap reprints designed for railroad reading. Confidence in its success was predicated on the assumption that he who runs may read. Fireside companions were now traveling companions; hammock literature had a new name—railroad literature. One publisher after another—A. K. Loring of Boston with his Railway Companions Series; Peterson of Philadelphia; the Putnams and Appleton of New York—all published individual titles, series, or libraries for travelers on the rails. The colorful New York publisher Frank Leslie made a flamboyant transcontinental rail journey in 1877 which made him keenly alive to the need for appropriate reading matter for the masses of people enjoying train travel during the silver seventies. Better than most, Leslie understood the impact of railroads upon national literary consumption. Between 1876 and 1877, when railroad expansion was at a height, he tripled his book production of preceding years, catering to the developing mass market for cheap reprints to read aboard trains. And so such delectables as Rhoda Broughton's *Good-by, Sweetheart!* and *Granville de Vigne* by "Ouida," along with the more classic works of Charles Reade and Bulwer-Lytton, Victor Hugo and Wilkie Collins, were carried by rail to the western plains and the solitary reaches of the continent.[33]

Summing up its methods of distribution, another publisher, Fowler & Wells of New York, announced grandiosely that its publications were sent "by Express, or as Freight, by Railroad, Steamships, Sailing Vessels, by Stage, or Canal, to any City, Town, or Village, in the United States." From that house's "great Metropolitan Emporium" its books passed along the "iron tracks of the locomotive and the watery pathways of the steamer," "in wagons and buggies, and on horse-back . . . into every . . . corner of the continent."[34]

Still another means of distribution was available to nineteenth-century American publishers, a means that had its own peculiar advantages and disadvantages. If the railway gave a name to popular reading matter, the post office gave it a shape and affected its quantity.

During the 1830s and early 1840s, special postal rates were in effect for the newspaper—or anything that looked like the newspaper. Therefore publishers of periodicals issued cheap books as "extras" in octavo format, printed in double columns. The "Brother Jonathan Extras," for example, offered pirated serials of British authors. The story goes that, as the *Great Western* approached its berth at the foot of New York's Clinton Street, the purser threw out a package containing a Dickens book hot from the English press. Printer James G. Wilson was waiting to catch it and hastened to his office where the volume was "stripped" within twenty-five minutes, distributed among forty-eight compositors, and published the next day as a "Brother Jonathan Extra." In this shape such reprints were allowed to pass as newspapers by the Post Office Department, and it is not surprising that at least one literary historian has described the postman of the period as "America's leading literary sales agent."[35]

In May 1845 Congress passed a Post Office Act that lowered the rates for mailing books, so the incentive to publish cheap books not as "extras" but as volumes in cloth or paper covers was intensified. Such books were usually sold directly by publisher to customer. The mail-order publishers Dick and Fitzgerald, for example, announced somewhat querulously, "We have done a large book trade through the mails. . . . We receive so many letters every day that it is impossible for us to remember the Post-Office, County, and State where any particular person receives books. . . . Put on a plain direction." The firm added, "It is easier and cheaper to get books from New York than people generally imagine. You have only to write a few words . . . and the book comes free of postage, and arrives by return mail."[36] Just so the Fowler firm posted from its Phrenological Depot guides for emigrants planning to cross the country. In 1882, thanks to the efforts of John Lovell—known, from the frequency of his publications, as "Book-A-Day Lovell"—a second class postal rate was applied to the books in Lovell's Library, so they could now be mailed at the same price as newspapers. Lovell boasted a yearly sale of seven million cheap books, carried four million in stock, and actually did publish a new book each day. John Alden and his American Book Exchange practiced mail-order selling; the House of Leslie addressed 1,500 wrappers an hour in its mailing department. The *Baltimore Sun,* defending cheap postage, was moved to state in 1890: "There is a vast amount of good reading scattered through the mails all over the country at prices ranging from 20 to 50 cents a volume, and it serves to lighten many lonely hours in the solitude of the country, in farmhouses and villages, and in towns where workingmen and their families congregate."[37]

When, perhaps as a result of such enthusiasm, there ensued a glut on the market for cheap foreign reprints, books were offered free with cakes of soap or bottles of patent medicine. According to Raymond Shove,

"The combination of books and soap seemed to work the best," and one manufacturer actually purveyed a product trademarked "Book Soap."[38]

Distribution by mail did not always run smoothly. In the early 1860s considerable pressure was placed upon the Post Office to levy a stamp tax on periodicals. It was then that many publishers of cheap books turned, as we shall shortly see, to another major means of book distribution. And it was then that a pleader for low postage rates for printed matter clearly equated those lower rates with literacy: "Perhaps there is no country in the world," he remarked in 1865, "that has so few persons unable to read, in proportion to the entire population, as our own, and this universal ability to read is traceable, in a great degree, to the cheapness with which the ability to read can be made useful by means of an unrestricted and cheap press."[39] Although the proposed stamp tax was not levied, distribution by mail was never without its problems. One problem emerged in the 1870s when Anthony Comstock, as special agent of the Post Office Department, made his rampages against evil. Despite the threat of censorship, despite the continued struggle for low book rates, it is clear that, as James Gilreath has said, "The use of the mails to deliver books may have played a far larger role in history than has been realized. . . . The flow of publications may be more properly traced along . . . post roads . . . than rivers and railroads."[40]

Aboard canal boats or steamships, on trains, through the postal system, literature was disseminated to Midwest and Far West. Concurrently, publishers experimented with other operational means of book distribution. One such method was a kind of barter system originally developed by Mathew Carey, a system of exchanged imprints whereby publishers and their correspondents swapped lists from which each ordered desired titles. Payment was made at year's end, and through the exchange system, besides extending the range of their stocks, publishers achieved a wider market for their imprints. The exchange was basically a form of distribution.[41]

So too was the trade sale. Begun in 1824 through the influence of Carey and Lea, the trade sale developed into a semiannual eight-day auction held in Philadelphia, New York, Boston or, for a time, Cincinnati. Lasting from eight o'clock in the morning until late evening, it was presided over by an auctioneer who provided not only wit and wisdom but meals. At trade sales, books were auctioned in job lots whose sizes varied from five books to several thousand. In addition, sheet stock, plates, and even printing presses and binding machinery went under the hammer. Obviously publishers could dump here their slow-moving titles, while others could extend their inventory by picking up at the lowest possible price the complete printing plates of some mediocre book. The trade sales peaked just before the Civil War. By the 1880s they had so disrupted the price system, especially of remaindered titles, that they were castigated as pernicious, and by 1891 they were out of existence. Despite their disadvantages, trade sales did serve to bring together publishers and retail booksellers, and to distribute books. The Cincinnati bookselling firm of U. P. James, for example, could purchase at such a sale large quantities of cheap publications consigned by eastern publishers. Thus money changed hands, stocks were enriched, and books were moved from one part of the continent to another. East and West were brought together, and in a sense distance was annihilated.[42]

A different attempt to annihilate distance was made by a business whose operations impinged upon the book trade. The express business literally had its beginning in a carpetbag—a carpetbag that belonged to William Frederick Harnden of Massachusetts. In 1839, Harnden established a carriage delivery service for small packages on the "Boston and New York Express Package Car." Within two years his carpetbag had become a trunk, and the express business was on its way. It is interesting to note that the future writer and publisher of cheap novels Maturin M. Ballou early in his career clerked for Harnden & Company. The express business was developed not by Harnden, who died in 1845, but by his competitor Alvin Adams, who in 1840 launched what would become the Adams Express Company. Acting as messenger, cashier, receipt clerk, label boy, and porter, Adams expanded the firm until his agencies extended as far west as St. Louis, where Wells and Fargo were operating, and by 1849 they reached California. In 1854 Adams Express absorbed Harnden & Company.

The express companies might use horsedrawn stages, locomotives belching sparks and smoke, or steamers. Packages had to be waterproof, and their transport westward was, to say the least, circuitous. "Upon the arrival of the steamer at Chagres with the Express, freight was sent ashore in boats that were frequently swamped by high seas; at Chagres it was transferred to river canoes and propelled to Cruces, where it was transferred to the backs of mules to Panama, where the Pacific steamship awaited to convey it to San Francisco."[43]

The advertisement with which William Frederick Harnden had initiated his express business was headed: "Important to Merchants, Brokers, Booksellers, and All Business Men." The packages carried in the care of express companies might contain gold, or letters, or books. The Adams charge for freight from New York to San Francisco amounted to seventy-five cents a pound for packages of fifteen pounds or less, and, as we shall see, the express companies were heavily relied upon by the firm that would become the nation's major single nineteenth-century book distributor. The good news carried from Ghent to Aix was carried in care of the express, and so too was a large part of the nation's reading matter.

If the express companies began in William Harnden's carpetbag, that giant wholesale jobber known as the American News Company began in the self-taught mind of a self-made man, a Civil War veteran named Sinclair Tousey.[44] Born in New Haven in 1815 and orphaned early, Tousey at age ten worked in a cotton factory in central New York State; at thirteen he was bound out to a farmer. To obtain winter gloves he had to trap fox and muskrat and sell the pelts. Determined to return to Connecticut, he took a hundred-mile walk back to his native state and apprenticed himself there to a carpenter. By the time he had reached his late teens, Tousey was a grocery clerk in New York. Noting the high prices fetched by quinces, he invested his wages in that fruit when he returned to Connecticut and subsequently sold them to the New York market at double the cost. Later on he varied his already checkered career by serving as carrier boy, delivering popular serials and British reprints to subscribers and setting up newspaper routes. The future tycoon allowed himself at that time six cents a day for lodging and ten cents for food.

Tousey's industry and innovativeness were rewarded, and his many-faceted apprenticeship given a channel, in 1853 when he entered the firm of Ross & Jones, wholesale news agents and booksellers on New York's Nassau Street. There his rise was swift. In 1856 the firm became Ross & Tousey; four years later Tousey bought out his partner. Working from three or four o'clock in the morning until six in the evening every day, he expanded the firm's scope from being an uptown delivery service to being an interstate carrier and increased its gross receipts from $150,000 a year to $1 million. A period of war service in the 14th New York Regiment of Volunteer Engineers interrupted his passage from rags to riches, but on 1 February 1864 Sinclair Tousey was ready for the climactic step that would determine for decades much of the nation's book distribution.

On that day the news depot of Tousey & Company and the competing Dexter & Brother were united to form the American News Company. The *American Literary Gazette* announced: "Messrs. Sinclair Tousey and Dexter, Hamilton & Co., the enterprising and rival newsdealers of New York city, have formed a co-partnership, and will carry on the same business under the name of 'The American News Company,' at the stand of the former, No. 121 Nassau Street."[45]

Tousey, who was the president of the American News Company, had timed the venture well. The Civil War was still raging, but Grant had begun the campaigns against Lee that would spell its end. Moreover, the war itself had created an enormously increased demand for pictorial and story papers, whose circulation rose accordingly. The proliferation of railroads, the roles of steamboat and telegraph, the growth of population and of literacy—all joined in necessitating an improved distribution of printed matter. At the same time, the threatened stamp tax soured publishers from delivery by mail. The time had come for a central jobbing agency that would remove from the office of the publisher the incessant problems of distributing his wares.[46]

As astutely as Sinclair Tousey had chosen his time had he chosen his partners. Henry Dexter had been apprenticed in a Boston printing office before joining his brother George in a wholesale news depot; John Hamilton had begun as a newsboy; Patrick Farrelly had also worked as a newsboy on the Canandaigua and Elmira Railroad and was fast becoming an expert on publishing and postal laws. As for President Tousey, he could double the cost of a quince, and he knew the road that led from rags to riches.[47]

A description of the American News Company's plant in 1866 helps to elucidate its operations. The building at 119 and 121 Nassau Street, New York, at the junction of Nassau and Fulton, extended back to Theatre Alley. It was open all night long. Visitors to the area could see heavy vans rumble up to the rear doors where they were speedily loaded before starting off to catch the early outbound trains. Meanwhile, porters arrived with heavy bundles of printed matter still damp from the press. These were distributed among a crowd of newsmen who waited at a broad counter to fold the papers. In the basements of Nos. 119 and 121, enormous counters and tables were laden with parcels being packed and labeled, those destined for the East separated from those destined for the West. Some parcels would be sent by express over the Hudson River Railroad to the West; others would be expressed on the New Haven Railroad to Boston and the East; still others would be consigned to the New Jersey express, Pennsylvania, and as far south as New Orleans. The basement rooms were walled around with customers' bins for holding papers, and printed address labels for each customer were kept on hand. The first floor of the building was occupied by the retail department and housed a miscellaneous stock of books, stationery, and related materials.[48]

In the bustle and seeming madness of the American News Company's premises there was considerable method. The company specialized in the distribution of newspapers and periodicals, but soon branched out into the distribution of other types of printed matter. It served as middleman, as jobber, buying publications from publishers at discounts variously reported as 40, 45, or 50 percent, and selling them to local dealers. Its basic operation was distribution—a gigantic task from which it relieved the publisher even as it supplied the retailer. The task involved gathering publications from publishing offices, packing them for a variety of destinations, conveying them to the place of shipment, forwarding them by express, and arranging for their safe arrival. Sinclair Tousey described some of the difficulties involved: "Many ... parcels are thrown from the train while in motion ... at places where the train does not stop; ... I have known but half an hour allowed for bringing in some twenty thousand papers, counting them out among some one hundred and fifty different parcels, tying up these parcels, and carting them nearly a mile to the place of shipment." Such labors obviously were beyond the interest or the ability of newsdealers, who "found that they could better afford to pay someone to assemble their newspapers and magazines than to go to the various publishing houses and slowly gather their bundles together."[49]

As for publishers of cheap series, they too resorted to Tousey's American News Company to distribute their publications. For several decades of the nineteenth century the American News Company was the primary distributor for the publications of dozens of publishers, and it was through its office that story papers and sentimental romances, sensational thrillers and society novels, adventure stories and parlor entertainments, produced wholesale and priced cheaply, reached a mass readership in the Midwest and Far West. As early as 1866, in addition to daily papers and magazines, the American News Company distributed about 225,000 cheap publications each month.[50] Thus it served not only the publisher and the retailer but the reading public.

By 1888, a year after Sinclair Tousey's death, a tourist observed in *Publishers' Weekly*, "The writer has traveled extensively in the United States, and has seen George Eliot, Carlyle, Scott, Victor Hugo, Emerson, Edwin Arnold, Homer, Goethe, Dante, and Shakespeare read in the backwoods of Arkansas and in the mining camps of Colorado, in the popular 10 or 20 cent editions."[51] While the writer credited this phenomenon to the low price of the paperbacks, he might also have credited it to the book distributor. How many "libraries," series of cheap books, were distributed by the American News Company! The Beadle firm, which had bundled Ann Stephens's *Malaeska* in carloads to Union soldiers in army camps, now arranged with the American News Company for distribution of its dime novels. Indeed, the American News Company name, as well as Tousey's, were actually used in the imprints of some Beadle American Tales and other books. Incidentally, the American News Company's attorney Edward H. Spooner was at one time a partner in Beadle & Co. Just so, George Munro's Seaside Library, Frank Leslie's railroad literature, Street and Smith's hundred thousand titles, and indeed most of the cheap paperbacks turned out in mass production for mass readership were distributed through the facilities of the American News Company.

Its enterprise expanded with its expertise. In one year (1865) the company spent over $12,500 for twine and paper alone. The next year it was receiving some 250 letters, in addition to telegrams, daily, and it was said that

> Along the line of every car, stage, or steamboat route, and in every large city and town, it has its agents and correspondents, from whom every paper, book, or pamphlet can be obtained as soon as published, and who are the distributing points from which dealers and customers in the surrounding country are supplied. As new railroads are extended, the news and the express companies open up their routes hand-in-hand, and where the road temporarily stops on lines in process of construction, the News Company's packages are pushed yet further beyond by means of wagons or stage. . . . The American News Company ranks as one of the most important literary agencies of our country.[52]

As the American News Company stretched across the continent, it spawned branches and subsidiaries. One of the latter, the Railroad News Company, bought an interest in the leading newsstand owner, the Union News Company. The Western News Company, established as a branch in Chicago, was destroyed in the 1871 fire, and, without losing a day, resumed distribution from a circus tent pitched along a railroad track where shipments could be easily handled. The American News Company's branches or regional depots dotted the country—in Cleveland and Cincinnati, Detroit and Kansas City, St. Louis and San Francisco. At the time of the earthquake in the city of the Golden Gate, a substitute branch was set up without delay in Oakland. The giant was on its way to becoming a monopoly. Eventually it boasted thirty-two branches. By the 1880s its annual business amounted to $17 million, and from a four-story building on Chambers Street, "publications streamed forth, shipped express by rail and boat . . . all over the country." In 1909, atop its new premises on Park Place, the figure of a newsboy stood triumphant. For much of the nineteenth century, the American News Company had been a dominant force in the distribution not only of newspapers but of literature for mass consumption.[53]

The company endured until 1969 when it was merged with Ancorp National Services, Inc. Subsequently it filed for bankruptcy, and still later Ancorp was bought by Sodexho, a company headquartered in Marseilles. Curiously enough, Ancorp National Services, Inc., lingered on in the Manhattan telephone directory where, until 1985–86, it was listed at 21 East 40th Street. Eager to unearth the old files of the American News Company—surely an invaluable record of nineteenth-century American book dissemination—I contacted Ancorp, or what remained of Ancorp. The reply by letter was succinct: "The above Companies are no longer in existence. Anything that is of public record can be found in the Library or the S.E.C." The reply by telephone was not only succinct but devastating: "There are no American News Company files left," I was told, "but even if there were, we couldn't possibly let you see them—just for a book!"[54]

The story of book distribution must end with the agency that sells the book to its ultimate recipient, the consumer. Who unwrapped the parcels carried by express or rail to Chicago or St. Louis? Who opened the crates of books that lined San Francisco's teeming wharves? Where did the long journey of the paperback have its destination? The answer is obvious. The final link in the long chain of book distribution was the local branch or bookstore which took on the ultimate disposition of this much-traveled merchandise.

The story of those bookstores is a history in itself, a history that begins with the sale of books even before there were formal bookstores, for books published in the East were part of almost every frontier inventory. Here there is room for only a few words about the bookstores that dotted the country and ended the line of distribution, room only to summon up a few images and venture a few comments:

Place: Columbus, Ohio. Time: 1841. The bookstore of H. W. Derby carries a full line of publications from the East, along with Currier prints and Macassar hair oil. From time to time Derby and his assistant take a load of surplus stock and travel into the country to sell books at auction from the tail of a wagon. Derby, who once served as an express agent in Ohio, finds that while much of his stock comes from the East, his best market is Cincinnati to the west.[55]

Place: Cincinnati, Ohio. Time: 1827. E. H. Flint, having opened a bookstore, announces that "He intends . . . to import from Boston and Philadelphia a complete assortment of books. . . . Having recently commenced the business of sending books to all the chief towns and villages in the valley of the Mississippi, he will be able to make up packages with neatness, and transmit them with safety and dispatch to any town in the Western and Southwestern country."[56] By 1862, it is a Cincinnati firm, Applegate & Company, that orders from George W. Childs of Philadelphia forty thousand copies of *Parson Brownlow's Book*—at that time the largest single order ever placed for one book.[57]

Place: Chicago. Time: 1856. By the middle of this year, one-tenth of all the existing copies of Longfellow's *Hiawatha* have been consigned to one Chicago jobber. In the "Elegant Book Establishment" on Lake Street founded by D. B. Cooke, a large stock of books are offered "at Eastern prices." It is said, in fact, that "He had such a stock as was suited to Eastern cities, but was told that he could not sell such expensive books here. But he did sell them readily, showing that the tastes of Western people were not different from those of Eastern people."[58]

Place: St. Louis. Time: 1820. The first actual bookstore established in St. Louis, opened by Thomas Essex and Charles E. Beynroth, is anticipating the "early arrival of a stock of books from Philadelphia," and with the chauvinism of frontier settlers the proprietors claim to be able to furnish "any book that can be had in Philadelphia" tagged "at Philadelphia prices, with the addition of carriage."[59]

Place: Kansas City. Time: the 1890s. Patrick McArdle has opened a bookshop where, it is observed, "Drays unloaded bundle after bundle of gorgeous-backed dreadfuls on the sidewalk. . . . Farmer boys crowded around his windows and, tempted by the colorful Nick Carter and Frank Merriwell titles, entered to buy. Stockmen bought up a winter's reading material." The Nick Carters and Frank Merriwells have, of course, journeyed from the publishing offices of Street and Smith, through the facilities of the American News Company, to arrive at the city on the great bend of the Missouri.[60]

Place: Salt Lake City. Year: 1868. The firm of Savage and Ottinger have launched the Rocky Mountain Book Store. One of the partners has visited publisher Samuel Wells of Fowler and Wells, New York, and fitted up a supply wagon with their publications for the return to Salt Lake. The *American Phrenological Journal* reports, "Here is a store ... three thousand miles west from New York, in the center of a vast Territory teeming with life, enterprise, education, and Mormonism ... one of its first book stores." It handles eastern imprints, and the same year Ottinger writes to his supplier Wells, "The CP.RR is drawing close to our doors and in a few months we shall be linked to civilization."[61]

The final scene: San Francisco in the 1850s. A bearded Bavarian, Anton Roman, who has migrated to America and crossed the plains to California, strikes rich diggings at Scott Bar, and in December 1851, at age 23, he appears in San Francisco and exchanges his gold dust for books. Later he sets up a stand in Shasta where his stock includes *The Necromancer; or, the Mysteries of the Court of Henry the VIII; The Parricide or the Youth's Career of Crime;* and *Amy Laurence; or, the Freemason's Daughter*—titles originating in the East, the first two from the press of T. B. Peterson, the third from that of Garrett & Co. When, in 1857, Roman establishes himself in San Francisco, his stock of standard and miscellaneous books also hails from eastern cities. His *Catalogue raisonné* of 1861 offers books "for the million" and includes the works of eastern publishers, G. W. Carleton and T. B. Peterson, D. Appleton and Harper, Loring and Lee & Shepard. They have been carried by semimonthly steamer and later by overland railroad, having been forwarded to him by his New York purchasing agent, William J. Widdleton.[62] Roman's New York agency is a factor of enormous interest in the many-faceted history of book distribution, for the California dealer used that agency as a two-way channel, not only east to west but also west to east.

Distribution east to west has been adumbrated. The methods of distribution, determined by geography, climate, and human invention, moved the literature published or reprinted in the East to the Middle and Far West and, in so doing, helped develop a popular readership. If those methods also developed systems of price cutting and wretched bookmaking, a spate of cheapjohns and a glut of libraries or series, if those methods were flawed and seldom fully effective, nonetheless they played an important role in America's transition to mass production, urbanization and, especially, literacy.[63]

Everywhere threads must connect to make a fabric, and the methods of distribution resorted to in nineteenth-century America were connected and often used simultaneously or in combination: the peregrinations of book agents, the role of canals and waterways, the proliferating railroads, the postal system, exchanges and trade sales, express companies and the great jobbers, and the branch and local bookstores that cropped up near mountain ranges and desert plains. Despite the inadequacies of distribution, it did disseminate literature and supply the western market.

A corollary suggests itself. Did the taste of the West in any way shape the literary products of the East and so influence the nature of the nation's reading matter? The question is a provocative one that moved William Charvat to state, "The taste of the West determined to some extent the literary fare offered to readers in the East."[64] That the western reader was indeed a cultural influence may be difficult to prove with scientific exactitude, but it is certainly a strong probability. The overland railway not only expedited book distribution east to west, as we have seen, but heightened the interest in books about the West. Even before its completion, Anton Roman, through his New York agency, offered Bret Harte's *Condensed Novels* to G. W. Carleton of New York, who published the volume in 1867. (Roman's advertisements, incidentally, appeared on the back of Widdleton's lists in the *Publishers' Trade List Annual.*[65]) Later on, when A. K. Loring of Boston noted that Horatio Alger's popularity was declining in the East but increasing in the West, he advised his star author to reverse his usual procedure and write stories about the West for boys in the East. The result was the Pacific Series including *The Young Miner; or, Tom Nelson in California* and *The Young Explorer; or, Among the Sierras.*[66]

As the methods of book distribution were determined by the nation's geography, the results of book distribution helped determine the nation's reading tastes and hence its literary history. And so, as James Gilreath has put it, "To fully appreciate the impact of the book on American culture, book dispersal must be part of intellectual and cultural history."[67]

Notes

1. *Diary of Cotton Mather 1681–1708* (Boston: Massachusetts Historical Society, 1911) 1: 65; Downing Palmer O'Harra, "Book Publishing in the United States to 1901," *Publishers' Weekly,* 11 May 1929, 2252–54.

2. William Charvat, *The Profession of Authorship in America, 1800–1870* (Columbus: Ohio State University Press, 1968), 18.

3. Richardson Wright, *Hawkers & Walkers in Early America* (Philadelphia: Lippincott, 1927), 162.

4. Mary Noel, *Villains Galore . . . The Heyday of the Popular Story Weekly* (New York: Macmillan, 1954), 2; O'Harra, "Book Publishing to 1901"; Wright, *Hawkers & Walkers,* 50, 162.

5. John W. Moore, *Moore's Historical, Biographical, and Miscellaneous Gatherings . . . relative to Printers, Printing, Publishing, and Editing* (Concord, N.H.: Republican Press Association, 1886), 23.

6. Charvat, *Profession of Authorship,* 40; Michael Hackenberg, "Hawking Subscription Books in 1870: A Salesman's Prospectus from Western Pennsylvania," *Papers of the Bibliographical Society of America* 78 (1984): 137–53; Donald Sheehan, *This Was Publishing: A Chronicle of the Book Trade in the Gilded Age* (Bloomington: Indiana University Press, 1952), 145; John Tebbel, *A History of Book Publishing in the United States,* vol. 2 (New York: R. R. Bowker, 1975), 102.

7. Quoted by Wright, *Hawkers & Walkers,* 52.

8. William Garretson & Co., *Confidential Circular to Agents* (Nashville: Garretson, 1868), 5.

9. Elizabeth Lindley, *The Diary of a Book-Agent* (New York: Broadway Publishing Company, 1911), 23.

10. J. H. Mortimer, *Confessions of a Book Agent* (Chicago: Co-operative Publishing Company, 1906), 172; Madeleine B. Stern, *Heads & Headlines: The Phrenological Fowlers* (Norman: University of Oklahoma Press, 1971), 139.

11. "Sketches of the Publishers: The American News Company," *The Round Table,* 14 Apr. 1866, 234.

12. *American Literary Gazette,* 1 Sept. 1869, 249, quoted by Sheehan, *This Was Publishing,* 151.

13. James Gilreath, "American Book Distribution" (unpublished typescript, courtesy of the author); Herbert Mitgang, "The Book Travelers: 100 Years on the Road," *New York Times,* 1 Dec. 1984, 15; *Publishers' Weekly,* 2 Jan. 1897, 7; Sheehan, *This Was Publishing,* 159, 164f.; Tebbel, *History of Book Publishing,* 2: 106.

14. Horatio Alger, Jr., *The Young Book Agent; or, Frank Hardy's Road to Success* (New York: Stitt Publishing Company, 1905); Charvat, *Profession of Authorship,* 299; J. C. Derby, *Fifty Years among Authors, Books, and Publishers* (New York: Carleton, 1884), 577; J. R. Dolan, *The Yankee Peddlers of Early America* (New York: Clarkson N. Potter, 1964), 210f.; O'Harra, "Publishing to 1901" (quoting Boston *News-Letter* of 9–16 Apr. 1705); Madeleine B. Stern, ed., *Publishers for Mass Entertainment in Nineteenth-Century America* (Boston: G. K. Hall, 1980), 68, 245; Wright, *Hawkers & Walkers,* 53.

15. Charvat, *Profession of Authorship,* 285.

16. Dolan, *Yankee Peddlers,* 210; Madeleine B. Stern, *Antiquarian Bookselling in the United States: A History from the Origins to the 1940s* (Westport, Conn.: Greenwood Press, 1985), 31; Wright, *Hawkers & Walkers,* 52f.

17. James Henry Foss, *The Gentleman from Everywhere* (Boston: the author, 1902), 279.

18. Louisa May Alcott to Samuel Sewall, 6 June 1880, Massachusetts Historical Society.

19. Garretson, *Confidential Circular to Agents,* 12.

20. Joshua Wright [Titus K. Smith], *The Book Agent: His Book* (New York: Thomson and Smith, 1904), 140.

21. Madeleine B. Stern, *Books and Book People in 19th-Century America* (New York: R. R. Bowker, 1978), 38. See also William Charvat, *Literary Publishing in America 1790–1850* (Philadelphia: University of Pennsylvania Press, 1959), 17.

22. Charvat, *Profession of Authorship,* 36.

23. "Sketches of the Publishers," *Round Table,* 21 Apr. 1866, 250; Stern, *Antiquarian Bookselling,* 109; John Tebbel, *History of Book Publishing in the United States,* vol. 1 (New York: R. R. Bowker, 1972), 110.

24. Charvat, *Literary Publishing,* 19. See also Stern, ed., *Publishers for Mass Entertainment,* 78.

25. Walter Sutton, *The Western Book Trade: Cincinnati as a Nineteenth-Century Publishing and Book-Trade Center* (Columbus: Ohio State University Press, 1961), 256–57.

26. Charvat, *Profession of Authorship,* 36; Stern, *Antiquarian Bookselling,* 64; Stern, *Books and Book People,* 30; Sutton, *Western Book Trade,* 255–56; Wright, *Hawkers & Walkers,* 53, 162.

27. *Alta California,* 8 Mar. and 18 June 1851, quoted by Stern, *Antiquarian Bookselling,* 132.

28. Charvat, *Literary Publishing,* 8; Charvat, *Profession of Authorship,* 285; Stern, *Antiquarian Bookselling,* 81, quoting the *Cincinnati Enquirer,* 25 Jan. 1979; Stern, "The Role of the Publisher in Mid-Nineteenth Century American Literature," *Publishing History* 10 (1981): 6; Sutton, *Western Book Trade,* 279–80, 284–85.

29. Quoted by Stern, *Antiquarian Bookselling,* 113; see also 120.

30. *Facts By a Woman* (Oakland: Pacific Press Publishing House, 1881), 134, 136–37.

31. The American News Company, *Serving the Reading Public* (New York: American News Company, 1944), unpaged; Roy Quinlan, "The Story of Magazine Distribution," *Magazine Week,* 19 Oct. 1953, 4.

32. Louisa May Alcott, "Letters from the Mountains," *The Commonwealth,* 24 July 1863, 1; Derby, *Fifty Years among Authors,* 573; Madeleine B. Stern, "Keen & Cooke: Prairie Publishers," *Journal of the Illinois State Historical Society* 42 (1949): 440; Stern, *Louisa May Alcott* (Norman: University of Oklahoma Press, 1971), 199.

33. Charvat, *Profession of Authorship,* 299; Madeleine B. Stern, *Imprints on History: Book Publishers and American Frontiers* (New York: AMS Press, 1975), 221, 223, 227–29; Stern, ed., *Publishers for Mass Entertainment,* xix, 184–86, 193, 234.

34. Stern, *Heads & Headlines,* 140.

35. Noel, *Villains Galore*, 3. See also "Sketches of the Publishers," *Round Table*, 14 Apr. 1866, 234.

36. Stern, *Books and Book People*, 280–81. See also Frank Luther Mott, *Golden Multitudes: The Story of Best Sellers in the United States* (New York: Macmillan, 1947), 79; Frank L. Schick, *The Paperbound Book in America* (New York: R. R. Bowker, 1958), 50.

37. Quoted by Raymond Howard Shove, *Cheap Book Production in the United States, 1870 to 1891* (Urbana: University of Illinois Press, 1937), 49. See also Stern, *Books and Book People*, 249; Stern, *Imprints on History*, 265; Stern, *Purple Passage: The Life of Mrs. Frank Leslie* (Norman: University of Oklahoma Press, 1970), 108; Tebbel, *History of Book Publishing*, 2: 484.

38. Shove, *Cheap Book Production*, 41. See also Tebbel, *History of Book Publishing*, 2: 487, 506.

39. Sinclair Tousey, *A Business Man's Views of Public Matters* (New York: American News Company, 1865), 28 and passim.

40. Gilreath, "American Book Distribution," 45. See also Heywood Broun and Margaret Leech, *Anthony Comstock: Roundsman of the Lord* (London: Wishart, 1928), 160.

41. For the exchange system, see Charvat, *Literary Publishing*, 47; Charvat, *Profession of Authorship*, 42; Sutton, *Western Book Trade*, 209; Tebbel, *History of Book Publishing*, 1: 110.

42. For trade sales, see Hellmut Lehmann-Haupt, *The Book in America* (New York: R. R. Bowker, 1951), 132, 258; Sheehan, *This Was Publishing*, 146–47, 150, 152, 156–57; Sutton, *Western Book Trade*, 202, 272–73, 275; Tebbel, *History of Book Publishing*, 1: 231, 237 and 2: 102–3, 105; W. S. Tryon, "Book Distribution in Mid-Nineteenth Century America Illustrated by the Publishing Records of Ticknor and Fields, Boston," *Papers of the Bibliographical Society of America*, 41 (1947): 223–24; Carl J. Weber, *The Rise and Fall of James Ripley Osgood* (Waterville: Colby College Press, 1959), 140.

43. A. L. Stimson, *History of the Express Companies: and the Origin of American Railroads* (New York, 1858), 112 and passim. For express companies, see also Anson L. Blake, "Working for Wells Fargo—1860–1863. Letters of Charles T. Blake," *California Historical Society Quarterly* 16 (1937): 31; Alfred L. Hammell, *Wm. Frederick Harnden (1813–1845) Founder of the Express Business in America* (New York, San Francisco, and Montreal: Newcomen Society in North America, 1954), 7 and passim; Frank Luther Mott, *A History of American Magazines*, vol. 3 (Cambridge, Mass.: Harvard University Press, Belknap Press, 1957), 8.

44. For details regarding Tousey, see *The American Bookseller*, 1 July 1887, 6–7; *Appletons' Annual Cyclopaedia . . . 1887* (New York: Appleton, 1888), 616; *Appletons' Cyclopaedia of American Biography* (New York: Appleton, 1889), 6: 144; *Publishers' Weekly*, 25 June 1887, 804; "Sketches of the Publishers: The American News Company," *The Round Table*, 7 Apr. 1866, 218; Stern, ed., *Publishers for Mass Entertainment*, 303–4 (an article by Nathaniel H. Puffer); *Dictionary of American Biography*, s.v. "Tousey, Sinclair."

45. *American Literary Gazette*, 15 Feb. 1864, 268.

46. *The American Bookseller*, 1 July 1887, 7.

47. Noel, *Villains Galore,* 107, 142; *Publishers' Weekly,* 30 Apr. 1904, 1183–84; "Sketches of the Publishers," *The Round Table,* 21 Apr. 1866, 250.

48. The plant is described in "Sketches of the Publishers: The American News Company," *The Round Table,* 7 Apr. 1866, 218, 21 Apr. 1866, 250.

49. Tousey, *A Business Man's Views,* 32. For the company's operations, see also the American News Company, *Serving the Reading Public,* passim; *Covering a Continent: A Story of Newsstand Distribution and Sales* (New York: American News Company, 1930), 13, 15; Lehmann-Haupt, *The Book in America,* 249; Tebbel, *History of Book Publishing,* 2: 393.

50. "Sketches of the Publishers," *The Round Table,* 21 Apr. 1866, 250.

51. Quoted by Shove, *Cheap Book Production,* 39–40. For the libraries or series distributed by the American News Company, see also Albert Johannsen, *The House of Beadle and Adams,* vol. 1 (Norman: University of Oklahoma Press, 1950), 47; Stern, *Imprints on History,* 228–29; Stern, ed., *Publishers for Mass Entertainment,* 45–46, 285.

52. "Sketches of the Publishers," *The Round Table,* 7 Apr. 1866, 218. See also 21 Apr. 1866, 250.

53. For the company's expansion and branches, see the American News Company, *Serving the Reading Public;* Mott, *History of American Magazines,* 3: 8 and 4: 18; Noel, *Villains Galore,* 291; *Publishers' Weekly,* 26 June 1909, 2057–58; Stern, ed., *Publishers for Mass Entertainment,* 304; Tebbel, *History of Book Publishing,* 2: 393.

54. For the company's later history I am indebted to information from James Gilreath and Michael Winship.

55. Stern, "Keen & Cooke," 425.

56. Stern, *Antiquarian Bookselling,* 66–67.

57. Stern, *Imprints on History,* 170.

58. Stern, *Antiquarian Bookselling,* 88; Stern, "Keen & Cooke," 432. See also Charvat, *Profession of Authorship,* 300.

59. Stern, *Antiquarian Bookselling,* 110.

60. Ibid., 121.

61. Stern, *Books and Book People,* 202–9.

62. Stern, *Imprints on History,* 136–54.

63. The *American Bookseller,* 1 Apr. 1889, 128, 1 Feb. 1890, 82; Mott, *Golden Multitudes,* 155; *Publishers' Weekly,* 26 Apr. 1913, 1493 ("The world . . . is still looking for a publisher who will 'discover or invent' a new method which shall be both practical and effective for the distribution of books of general literature"); Sheehan, *This Was Publishing,* 144; Tryon, "Book Distribution," 212.

64. Charvat, *Literary Publishing,* 25.

65. Stern, *Antiquarian Bookselling,* 137; Stern, *Books and Book People,* 222.

66. Stern, ed., *Publishers for Mass Entertainment,* 195.

67. Gilreath, "American Book Distribution," 2.

5. "Spiritual Cakes Upon the Waters": The Church as a Disseminator of the Printed Word on the Ohio Valley Frontier to 1850

Michael H. Harris

I had a number of reasons for writing this chapter. First, I wanted to report on what has been a long-term investigation into the role of the Church in book distribution in the West. I must admit that I have been seized of this project for rather longer than is my custom, having published my first thoughts on the matter in 1967.[1]

Second, I wanted to address briefly what I see as an unfortunate trend in the historiography of the antebellum era in American history. To be blunt, I am convinced that historians have increasingly lost sight of the significance of the book in the reform movements that swept the nation from 1820 to 1850. It seems to me that too much recent historiography of the era has generally misunderstood, or deliberately ignored, the nineteenth-century conception of the role of the printed word in the establishment of a civically virtuous republic.

I would contend that much recent work ignores the abundant evidence that illustrates the extent to which the intellectual elite in nineteenth-century America shared an unwavering conviction that the proper deployment of an army of well-selected books would prove of major consequence in the battle for the minds and hearts of ordinary Americans. This unwavering conviction explains the intense commitment of that elite to a wide range of voluntary organizations dedicated to the dissemination of printed messages as the key to controlling "public opinion" and thus ameliorating mankind.

However, by the 1950s, historians (who were relying heavily on empirical studies carried out by communications scholars on the impact of propaganda) came to view this unwavering conviction in the efficacy of the printed word to influence human behavior in predictable ways as anachronistic. That is, our advanced knowledge of the inability of printed messages to influence human behavior in predictable ways led us to dismiss the nineteenth-century conception of the role of the printed word as unrealistic, or worse, as hypocritical camouflage for more devious objectives.

In many ways, our more sophisticated understanding of how print communication "works" has dramatically revised and improved our understanding of eighteenth- and nineteenth-century America.[2] The work of Bernard Bailyn, Michael Wood, and Lance Banning illustrates this point nicely.[3] At the same time our desire to assess the real impact of "ideology" on public opinion has led us to ignore or underestimate the conception of the impact of print which informed the great book crusades of the nineteenth century.[4]

What emerges is a much fuller picture of how print actually contributed to the coming of the Revolution, for instance, but what is lost is an understanding of the central position that the printed word played in any battle plan devised by reformers during the first half of the nineteenth century. It is my contention that recent studies of the reform movements of the era in question tend to slight, or misunderstand, the pivotal role of nineteenth-century conceptions of the impact of print on human behavior and thus tend to ignore the centrality of the book to every one of the major reform movements of the period. This blind spot, I conclude, leads historians to slight, or misunderstand, the structural and functional characteristics of nineteenth-century reform movements premised on the "bullet theory" of the impact of print on human behavior. Hopefully what follows, which simply lets the subjects speak for themselves, will illustrate my point.

Finally, I will conclude this chapter with some brief reflections on the nature of the revived interest in the history of the book as evidenced in conferences like the Chicago conference. While I feel historians of the nineteenth-century reform movements underestimate and misunderstand the role of the book in those great book crusades, I will also contend that historians of the book tend to misunderstand that same question.

My object, then, is to illustrate my case by exploring the Church's efforts to establish itself on the frontier, while at the same time saying something about the nineteenth-century conception of the significance of the printed word in establishing an ordered Christian society in America.

The Ohio Valley's first settlers, when they felt the need of new reading matter, could seldom turn to a nearby bookstore. Bookstores were scarce on the frontier, and those sources of the printed word were scattered and difficult to reach in the days of bad roads and expensive travel.

Fortunately, many books traveled by horseback, carefully packed in the saddlebags of itinerant ministers serving their flocks through the valley. These men were representatives of an eastern elite which, as Bernard Weisberger points out, held a threefold indictment against the American people:

> The first charge was intellectual: the nation had succumbed to Beelzebub in adopting newfangled and "infidel" doctrines. The second was social and political: it had thrust the church out of its rightful place at the head of society. The third was harder to characterize, but exclusively American. Those who had gone west were abandoning old churches and showing no enthusiasm for building new ones. The frontier was destitute of religion.[5]

Of all the charges against Americans, the last seemed the most serious and the most immediately in need of attention. The clergy saw a vital need to convert the West, for as that section of the nation grew, its power grew concomitantly. What would be the fate of the country if the West did not hold to Christian principles? It was imperative to get on with the job of saving the West for Christ for, as one agent of a national missionary society argued in 1830,

> Look at . . . the "valley of the Mississippi." In twenty years if it should continue to increase as it has done . . . it will contain a majority of the people of the United States. . . . The destinies of the Union will be in their hands. If that portion of the country be not brought under the influence of religion *now,* it cannot, to human view, be done at all. . . . *Now or never* is the watchword . . . in reference to that religion.[6]

This sentiment was still being echoed as late as 1847, when Henry Ward Beecher, in a report dispatched from Indianapolis to the American Home Missionary Society of New York, wrote, "It should be burned into the minds of Christians in the East, that the work of the age, for the American Church is the care of the new states of the West."[7]

But how was this "care of the new states of the West" to be effected? It was really all quite simple, too simple perhaps, for modern historians to believe. It must be remembered that the eastern elite that provided the dynamic force to these crusades subscribed to the view that sin, poverty, intemperance, and bigotry were personal rather than social ills, and that the cure lay in reforming the individual through moral instruction.[8] It was, in short, a cognitive problem.

This understanding of the problem makes it clear how an essayist in the *Quarterly Register* for 1828 could identify the problem of the West as that of a "mighty mass of unsanctified intellect." The same sentiment led

Edward Everett to note that "the mind of the West" was at risk; the question was simply whether that "mind" "shall be a power of intelligence or of ignorance; a reign of reflection and reason, or of reckless strength; a reign of darkness, or of light."[9] Mr. Everett and his friends were determined that the mind of the West should adhere to the principles of intelligence, reflection, reason, and light.

But then how did one attack the problem of enlightening this "mass of unsanctified intellect?" Once again the answer was quick to the lips of the reformers—with the word, especially the printed word. As Daniel Walker Howe has noted, the book crusaders were of one mind in believing that "reading could make a Christian."[10] For they generally agreed in what is now jokingly referred to as the "bullet theory" of communication. Simply put, if you intelligently prepare your ammunition, load and aim it with care, and then hit your target with it, you can predict that the target will fall down. To these reformers the printed word was felt to be an especially potent bullet, and the firing of these "silent monitors" at the mind of the West determined to a considerable degree the structural and functional characteristics of the wide-ranging but interlocked endeavor to Christianize the West.[11]

The organizational problem posed by the need to deliver a printed bullet from the East to a living target in the West was met through the expedient of forming voluntary organizations.[12] These voluntary organizations—missionary, tract, Bible and Sunday School associations—have been frequently discussed, but what is rarely remarked was that most of the movers in the "Great Crusade" felt that the delivery of the printed word to the West was as significant, if not more significant, than the delivery of missionaries to the West.[13] The printed word was simply seen as the most effective and cost-efficient way to ameliorate the western problem, for as one executive of the American Home Missionary Society noted in 1839, "the Gospel is the most economical police on earth."[14]

Before the end of the eighteenth century, home missionary societies were formed for the express purpose of sending ministers, Bibles, and religious tracts into the backwoods of the West in hope of converting its wild and irreligious inhabitants to Christianity. Recruiting, dispatching, and supporting itinerant ministers in their missionary endeavors garnered much attention among the founders of the home missionary movement. But the publication and distribution of God's word, and that of his most respected earthly representatives, drew as much attention. Soon thousands of Christians were stimulated to give financial support for the effort to provide the West with good religious literature. Even children were encouraged to help, as evidenced by the following excerpt from the *Gospel Kite,* number forty-four in "Aunt Celia's Library" and a frequent inhabitant of Sabbath School library shelves:

A boy in Connecticut, eleven years of age, was one day busily engaged in his play. . . . Well, the amusement in which this lad was so busily occupied was that of making a little *kite*. But, while his hands were actively engaged in his play, his thoughts were towards the benighted heathen, and he was studying ways to send them relief. By-and-bye he looked up to his father and said very seriously, "Father, I wish I had a string to my kite that would reach clear to the heathen." "Why, my son," said the father, "what would you do with it if you had?" "I would send the gospel to them," quickly replied the boy. "How *could* you do that?" inquired the father. "I would make a *great* kite," said he, "and then I would tie a little Testament to it, and if I only had a string long enough, I would send it away to the heathen!" Now, young readers, what say you to this kind of amusement? Would not every boy who reads this be glad to make a little kite and send a Testament to some poor heathen child? And would not several of you be willing to unite in making a kite large enough to send out a Bible with large type, so that some of the old heathen, who have poor eyes, if they have learned to read, may read the story of the Savior? Would you not love to do it? . . . We suppose our readers all understand what we mean by the *Kite*. It is the little *money* you will contribute to buy books; and the more money, the bigger the kite. . . . And the string is the MASS. S.S. SOCIETY. And there is not a longer, safer, or more beautiful *kite-string* in the land.[15]

Whether this project inspired many children to donate their small allowances for the purchase of books is not known, but the fact remains that millions of Bibles, testaments, and religious tracts were sent west during the first half of the nineteenth century.[16] These books were purchased, packed, and shipped from Boston, Philadelphia, and New York to Cincinnati, Louisville, or the headquarters of the various ministers. They were then carried in saddlebags into the backwoods of the valley to be sold or given away to families in need of God's word.

The men who carried these religious works throughout the valley differed in many respects, but they all had access to books. Although the books were limited in number and scope, they were carefully read as the itinerants rode through the wilds or sat at night near their lonely campfires. All types of men could be found distributing the message of Christianity on the frontier. There were some like the eccentric John Chapman, better known as Johnny Appleseed, who traveled throughout the West sowing the seeds of the "New Jerusalem" in the form of the works of Emanuel Swedenborg, as well as the better-known apple seeds.[17] Although Chapman was never an ordained minister, he did gain support and acknowledgment from the New Churchmen. In the *Journal* of the fifth General Convention of the New Churchmen, held in Philadelphia in 1822, the following bright description of Chapman and his work was printed:

> His temporal employment consists in preceeding the settlements, and sowing nurseries of fruit trees, which he avows to be pursued for the chief purpose of giving him the opportunity of spreading the doctrines throughout the western country.
>
> In his progress, which neither heat nor cold, swamps nor mountains, are permitted to arrest, he carries on his back all the New Church publications he can procure, and distributes them wherever opportunity is afforded. So great is his zeal, that he does not hesitate to divide his volumes into parts, by repeated calls, enabling the readers to peruse the whole in succession.[18]

Others like the Reverend John Strange, one of Indiana's most popular camp meeting preachers, exhibited a deep-seated anti-intellectualism and placed little stock in book learning. But even men like Strange, who proudly claimed as his alma mater, "Brush College, more ancient though less pretentious than Yale or Harvard or Princeton," were quick to acknowledge that "the word of God, the discipline and the hymn book," were necessary items in any Christian home.[19]

But more numerous than the eccentrics like Chapman or the anti-intellectuals like Reverend Strange were the hardworking and devout itinerants who considered the distribution of books and tracts as one of their most sacred duties. Peter Cartwright, perhaps the best known of the Methodist circuit riders, exemplified this feeling when he wrote:

> It has often been a question that I shall never be able to answer on earth, whether I have done the most good by preaching or distributing religious books. . . . For more than fifty years I have firmly believed, that it was part and parcel of a Methodist preacher's most sacred duty to circulate good books wherever they go among the people.[20]

Especially active in the establishment of programs to serve the religious needs of the frontiersman were the New England Congregationalists who had formed many state and local missionary societies for the purpose of sending missionaries and books into the West. During the War of 1812 the missionary societies of Massachusetts and Connecticut rendered significant service to this cause by underwriting two missionary tours of the Mississippi Valley.[21] The reports that resulted from them surveyed the moral and religious conditions prevalent on the frontier and found them desperately in need of attention. It is generally agreed that the report issued in 1815 more than anything else was responsible for uniting the small local and state societies into national organizations that were then able to design and implement a national strategy, and that it stimulated many denominational groups to develop vigorous and rapidly increasing programs in the West.[22]

During the latter part of 1812 and the first few months of 1813, Samuel J. Mills and John F. Schermerhorn undertook a tour of the Mississippi Valley on behalf of New England's two leading missionary societies. Their specific task was to investigate the religious and moral condition of the West, "ascertain the number of Bibles available, the number of clergymen serving each community, search out profitable areas of missionary endeavor, and assess the general characteristics of the inhabitants."[23] About six months were required for them to make the journey down the Ohio to Indiana, across Kentucky and Tennessee to the Mississippi River, and then on to New Orleans. Their report, published in 1814, contained much useful and provocative information about the extent and nature of religion in the West. Particularly distressing to the authors was the obvious lack of Bibles and other religious works among the inhabitants of the "Great Valley."[24]

As a result of this report, Mills and Daniel J. Smith were commissioned by the Massachusetts Missionary Society, the Philadelphia Bible Society, and the Philadelphia Missionary Society to go into the West to distribute Bibles and religious tracts and to encourage the establishment of Bible societies.[25] Charged with the responsibility of distributing some fifteen thousand tracts selected from those published by the New England Tract Society, and thousands of Bibles, they set out from Philadelphia in the summer of 1814. The two missionaries headed down the Ohio River to Indiana and proceeded overland to Illinois and Missouri. From St. Louis they returned through Illinois and Indiana and entered Kentucky, from which they descended the Ohio and Mississippi rivers to New Orleans.

In Indiana, Mills and Smith visited Vincennes, New Albany, Charleston, and Vevay, distributing Bibles and tracts and attempting to establish Bible societies as they proceeded. Their report shows that they deposited nine hundred tracts and several hundred Bibles in the state. Their custom was to leave a set of tracts with the clergymen they met along the way.[26]

The missionaries left twenty-five Bibles and a number of tracts with Governor Thomas Posey at Jeffersonville, and in 1815 Posey wrote that he had given nearly all of them away.[27] While in Indiana, Mills sent ten copies of the French New Testament to Mr. Daniel Dufour in Vevay, the site of a Swiss colony in southeastern Indiana. On 20 June 1815, Dufour wrote Mills, "In the beginning of May, I received your very acceptable letter, dated January 3, 1815, with ten copies of the French New Testament, printed by the Philadelphia Bible Society. The reception of the Testaments has afforded real pleasure, both to me, and the Swiss families, among whom I have distributed them." Dufour was somewhat disturbed "that a book so sacred as the New Testament had not been printed with greater care," for the binder had cut off words, even lines, in folding the sheets. Despite these defects he wrote that all the Bibles had been received with "much joy; and all the families, which have received copies, have charged me to present to you their cordial salutations, and sincere thanks."[28]

At New Albany, the missionaries found that they had been preceded by an agent of the Newark Auxiliary Bible Society, Nathaniel Scribner, who had distributed fifty Bibles in that town. Mills was impressed by the enthusiasm with which the Bibles had been received and glowingly described what had transpired:

> Two young men, having heard of the circumstance, came on the Sabbath—a stormy and uncomfortable day, twenty miles, to obtain Bibles. When they received them, they placed them in their bosom. They were induced to tarry and hear a sermon; and then went home in the night, rejoicing that they had obtained such a treasure. In a few days the Bibles were all gone; and Mr. Scribner said he could immediately distribute a hundred more, if he had them.[29]

Mills and Smith had some success in fostering the establishment of Bible societies which would carry on their work after the two missionaries had departed. On 27 January 1815, Governor Thomas Posey wrote from Jeffersonville,

> Agreeably to my promise, I can inform you, that the Bible Society, which we have made some progress in exertions to establish, is not yet matured. At New Albany and this village, there are subscribed about two hundred dollars. Judge James Scott informs me, that at Charleston the subscription is small—does not say to what amount, but expects, that the people, when they come to understand the true principles of the Society will subscribe liberally.[30]

Mills and Smith had similar successes all along the route they traveled. By the time they reached New Orleans the War of 1812 was over, and Jackson's militia had triumphed over the British troops sent to capture that city. The two missionaries found that the militia were eager to receive copies of the Bible, and "many of the Tennessee detachment said that they would carry them all the way home in their knapsacks, even though they should be obliged to leave a part of their baggage."[31]

The two tours undertaken by Samuel Mills and his companions had a great impact upon the future missionary endeavors of religious bodies, especially the Congregationalists and the Presbyterians, in the West. The needs for, and the potential of, missionary programs in the West had been vividly portrayed. Thousands of Bibles and other religious works had been distributed in the West to people who seemed overjoyed at receiving them. The time had certainly come for a determined effort at converting the West to Christianity. Soon national organizations such as the American Education Society (1816), the American Bible Society (1816), the American Sunday School Union (1824), the American Tract Society (1825), and the American Home Missionary Society (1826) were aiding the cause. Evangelicals all, the members of these groups subscribed to the view that any rational man, properly instructed, could see the superiority of the Christian system. Many denominational groups also rushed into the fray; but most notable were the Methodists and Presbyterians.

From the beginnings Methodism was a bookish religion. Wesley himself was a firm believer in the power of the printed word and began early his efforts to provide cheap books and pamphlets for his flock. In 1790, he wrote a friend that

> It cannot be that the people should grow in grace unless they give themselves to reading. A reading people will always be a knowing people. . . . Press this upon them with all your might; and you will soon see the fruit of your labours.[32]

His exhortation to "take care that every society be duly supplied with books" was not lost on his American brethren. To the Methodist circuit riders the distribution of books was a sacred and glorious duty. It was with a full appreciation of the significance of books that Wesley wrote to Richard Rodda,

> You should take particular care that your circuit be never without an assortment of all the valuable books, especially the *Appeals,* the *Sermons,* Kempis, and the *Primitive Physick,* which no family should be without. . . . You are found to be remarkably diligent in spreading the books; let none rob you of this glory.[33]

Methodist works were published in America for several decades before the historic Christmas meeting in Baltimore in 1784, when the Methodist Episcopal Church in America was formally organized. The first bishop of the Methodist Church in America, Francis Asbury, desired an organized approach to book publishing and distribution. Between 1773 and 1782, a plan was formed to publish and sell books, with the profits from their sales going to the support of Methodist ministers. In 1782 this plan was approved, and before long the Methodist Book Concern was operating, taking as its motto: "The advancement of the cause of Christianity through the printed word."[34]

Asbury, like most early Methodist ministers, had little formal education, but he shared their interest in the distribution of books among the people.[35] In the *Discipline* of 1796, the bishop wrote:

> The spreading of religious knowledge by the press is of the greatest moment to the people. The books of infidelity and profaneness with

which the States at present abound demand our strongest exertions to counteract their pernicious influence; and every step shall be taken which is consistent with our finances to furnish our friends from time to time with the most useful literature available.[36]

Unfortunately, the early sales of books by Methodist circuit riders brought them only a negligible return, and therefore they sometimes faltered in their efforts to sell them. In 1800 the general conference provided some real stimulus to the sale of books by allowing the preachers to retain a certain percentage of the cash they received from book sales. This practice greatly encouraged the sales of books on the frontier, for as one Methodist historian has pointed out, it provided "the source of the only cash some Methodist preachers ever saw."[37]

Given the stimulus of profits from their bookselling efforts, Methodist circuit riders devoted themselves to the task with vigor. Indeed, at times their interest in the money-making book business became too obvious, and in 1824 the *Methodist Magazine* warned, "Let it be known that you do not do this selling on account of the profits of sale. A just suspicion of this motive will destroy your dignity, and usefulness."[38] Despite this cautionary note, Methodist circuit riders steadfastly traveled their circuits selling books to those they met on the way.

By 1814, when Mills and Smith toured the "Great Valley," the Methodists had already gained the forefront of the business of spreading books across the frontier. Mills was highly impressed with the success of the Methodists' venture and described what he found at length:

> The leading characters of the Methodist Society are very active in supplying the western country with books. . . . It is generally said in the western country, that the members of that connexion are expected to purchase all their books of the preachers and other agents of the Society. . . . The impression seems also to be general, that the books are sold very low—at cost. . . .
>
> This energetic Society sends out an immense quantity of these books. We found them almost everywhere. In the possession of the obscurest families, we often found a number of volumes. . . . It puts to the blush all the other charitable institutions in the United States.[39]

The Methodists did not have to await the formation of a national society aimed at the distribution of books in the West, for, as William Warren Sweet noted, "the whole Methodist system was missionary in purpose and in a real sense every circuit rider was a missionary."[40] The Methodist circuit rider did not set out looking for settlers who were already members of his denomination, as did the Presbyterian ministers, but instead threw his net wide and visited everyone he could find along his circuit. Consequently he had a much larger market for his books.

One of the most successful Methodist booksellers was the Reverend Joseph Tarkington who, after his conversion at a camp meeting five miles west of Bloomington, Indiana, on 27 August 1820, rode circuits all across the southern half of Indiana. In that time he sold thousands of books. His most successful year was probably 1835 when he was riding the Charleston circuit:

> I sold five hundred dollars' worth of religious books in the circuit. Getting books among the people stirred them up wonderfully. They could read at all times. One can judge of the religious standing of a family by the books they read. Going the first round of the circuit, I would look to see what books were read.[41]

Tarkington and his colleagues rode their circuits bringing large quantities of books to people who had lost most other ways of "following cultural pursuits when the great migration to the West had occurred." As one historian of the Methodists' bookselling efforts in the West has concluded, "Surely many of the frontier homes would have been without books of any kind if the circuit rider had not insisted that a need for them existed in the home."[42]

The Presbyterians were the only denominational group which was equipped, by training and motivation, to compete with the Methodists in the matter of distributing Bibles and other religious works among the settlers prior to 1850. Interestingly, the clergy representing the Methodists and the Presbyterians in the West differed markedly in almost every essential aspect. The Methodist circuit rider was not as well educated and very seldom commanded a college degree. The Presbyterian clergy were required by church law to hold a bachelor's or master's degree from a college or university, or at least to present testimonials of having completed some regular course of learning.[43] Thus the Presbyterians were responsible for sending many of the first college-educated men into the West.

The approach of the two denominations to their work differed too. The Presbyterian minister was usually called to the West by the people; while the Methodist circuit rider was sent to the people. The Presbyterian itinerants usually "located" in one place, although they did travel circuits on occasion, while the Methodist circuit rider rode his long and difficult circuits from the beginning, and thus reached a much larger number of people. The result, as Sweet has pointed out, was that

> The frontier Presbyterian minister seldom or never ministered regularly to more then three congregations, and usually to not more than two, with the result that the Presbyterian influence tended to be more or less localized, whereas Methodist influence, through their circuit system, was spread broadcast throughout the frontier, one minister often serving as many as twenty-five communities.[44]

All of these reasons explain why the Methodists had a broader success than their Presbyterian counterparts in the West. But in one essential area, the distribution of Bibles and religious tracts among the settlers of the West, they labored with equal determination for years. In this area only were the Presbyterian ministers able to point to successes equal to, sometimes greater than, those of the Methodists.

One of the first Presbyterian missionaries to work in the valley was the Reverend Isaac Reed, a representative of the Connecticut Missionary Society, who settled in Owen County, Indiana, on the West Fork of the White River in 1822. Reed traveled more than was generally expected of the Presbyterian missionaries, and he considered the distribution of books to be of only slightly less importance than his duties as a preacher. It is from Reed that we get some of the first descriptions of a Presbyterian minister's effort to distribute God's word along the frontier. In 1825, we find him writing to the Connecticut Missionary Society:

> You wrote me of the books, that they would soon be shipped; you also inform me, that I am to be intrusted with the distribution of 200 Bibles. . . . Thank the Directors of the Connecticut Bible Society. . . . Their benefaction is needed, and greatly needed, in this new country. Many are without the Scriptures—many have the New, and not the Old Testament; and most unfortunately, many cannot read either. Were their benefaction 2000, instead of 200, it would not be sufficient supply for the fourth part of this state.[45]

Reed went throughout the valley distributing tracts and Bibles to "destitute families." In another letter he interestingly described a problem that must have plagued all those involved in the distribution of religious works on the frontier:

> The state of learning is also on the advance. But there are many people without even a common school education. When I began first to distribute Religious Tracts, in different parts, I found I often gave, or was about to give tracts, to persons who could not read. Afterwards, when I was about to give tracts to strangers, I first asked them whether they could read, before I offered them the tracts.[46]

Missionaries like Reed did their best to serve the religious needs of the rapidly growing population of the West, but their numbers were too small and their support too unreliable to allow them widespread successes. At the same time, the significance of the rising West was growing more and more apparent to eastern churchmen. As one Andover student put it,

> The hundreds and thousands of populous towns and cities which stretch along the shores and cover the hills and vallies of the Atlantic

states will soon cease to characterize our nation and sway its councils. They will soon come to be but a small minority compared with the millions that shall roll in wealth and luxury beyond the Alleghany, and even beyond the Mississippi. Already is the influence of the West beginning to be strongly felt in our halls of national legislation. A few years and of those who represent our nation in our council chambers, the majority will come over the Alleghany: —few years more and that majority will cross the Mississippi on the way. And with what character shall they come.[47]

"And with what character shall they come?" As Goodykoontz has pointed out, it was in hopes of providing an acceptable answer to this question that a large number of Christian Americans conceived of and put into motion the American home missionary movement.[48]

The desire to see the West develop in a way acceptable to God-fearing Americans gave rise to a number of national societies pledged to send missionaries and books to the frontier. The most prominent and influential of these groups established prior to the Civil War was the American Home Missionary Society (AHMS), formed in New York in 1826.[49] The AHMS grew out of an earlier organization, the United Domestic Missionary Society, which had been created out of an amalgamation of a number of local societies. The United Domestic Missionary Society, an interdenominational group controlled and financed primarily by Presbyterians, but with close relationships with the Congregationalists, enjoyed a certain amount of success, and by 1826 supported 127 missionaries in the field, most of them in New York. Despite its successes there was a feeling among many interested in the movement that the United Domestic Missionary Society was not organized on a broad enough base to meet the needs of the West adequately. One of these men, John Maltby, expressed this belief when he wrote that a system was now needed "which shall have no sectional interests,—no local prejudices,—no party animosities;—no sectarian views; a system which shall bring the most remote parts of our nation into cordial cooperation, awaken mutual interest in the same grand and harmonious design, produce a feeling of brotherhood, and thus bind us all together by a new cord of union."[50] Furthermore, Maltby shrewdly realized that such a system would be one "which in its operation, shall have but one treasury, and that, as it were, the treasury of the nation."

John Maltby's "system" became a reality on 10 May 1826, when representatives of the Presbyterian, Congregationalist, Dutch Reformed, and Associate Reformed churches in the United States met and formed the American Home Missionary Society. The society's constitution (article II) stated that: "the great object of this Society shall be to assist congregations that are unable to support the Gospel Ministry, and to send the Gospel to the destitute within the United States." The society was an immediate success, and its funding grew steadily, from $18,000 in 1826 to more than $100,000 in 1836.[51] Most of this support was drawn from Presbyterians and Congregationalists, and members of these two religious bodies controlled the organization.

In a short time hundreds of missionaries had been sent west. Frequently they were the best-educated men in their respective districts, and yet rarely did they despair or waver in their conviction that the deployment of an army of well-selected books would win the day for Christ. An examination of the thousands of letters from the missionaries to the home office in New York yields only an occasional example of utter despair. For example, in 1833, John Parsons wrote a vitriolic letter to Absalom Peters, in which he described southern Indiana as being characterized by a "universal dearth of intellect" and noted that "total abstinance from literature is very generally practiced."[52] But for every example of such despair at ever getting books to people, there are hundreds like that of the Reverend John Todd, also writing to Peters in 1833, who noted that while the "riding generation have very little knowledge of letters, very many none at all" he had distributed a number of "valuable tracts" and eagerly awaited a new supply.[53]

The Presbyterians were less likely to be involved in the colportage or subscription efforts characteristic of the aggressive Methodist book distribution program, and thus they appear to have been more willing to distribute their books and tracts gratis. One gets the impression from their letters that they literally papered their respective districts with free religious materials.

They received these materials from the American Tract Society, the American Bible Society, or the Sunday School Union, and when books did have to be paid for, the American Home Missionary Society frequently picked up the bill.

The missionaries were often deeply moved by the generosity of their friends in the East. In 1830, the Reverend Archer Craig wrote from Franklin County:

> When I received the box of books from my good friends in New York it excited feelings of gratitude bordering on astonishment. The works are valuable and well selected but the feelings of attachment and esteem that the donation displays is the thing that more than all increases its value [.] These I distribute carefully as I ride through the country [.] It is truly gratifying to find them so thankfully received. Very seldom I gave away one without receiving an expression of thanks with a bow or a courtsy. I have now cast upwards of 400 of these spiritual cakes on the waters and I entertain a hope that it will cause sinners to return weeping to the Savior.[54]

Missionaries like Craig sold or gave away thousands of pages of tracts over the years, and one minister reported having distributed forty thousand pages in a two-year period.[55] Allowing for exaggeration in their reports, one must still be impressed with their prodigious exertions in the distribution of the printed word on the frontier.

The ministers would often encounter special problems and would request help from the home office in New York. A case in point is found in a letter from the Reverend James Alexander, who wrote from Vincennes in 1830, that

> infidelity is becoming consolidated in Vincennes—Thomas Payn & Exec Homo are industriously circulated here,—there are thirty-six subscribers here for a periodical published in your city entitled *Priest-Craft Unmasked:* if you have anything to meet this work please send it to us immediately.[56]

The enthusiasm with which the Presbyterian missionaries cast their "spiritual cakes upon the waters" continually left them with a shortage of religious works to pass out along the frontier. Their letters are full of complaints that "tract distribution is entirely suspended for the want of tracts, which are not to be found in the depositories."[57] In 1837, Lewis Pinnel wrote from Mount Vernon:

> I have felt very greatly the want of tracts, Bibles and other religious books here. I have scarcely a tract to distribute since I have been here. There is no depository nearer than Cincinnati, 300 miles, or Terre Haute, 200. We are in a very great need of a book store & repositories of religious books in this area. ... We hope for a supply of religious books in this region before long. I could have disposed of a great number of books of the Tract Soc. if I had them.[58]

In addition to the shortage of tracts available for distribution in certain areas, the ministers ran into another problem in the late thirties and early forties; it was growing more and more difficult to get material gratis from the tract and Bible societies.[59]

The shortage of tracts forced many of the missionaries to initiate novel approaches to the distribution of religious reading materials among their charges. One of the most ingenious solutions to the problem was described by the Reverend Ransom Hawley, an American Home Missionary representative in Washington, Indiana, who wrote in 1831,

> I have put in circulation a large number of Tracts and my stock is now nearly exhausted. I have recently introduced a new plan in sending out these little heralds of salvation. It is this. After preaching I announce to the congregation that I will lend to each one a Tract

until I preach there again; when I shall expect them to be returned and lend them others. On this plan there is more certainty of their being read, they will be better preserved, and benefit a greater number than by donating them. . . . The tracts have been received with thankfulness, read with attention and punctually returned.[60]

What we have discovered thus far illustrates our principal point— that is, the incredible commitment evidenced by the majority of the book crusaders to a vision of Christianizing the West by means of shooting printed messages throughout the valley. One could add quotation upon quotation supporting this contention. However, what requires emphasis is the sense of disbelief that sweeps over us as we read the thousands of letters written by the book crusaders in the valley. How could they be so naive? Did they really believe that these printed messages, distributed so vigorously over nearly thirty years, could dramatically alter "this sin-stricken world"? How could intelligent, dedicated, and experienced ministers like Peter Cartwright remain convinced after fifty years of laboring in the valley that "nothing but the principles of the Bible can save our happy nation or the world and every friend of religion ought to spread the Bible to the utmost of his power and means"?[61]

While we may have difficulty comprehending what Paul Boyer has described as the "supreme—or perhaps desperate?—faith in the power of the printed word to reshape social reality," it now seems clear that we must sympathetically attend to this "supreme faith" if we want to understand fully the structural and functional characteristics of nineeenth-century American reform movements.[62] They were, no matter what their ultimate objective, print dissemination agencies. We ignore that essential, and incredible, truth at the risk of misunderstanding the movements.

While I am bothered by the evidence of this blind spot in the historiography of the antebellum reform movements, I am equally con-cerned by a certain tendency in the historiography of the book. Let me take as my text a paper by James Carey entitled the "Paradox of the Book."[63] Carey notes there the revived interest in the book and provides us with a brilliant and provocative interpretation of the new scholarship. He concludes that the intensified interest in the book divides nicely into two categories. The first large body of work is that in which most of us are engaged, a project that Robert Darnton has suggested might result in the emergence of a distinctive new field in the humanities.[64] And Carey goes right to the heart of this project when he notes that it is focused on the book just at the moment "when we are about to lose it" and is "simultaneously an episode in nostalgia and a way of finding our bearings in a world that seems to be shifting under our feet." He further notes that in this "whiggish" interpretation of history, "the history of the book is everywhere connected to a particular view of history in which the book aids in the realization of both a more democratic and a more rational form of political life."[65] Then, in a passage of particular relevance to our concerns, he argues that "in this conventional narrative the book does not refer so much to the wide range of materials produced by the printing press . . . but to an artifact that is an abstraction, a volume transmuted to a symbol." According to Carey, in this whiggish history, "Book refers less to a manufactured object than to a canon: a selective tradition of the best that has been thought and written in the Western tradition. . . . It condenses, as well, certain skills and values . . . and a certain way of life in which the intercourse with books connects to wider habits of feelings and conduct"— habits that Carey identifies as bourgeois, "in the honored sense."[66]

The literature in this whiggish tradition of book history is full of alarm for the fate of the book and celebration of the book's vital role in civilized life. It is widely in evidence at the many recent conferences on the book sponsored by the Center for the Book in the Library of Congress.

Carey notes that he has no desire to be a skeleton at these banquets for the book, but he forcefully notes that there is another category or tradition of research focusing on the book, a tradition he precisely defines as "anti-canonical."[67] In this tradition, "the equation linking the book and literacy with wisdom and progress is seen as part of a complex ideology that justified the technology of printing as it served the interest of those who controlled it."[68] The anti-canonical research is driven by a desire to "incorporate the book into the central theme of contemporary scholarship, namely the acquisition and experience of power."[69]

In a book that might serve as the manifesto of the anti-canonical spirit, Frank Lentricchia notices that the book—the canon—is created, produced, and reproduced by individuals involved in "the systematic act of tradition-making," which he defines as the "cultural mechanism that ideologically reproduces social hierarchy and political domination by passing along a dominant culture."[70] For Lentricchia, these canon-makers are located in vital institutional sites where "for better or worse the cultural future is decided," and that the book community is involved in manipulating the "productive force of ideology."[71] In short, the anti-canonical spirit is premised on Claude Levi-Strauss's insight that from the beginning books have been "first and foremost connected with power, . . . power exercised by some men over other men and over wordly possessions."[72]

I would like to conclude by suggesting that that certain tendency in book history that I find troubling is our nearly total commitment to writing "whiggish" histories of the book and our lack of interest in the large body of research now reflecting such startling light on the connection between books and power. A discussion of the full implications of the anti-canonical research for the writing of history will have to await another time and place, but it should be emphasized that there is a good deal more to the revived interest in the book than would be apparent to those attending conferences like the Chicago Conference.[73]

Notes

1. The evolution can be traced in my "A Methodist Minister's Working Library in Mid-19th Century Illinois," *Wesleyan Quarterly Review: A Methodist Historical Magazine* 4 (1967): 210–19; in chapter seven of "The Availability of Books and the Nature of Book Ownership on the Southern Indiana Frontier" (Ph.D. diss., Indiana University, 1971); and in two lectures, both having the same title as this chapter: The Ryan Lectureship, Asbury Theological Seminary, 22 Oct. 1975; and a Symposium on Appalachian Studies, East Tennessee State University, 21 Apr. 1978.

2. I have discussed this changing historiographical emphasis in my "Historians Assess the Impact of Print on the Course of American History: The Revolution as a Test Case," *Library Trends* 22 (1973): 127–47; and see Roger Haney, Michael H. Harris, and Leonard Tipton, "The Impact of Reading on Human Behavior: The Implications of Communications Research," *Advances in Librarianship* 6 (1976): 139–216, for a summary of the work in communications.

3. Bernard Bailyn, *The Ideological Origins of the American Revolution* (Cambridge: Harvard University Press, 1967); Gordon S. Wood, *The Creation of the American Republic, 1776–1787* (Chapel Hill: University of North Carolina Press, 1969); and Lance Banning, *The Jeffersonian Persuasion: Evolution of a Party Ideology* (Ithaca: Cornell University Press, 1978).

4. This judgement cannot, given the principle object of our paper, be fully documented here, and I will be content if my readers simply give the idea serious consideration. However, several examples would seem in order. Consider first, Daniel Boorstin's award-winning trilogy *The Americans,* the first volume of which devotes nearly a hundred pages to books, reading, and the press in Colonial America, while the second treats the subject only in passing. Note also Robert H. Wiebe's *The Opening of American Society: From the Adoption of the Constitution to the Eve of Disunion* (New York: Knopf, 1984), which overlooks the great "book crusades" completely.

5. Bernard A. Weisberger, *They Gathered at the River: The Story of the Great Revivalists and Their Impact Upon Religion in America* (Chicago: Quadrangle Books, 1966), 5–6.

6. Extract from a form letter issued from the office of the American Home Missionary Society, August 20, 1830, by order of the Executive Committee and signed by Knowles Taylor, published in William Warren Sweet, *Religion on the American Frontier: 1783–1840,* vol. 2, *The Presbyterians* (1936; reprint ed., New York: Cooper Square Publishers, 1964), 668–70.

7. Henry Ward Beecher to Milton Badger, July 1847, American Home Missionary Society Papers, film copy, Indiana University Library, Bloomington, Indiana. These papers will be cited hereafter as AHMS.

8. We are fortunate to have a number of works that clearly delineate the world view of the elite that dominated the book crusades. Foremost are Daniel Walker Howe's *The Unitarian Conscience: Harvard Moral Philosophy, 1805–1861* (Cambridge: Harvard University Press, 1970) and his *The Political Culture of the American Whigs* (Chicago: University of Chicago Press, 1979). Two works that are good on the religious values of the book crusaders are one by George M. Marsden, *The Evangelical Mind and the New School Presbyterian Experience* (New Haven: Yale University Press, 1970), and, especially, another by Fred J. Hood, *Reformed America: The Middle and Southern States* (University: University of Alabama Press, 1980). For a brilliant discussion of the Evangelicals that laid "Spiritual Siege to the West," see Ronald P. Formisano, *The Birth of Mass Political Parties: Michigan, 1827–1861* (Princeton: Princeton University Press, 1971).

9. Both quoted by Rush Welter, *The Mind of America, 1820–1860* (New York: Columbia University Press, 1975), 310, 311–12.

10. Daniel Walker Howe, *The Unitarian Conscience,* 195.

11. The phrase is that of missionary John Mason Peck, who is quoted (and whose idea is discussed) by Russell B. Nye, *Society and Culture in America, 1830–1860* (New York: Harper and Row, 1974), 294.

12. Alexis de Tocqueville noticed this most clearly when he noted that "Americans . . . are forever forming associations" whenever "they want to proclaim a truth" or "distribute books" or "send missionaries to the antipodes" (*Democracy in America,* ed. J. P. Mayer and Max Lerner, New York: Harper and Row, 1966, 485). For a more recent analysis see Gregory Singleton, "Protestant Voluntary Organizations and the Shaping of Victorian America," in *Victorian America,* ed. Daniel Walker Howe (Philadelphia: University of Pennsylvania Press, 1976), 47–58. The most recent survey of the reform movement is Ronald G. Walters, *American Reformers, 1815–1860* (New York: Hill and Wang, 1978).

13. The best overviews remain those by Charles I. Foster, *An Errand of Mercy: The Evangelical United Front, 1790–1837* (Chapel Hill: University of North Carolina Press, 1960), and Clifford S. Griffin, *Their Brothers' Keepers: Moral Stewardship in the United States, 1800–1865* (New Brunswick: Rutgers University Press, 1960). The "social control" thesis central to these two works has come under considerable fire; see Fred Hood's *Reformed America* for a clear analysis of the controversy and a treatment of the book crusades that avoids the excesses of the contending schools of historiography.

14. Griffin, *Their Brothers' Keepers,* 111.

15. The *Gospel Kite* is quoted by Alice B. Cushman, "A Nineteenth Century Plan for Reading," *Horn Book* 33 (1957): 160–61.

16. For instance, in 1829–30 the American Bible Society sent 14,408 Bibles to Indiana, 23,171 to Ohio, and 10,000 to Tennessee. During the same period the American Tract Society shipped $14,927.13 worth of tracts west of the Alleghenies. The Baptist General Tract Society was publishing some 5 million pages of tracts a year in 1829—most of them finding their way to the West. See Winthrop Hudson, *American Protestantism* (Chicago: University of Chicago Press, 1961), 81–82. In 1855 the American Bible Society published some 900,000 volumes, and the American Tract Society printed 961,863 items. See John Tebbel, *A History of Book Publishing in the United States,* vol. 1 (New York: R. R Bowker, 1972), 508.

17. He died in Fort Wayne, Indiana. Robert Price, *Johnny Appleseed: Man* *and Myth* (Bloomington: Indiana University Press, 1954), 124–34, treats his efforts to distribute books in the West.

18. Ibid., 132–33.

19. Quoted by William Warren Sweet, *Circuit-Rider Days in Indiana* (Indianapolis: W. K. Steward Co., 1916), 50–51.

20. Peter Cartwright, *Autobiography* (Nashville: Abingdon Press, 1956), 187.

21. Colin Brummitt Goodykoontz, *Home Missions on the American Frontier with Particular Reference to the American Home Missionary Society* (Caldwell, Idaho: The Caxton Printers, 1939), 139.

22. Hudson, *American Protestantism,* 85.

23. Goodykoontz, *Home Missions on the American Frontier,* 139.

24. The first report was J. F. Schermerhorn and S. J. Mills, *A Correct View of That Part of the United States Which Lies West of the Allegheny Mountains* (Hartford: P. B. Gleason, 1814).

25. Samuel J. Mills and Daniel Smith, *Report of a Missionary Tour Through That Part of the United States Which Lies West of the Allegheny Mountains . . .* (Andover: Printed by Flagg and Gould, 1815), 13.

26. Ibid., 41–42.

27. Ibid., 50–51.

28. Ibid., 56.

29. Ibid., 51.

30. Ibid., 50.

31. Letter of Daniel Smith, quoted by Goodykoontz, *Home Missions on the American Frontier,* 142.

32. John Wesley, *Letters,* ed. John Telford, 8 vols. (London: Epworth Press, 1931), 8: 247. The Methodist ministers' reliance on the printed word is discussed in Willard G. Roberts, "The Methodist Book Concern in the West, 1800–1870," (Ph.D. diss., University of Chicago, 1947), chap. 1. See also James Penn Pilkington, *The Methodist Publishing House: A History,* 2 vols. (Nashville: Abingdon Press: 1968), 1: 10–14. Peter Cartwright expressed the feelings of many Methodists when he wrote, "The religious press is destined, in the order of Providence, to give moral freedom to the perishing millions of earth" (*Autobiography,* 187).

33. Wesley, *Letters,* 7: 138.

34. The history of Methodist publishing is covered nicely in those items cited in note 32 above. The operation of the Cincinnati branch of the Methodist Book Concern is also dealt with by Walter Sutton, *The Western Book Trade: Cincinnati As a Nineteenth Century Publishing and Book Trade Center* (Columbus: Ohio State University Press, 1961), chap. 12.

35. L. C. Rudolph, *Francis Asbury* (Nashville: Abingdon Press, 1966), 132. Asbury was very much concerned with the book business, as his journals and letters show. See Francis Asbury, *Journal and Letters,* ed. Elmer T. Clark, J. Manning Potts, and Jacob S. Payton, 3 vols. (Nashville: Abingdon Press, 1958).

36. *Discipline of the Methodist Episcopal Church, 1796* (Phildelphia: Methodist Book Concern, 1797), 5.

37. Rudolph, *Francis Asbury,* 135. Near the end of his career Cartwright noted that he had sold more than $10,000 worth of books and had earned a commission of $1,000 on them (Cartwright, *Autobiography,* 338).

38. "A Letter to a Junior Preacher," *Methodist Magazine,* March 1824; quoted by Roberts, "Methodist Book Concern in the West," 29.

39. Mills and Smith, *Report of a Missionary Tour,* 49.

40. William Warren Sweet, *Religion in the Development of American Culture, 1765–1840* (New York: Scribners, 1952), 275.

41. Joseph Tarkington. *The Autobiography* (Cincinnati: Curts & Jennings, 1899), 129.

42. Roberts, "Methodist Book Concern in the West," 79–80.

43. Sweet, *Religion on the American Frontier, 1783–1840: The Presbyterians,* 70. A detailed analysis of the educational backgrounds of the Presbyterian clergy in Indiana is found in L. C. Rudolph, *Hoosier Zion: The Presbyterians in Early Indiana* (New Haven: Yale University Press, 1963), chap. 2.

44. Sweet, *Religion on the American Frontier: The Presbyterians,* 49–50. T. Scott Miyakawa, *Protestants and Pioneers: Individualism and Conformity on the American Frontier* (Chicago: University of Chicago Press, 1964), presents a detailed analysis of these differences.

45. Isaac Reed, *The Christian Traveller in Five Parts: Including Nine Years and Eighteen Thousand Miles* (New York: J. and J. Harper, 1828), 206.

46. Ibid., 224–25.

47. John Maltby, "Connection between Domestic Missions and the political prospects of our country," an address before the Society of Inquiry Respecting Missions, Andover Theological Seminary, 1825. Quoted in Goodykoontz, *Home Missions on the American Frontier,* 170–71.

48. Goodykoontz, *Home Missions on the American Frontier,* 171.

49. Ibid., 173.

50. Quoted, ibid., 176–77.

51. Ibid., 179–80. The history of the AHMS is treated in all of the items cited in note 13 above. For a detailed history of the AHMS in the Old Northwest see Frederick Kuhns, "The Operations of the American Home Missionary Society in the Old Northwest, 1826–1851" (Ph.D. diss., University of Chicago, 1947). Unfortunately, Kuhns has little to say about the book distribution process. My understanding of the great book crusade in the West is based especially on a detailed reading of the thousands of letters in the American Home Missionary Papers. The original papers, mostly letters from the missionaries to the New York Office of the AHMS, are in the Amistad Research Center in New Orleans. Photostatic copies of the Indiana letters are available in the Indiana Division of the Indiana State Library. A film copy is located in the Indiana University Library.

52. Parsons to Absalom Peters, 20 February 1833, AHMS.

53. John Todd to Absalom Peters, 2 November 1833, AHMS.

54. Craig to Peters, 14 August 1830, AHMS.

55. A. Maynard, Union County, Indiana, to Absalom Peters, New York, 8 December 1830, AHMS. Another minister reported some sixteen thousand pages of tracts distributed in his county, most of which were "read with great interest by young and old" (James Crawford, Jefferson County, Indiana, to Absalom Peters, New York, 5 November 1827, AHMS).

56. Alexander to Absalom Peters, 12 January 1830, AHMS.

57. Calvin Butler, Evansville, Indiana, to Absalom Peters, New York, 4 June 1833, AHMS.

58. Pinnel to Peters, 29 May 1837, AHMS.

59. T. B. Thornton, Boone County, Indiana to Milton Badger, New York, 27 August 1841, AHMS. It should be noted that after 1838, the Presbyterians had access to their own materials published by the Presbyterian Church. See Anna Jane Moyer, "The Making of Many Books: 125 Years of Presbyterian Publishing, 1838–1963," *Journal of Presbyterian History* 41 (1963): 124–25. For a study of the American Tract Society, see Harvey G. Neufeldt, "The American Tract Society, 1825–1865: An Examination of its Religious, Social, and Political Ideas" (Ph.D. diss., Michigan State University, 1971). Sunday school libraries have been extensively studied: see F. A. Briggs, "Sunday School Libraries in the 19th Century," *Library Quarterly* 31 (1961): 166–77; Alice B. Cushman, "A Nineteenth Century Plan for Reading: The American Sunday School Movement," *Horn Book* 33 (1957): 61–71, 159–66; Ellen Schaffer, "The Children's Books of the American Sunday-School Union," *American Book Collector* 17 (1966): 21–28. A surprisingly critical and insightful analysis of the whole movement can be found in Robert W. Lynn and Elliot Wright, *The Big Little School: Two Hundred Years of the Sunday School,* 2d ed. (Nashville: Abingdon, 1980), especially chap. 3, "In Every Destitute Place." The AHMS papers are replete with references to Sunday School libraries.

60. Hawley to Peters, 11 February 1831, AHMS.

61. Cartwright, *Autobiography,* 124–25.

62. Paul Boyer, *Urban Masses and Moral Order in America, 1820–1920* (Cambridge: Harvard University Press, 1978), 33. What we are calling for is an intellectual history of American "ideologies" of reading and an intellectual history of evolving conceptions of the impact of reading on human behavior. A great deal of work would be required before such an intellectual history could be written, but perhaps readers might find it useful to have some sense of how such a project might proceed. At this point all that can be offered is a list of works that I feel offer, in the context of larger concerns, exciting and provocative insights into the matter: Harvey Graff, *The Literacy Myth: Literacy and Social Structure in the Nineteenth Century City* (New York: Academic Press, 1979); Philip Gura, *The Wisdom of Words; Language, Theology, and Literature in the New England Renaissance* (Middletown, Conn.: Wesleyan University Press, 1981); Paul E. Johnson, *A Shopkeeper's Millennium: Society and Revivals in Rochester, New York, 1815–1837* (New York: Hill and Wang, 1978); Michael Paul Rogin, *Subversive Genealogy: The Politics and Art of Herman Melville* (Berkeley: University of California Press, 1985); and Mary P. Ryan, *Cradle of the Middle Class: The Family in Oneida County, New York, 1790–1865* (Cambridge: Cambridge University Press, 1981).

63. James W. Carey, "The Paradox of the Book," *Library Trends* 33 (1984): 103–13.

64. Robert Darnton, "What is the History of Books?" *Daedalus* 111 (Summer 1982): 65.

65. Carey, "Paradox of the Book," 105.

66. Ibid., 106.

67. Ibid., 108.

68. Ibid., 107.

69. Ibid., 108.

70. Frank Lentricchia, *Criticism and Social Change* (Chicago: University of Chicago Press, 1983), 141, 143.

71. Ibid., 104.

72. Quoted in Carey, "Paradox of the Book," 103.

73. I have attempted such an examination in "State, Class, and Cultural Reproduction: Toward a Theory of Library Service in America," *Advances in Librarianship* 14 (1986): 211–52.

6. Copyright and Books in Nineteenth-Century America

Alice D. Schreyer

In 1850, Sara Lippincott published a collection of essays under her pen name, Grace Greenwood. The volume contained a group of pastiches on the subject of copyright, including this exhortation:

> Ho, wielders of the mighty pen!
> Men of the rolling eye!
> Ye who have heaved around the world
> Thought's surges, vast and high,—
> Come mingle in a brother-band—
> Come, authors, great and small,
> In common cause join heart and hand,
> And throng to Faneuil Hall!
>
> Ho, ancient Harvard's youthful sage!
> Long-fellow of the Nine!
> Shall this day's sun's astonished rays
> On thy *short*-comings shine?
> Ho, Lowell, Pierpont, Emerson,
> We're friends and brothers all,—
> Ho, Taylor, Poe, Duganne and Read,
> Away to Faneuil Hall!
> . . . .
> Old Russia's proud and well-fed bards,
> Cast on us scoffs and jibes!
> And Turks bless Allah by the hour
> They're not poor Yankee scribes!
> Ho, on the spirits of our sires,
> On freedom, truth, we'll call!
> And for our rights, our copy-rights,
> We'll rock old Faneuil Hall!

121

Not pay us for the toils of thought!
The struggling of our brains!
By old George Fox, the indignant blood
     Is lava in my veins!
Shame on our country and its laws!
     Strike, let the Bastille fall!
Down with the tyrant Publishers!
     Hurrah for Faneuil Hall![1]

This poem, entitled "A Call for a Convention of Authors, at Faneuil Hall, to Discuss the Question of International Copyright," appeared over the initials "J. G. W." We do not know what Whittier—or Bryant, Poe, Oliver Wendell Holmes, or several others—thought of the parodies of their work, but they certainly shared Lippincott's views. Precisely at mid-century, sixty years after the first federal copyright act and forty years prior to the Chace Act, American authors maintained that lack of international copyright deprived them of the rights the law purported to protect. Moreover, they claimed that the act was impotent to achieve what the drafters of the Constitution had intended, namely, "To promote the progress of science and useful arts," and that it resulted in continued dependence on English letters and, consequently, culture.[2] Prominent English authors, of whom Dickens was the most vocal on this side of the Atlantic, also condemned this so-called "national disgrace."[3]

The failure of nineteenth-century American copyright law to extend protection to works by foreign authors was, unquestionably, a major factor in nineteenth-century publishing decisions and arrangements. It encouraged American publishers to reprint works by established foreign authors rather than risk publishing a new work by an unknown writer to whom a copyright fee must be paid. Lack of international copyright created some of the most dramatic tales in the annals of publishing history—of how publishers raced to be the first with an American edition, paying for advance sheets, hiring confidential agents, bribing British compositors, rushing plates across the ocean and running presses night and day, and of how American authors met requirements for residence or prior publication when these were sufficient to secure British copyright without losing their U.S. rights.[4]

Despite the importance of these activities in the history of authorship and the book trades, the widely held assumption that lack of international copyright was solely responsible for all of the difficulties suffered by nineteenth-century American authors may be based more on rhetoric than on established fact. The protection afforded by copyright stimulated the development of printing and publishing and the standardization of relationships between authors and publishers. Provisions of nineteenth-century American copyright law reflected and affected these relationships and those among members of the printing and publishing trades. The very concept of authorship, as it evolved over the course of the nineteenth century, was shaped by copyright legislation and litigation. Finally, one issue raised during this period, native manufacturing requirements, is still current and controversial. I will focus on each of these topics, with the understanding that the circumstances created by the international situation formed the background to the relationship between copyright and books in nineteenth-century America.

The "Act for the encouragement of learning" passed by the first Congress in 1790, modeled on state copyright laws and the 1710 English Statute of Anne, provided for "securing the copies of maps, charts, and books, to the authors and proprietors of such copies, during the times therein mentioned."[5] The initial term—for works already or not yet printed—was fourteen years. Authors were eligible for a fourteen-year renewal, but their widows and children were not. Copyright was restricted to citizens and residents, and the importation of works by foreign authors was expressly permitted, opening the door to the widespread reprinting that followed.

The requirements for copyright registration were: the deposit, before publication, of a printed title page with the clerk of the district court in which the proprietor resided; the publication of a notice in a newspaper within two months of publication, to run for four weeks; and the deposit of a printed copy of the completed work with the Secretary of State within six months of publication. These were simple procedures, but they presumed that the projected work would be sufficiently profitable to warrant taking precautions. We know from ghosts in the surviving copyright records—records of projected works that were never published—that registration also functioned as a statement of intent, a way to stake one's claim to a particular work.[6] And in the earliest extant copyright records from several frontier states, for example Michigan during the 1820s, the very high percentage of maps suggests that cartographers may have registered maps as a way, quite literally, to stake a claim to territory they had surveyed.

The 1790 act granted to authors and proprietors "the sole right and liberty of printing, reprinting, publishing and vending." This is how copyright prevented piracy of published works—by giving to the copyright holder the exclusive right to print, publish, and sell.[7] Authors could exercise these rights themselves by arranging and paying for manufacturing and contracting with a publisher who served as a distributor on commission. This way, the author retained control and reaped all but a small percentage (usually 10 percent) of the profit on sales. Washington Irving, who operated in this manner at first, observed in 1824 to James Fenimore Cooper's London publisher, John Miller, "Were I inclined to dispose of my copyright in America I know of no house that I would so readily treat with as the Careys; but I have determined to retain the controul over my writings on that side of the water, which can only be done by keeping the copy right of them in my own hands."[8] Although successful authors like Irving and Cooper were eager to preserve their rights, most nineteenth-century American authors who assumed the costs (and risks) of publishing had no choice. Unknown authors usually could not find a publisher who would consider any other arrangement, except perhaps outright sale of the copyright, which authors without the resources to foot the bills or in need of ready cash were forced to accept.

Authors could also keep close control over printing and sales by licensing those rights for short periods, preserving the option of rene-gotiating the contracts on more favorable terms. Noah Webster practiced this method and kept careful account of the number of copies printed by the licensees of his fabulously successful *American Speller.*[9] Other standard contracts were the "half-profits" system by which author and publisher shared costs and divided profits after the costs had been returned (when this had occurred was frequently a subject of dispute), and an arrangement wherein the author paid for and retained control of the stereotype plates and leased them to the publisher for a limited number of copies. William Prescott was committed to this scheme, and it was also used by Longfellow and Melville.[10]

The variety and complexity of author-publisher contracts in nineteenth-century America reflected the as yet tentative nature of the relationship between them. In the late 1860s Elizabeth Peabody, the sister of Nathaniel Hawthorne's widow, reviewed Ticknor and Fields's contract books and found "a most perplexing medley—a sort of contra dance between written contracts and verbal agreements with the rattling of stereotype plates for tambourines."[11] Each transaction enumerated terms on which the copyright was bought, sold, or leased. When publishers went bankrupt and their assets were taken over by another firm or when stereotype plates were sold at trade sales the copyright went along.[12]

As the century progressed and publishers increasingly assumed an entrepreneurial role, there was a gradual but not absolute trend toward standardization of the copyright clause in author-publisher contracts. The standard fee structure that emerged was payment to the author of a percentage of the retail price of copies sold, although a specified number of copies—sometimes the entire first edition—might be exempted. Later in the century a sliding scale was introduced, the percentage increasing with the numbers of copies sold. Sometimes a publisher, anticipating a rise in prices, would switch to a flat fee per copy sold. When this happened to Mary Abigail Dodge, her ire was aroused, and her subsequent corre-spondence with other Ticknor and Fields authors ultimately led to Elizabeth

Peabody's examination of the Ticknor and Fields records. Regardless of the terms, the payment, or royalty, was simply a percentage-based leasing fee by which publishers acquired the use of a copyright. It is important to remember that, although royalty and copyright were used synonymously as terms for payment in the nineteenth century, the law never prescribed or preferred any one of these contractual arrangements.[13] As a *Publishers' Weekly* editorial reminded its audience in 1886: "The Government has no more to do with the relations between author and publisher than between a miller and a baker."[14] Authors' terms were determined by the market value of their product, the law providing the framework for negotiations by giving authors something to sell. Copyright, a part of property law, protected the exclusive right of the proprietor or owner— author or publisher—to possess, enjoy, and dispose of a thing.[15]

Copyright protected publishers from unfair native competition, and so they were willing to invest money and effort into promoting works to which they had bought the rights. In dealing with foreign authors or works that lacked legal security, the trade resorted to informal traditions to regulate itself, usually called "rights in courtesy" or "courtesy of the trade."[16] This meant that once a firm had announced an intention to reprint a work, no other publisher would reprint it. An infringement was called "printing upon." The publisher who got out the first American edition therefore had a far more substantial advantage than simply the first day's sales. Another unwritten law was that a publisher would not offer better terms to an author already identified with a firm unless the author had expressed interest in a change. In 1834 Henry Carey warned Harpers that "If you choose to raise a storm we shall be greatly mistaken if we are not able to carry sail as large as you can."[17] The following year Harpers admonished Bulwer Lytton, who had allowed his novel *Rienzi* to be reprinted first by Carey & Lea after signing an agreement with Harpers,

> We have invested a large amount of capital in your productions, having stereotyped them all—an unusual measure by the way—and given assurances, both publicly and privately, . . . that they would be supplied by us with uniform editions of all you might write hereafter. For our own interest, as well as to redeem this pledge, we should be under the necessity of reprinting them upon the publisher to whom you might give the preference; and . . . we should, of course, put in requisition all our means of competition; from the magnitude of our disposable force, we could throw before the public one of your novels in twenty four hours after obtaining a copy—which no other house in the U.S. could do. . . .[18]

Many believed that little more could be expected from honor among thieves, and there does not seem to have been much "courtesy" when a publisher felt the code had been violated. During the cheap books war with newspaper competitors of the early 1840s, the system broke down completely, but by 1865 the "custom of the trade" was once again sufficiently operative to form the basis of a lawsuit by Smith Sheldon and others against Henry O. Houghton over a uniform edition of Dickens's works. Observing that "protection rests in the voluntary and unconstrained forbearance of the trade," the court ruled that the "alleged good will rests, therefore, upon no legal foundation, and, consequently, is not a partnership asset possessing any legal value."[19]

Most claims of infringement were fairly subtle, and they reveal that nineteenth-century copyright law served as a general umbrella policy, under which authors and publishers brought suit for a variety of unfair trade practices. The Cincinnati publisher U. P. James suffered three types of copyright infringement between 1859 and 1865, including appropriation of titles, text, and both.[20] Most outright piracies were probably not worth prosecuting, because they were sufficiently distant not to interfere with the authorized publisher's market. And of course, the legal record documents only disputes that went into the courtroom, and surely most were settled or abandoned in correspondence of a more or less "courteous" nature.[21]

The Philadelphia publisher T. B. Peterson engaged in a variety of reprinting practices on the borderline of copyright infringement, but on at least one occasion he was solidly within his rights and let everyone know it. In 1857 he published a two-volume work entitled *Frank Forester's Sporting Scenes and Characters,* which he presented as a new work, with new copyright dates, although it contained straight reprints of four previously published novels by Forester to which Peterson had bought the plates and the rights.[22] Henry William Herbert, the author, took out the following advertisement in *Porter's Spirit of the Times:* "Caution. . . . The Public are hereby notified by the author that this publication is a fraud on the community." Peterson's reply, which appeared in the same issue, announced,

> From the coarse style in which these four works were originally published . . . they had a comparatively small sale, and the copyright of them, which had been sold by the author to the original publisher, went begging in consequence, from one house to another, until the present publishers purchased them, and in hopes to extend the reputation of Frank Forester, has printed and published these sporting scenes and stories in a decent, becoming, and permanent style. . . . As the Author has once received what, at the time, he considered an equivalent for the copyright, it is hardly to be supposed that he wishes to be paid for them again, or is really otherwise than grateful that the four books are printed and published for the first time in a beautiful style handsomely illustrated from designs by Darley.

Herbert's complaint illustrates one of the arguments for perpetual copyright. Authors maintained that, based on the correspondence between literary and tangible property, they had a natural, unrestricted right to the fruits of their labors. The landmark 1824 case of *Wheaton* v. *Peters* established that although an author had a common-law right in unpublished works that existed in perpetuity, after publication the only rights were the ones that were granted by the copyright statute. The majority decision maintained: "That a literary man is as much entitled to the product of his labor as any other member of society, cannot be controverted; and the answer is, that he realizes the product in the sale of his works, when first published."[23] As Herbert's plight suggests, this was not always how the market operated. In 1831, after lobbying led by Noah Webster, whose efforts had been instrumental in the passage of the state copyright laws, the initial copyright term was extended to twenty-eight years, and widows and children were made eligible for the fourteen-year renewal.[24] These liberalized benefits substantially improved matters, for the forty-two-year period covered the profitable life of most works. Despite continued debate over perpetual copyright, the courts and the legislature upheld the principle that copyright did not *protect* already-existing natural rights, it actually created authors' rights by statutory privilege.[25]

Several aspects of Harriet Beecher Stowe's career reflect fundamental differences between nineteenth- and twentieth-century conceptions of author's rights. Foreign reprints, translations, dramatizations, and all other derivative uses—from songs to Staffordshire china—were outside Harriet Beecher Stowe's control. She denied consent to one playwright who sought permission to dramatize her novel, but could not prevent others from going ahead without her consent.[26] Although performance rights were granted to the author or proprietor of a dramatic composition in 1856, it was not until 1870 that "authors [could] reserve the right to dramatize or translate their own works."[27]

An 1853 case brought by Stowe against a German translation of *Uncle Tom's Cabin* turned on the question, "Whether a translation of a copyrighted work is an infringement of copyright?"[28] In order to decide whether the author's rights had been infringed, the court set out to define what constitutes literary property. A distinction was made between the "ideas" contained in a book and the "combination of words" used to represent them. Although both are creations or inventions of the author, and both are protected before publication, after publication the ideas become common property. The concluding statement dismissing Stowe's suit will shock twentieth-century ears attuned to the ring of "All rights reserved":

> By the publication of her book the creations of the genius and imagination of the author have become as much public property as those of Homer or Cervantes. Uncle Tom and Topsy are as much

publici juris, as Don Quixote and Sancho Panza. All her conceptions and inventions may be used and abused by imitators, playrights and poetasters. They are no longer her own—those who have purchased her book, may clothe them in English doggerel, in German or Chinese prose. Her absolute dominion and property in the creations of her genius and imagination have been voluntarily relinquished; and all that now remains is the copyright of her book, the exclusive right to print, reprint and vend it; and those only can be called infringers of her rights, or pirates of her property, who are guilty of printing, publishing, importing or vending without her license *'copies* of her *book.'* ... a translation may be called a transcript or copy of her thoughts or conceptions, but in no correct sense can it be called a copy of her book.

This narrow interpretation was undoubtedly extreme, but the language of nineteenth-century copyright law did prevent piracy better than plagiarism. The difference is one of degree: a pirate usually appropriates the whole work and gives credit, but not remuneration, to the original author, while a plagiarist takes part of a work, usually ideas, and does not give credit.[29] The 1909 copyright act added the exclusive right to "copy" to those of printing, publishing, and vending, opening the way for authors and others to claim protection for the ideas as well as their precise expression.

New editions or arrangements of reference or standard works such as the Bible, dictionaries, encyclopedias, grammars, textbooks, legal compilations, or treatises often brought claims of copyright infringement on grounds of plagiarism. It was widely acknowledged that such works were based on knowledge or ideas available to all and that "Any compilation may be the subject of a copyright, provided the plan, arrangement, and combination of the materials be new."[30] As one might guess, it was not always easy to decide what constituted a "new" arrangement. One of the longest, most complicated, and most bitter nineteenth-century copyright cases concerned this point. It involved an edition of Henry Wheaton's *Elements of International Law* prepared by lawyer, politician, and travel writer Richard Henry Dana. William Beach Lawrence, Dana's predecessor as Wheaton's editor, claimed the work infringed his copyright.[31] On evidence that included coincidence of citations and of errors, the court ruled that Dana had made improper use of Lawrence's notes and plan, and that Dana's work could not be defended as an abridgment which, if it involved "intellectual labor and judgment," would not be considered an infringement. The course of this case was probably determined by personal and political vindictiveness, and the 146 instances of "alleged gross plagiarism and servile copying" were reduced to fourteen points of technical infringement in a Master's Report filed with the court in 1881.

Lawrence v. *Dana* also established that "Copyrights to editions of a work other than the original one are granted for additions to or emendations of the work. . . . Subsequent editions with notes or improvements are new books within the meaning of the act." Authors of medical and legal works had always operated on this assumption, and publishers of *belles lettres* often added prefaces or illustrations, although the new copyright actually applied only to the new material.

A major deficiency in nineteenth-century copyright law was the failure to protect serial publication. After Oliver Wendell Holmes's death in 1894, three editions of *The Autocrat of the Breakfast Table* were announced. The work had appeared, first, in the *Atlantic Monthly* and, on its completion there in 1858, in book form. Houghton, Mifflin had renewed the copyright in Holmes's name and believed it to be covered through 1900. When they threatened suit, their lawyer advised them to withdraw, because no copyright had been taken out in any of the twelve issues of the *Atlantic Monthly,* and to advertise this defect might stimulate similar acts of piracy.[32] Holmes's son and heir, Oliver Wendell Holmes, Jr., brought a case that reached the United States Supreme Court in 1899. The decision of a lower court was upheld: "beyond dispute," an appearance in a serial was found to constitute publication. Since no title page had been deposited until after the last issue appeared, and the edition in question was taken directly from the periodical publication, in the public domain, the only possible infringement consisted in binding the individual numbers together into a single volume, which was not a legitimate subject of copyright. The presiding judge remarked, "We have not overlooked the inconvenience which our conclusions will cause, if, in order to protect their articles from piracy, authors are compelled to copyright each chapter or instalment as it may appear in a periodical; nor the danger and annoyance it may occasion to the Librarian of Congress . . . but these are evils which can be easily remedied by an amendment of the law."[33] Easily remedied the evils might be, but it was not until 1909, after Houghton, Mifflin appeared in court as the proprietor of Holmes's and Harriet Beecher Stowe's copyrights, that the law was changed so that "The copyright upon composite works or periodicals shall give to the proprietor thereof all the rights in respect thereto which he would have if each part were individually copyrighted under this Act."[34]

A few years before expiration of the copyright on *Uncle Tom's Cabin,* Houghton, Mifflin fought off another attempt to pirate an unprotected serial publication.[35] An article in the *National Advertiser* on March 1, 1892, announced "A Remarkable Discovery," namely that the original copyright was defective and that the book was common property. An agent, hurriedly dispatched by the publishers to the Copyright Office in Washington, confirmed that one of the installments in the *National Era* failed to state "Copyright secured by the author" in accordance with the requirement.

Houghton, Mifflin kept this knowledge to themselves and threatened to prosecute anyone who published or sold any but their authorized editions. Their offensive was successful.

By the end of the nineteenth century, authors and their heirs were looking to copyright for relief from a broad range of what they considered to be unfair trade practices. Claiming a trademark in Washington Irving's name, G. P. Putnam's and Irving's heirs sued Pollard & Moss in 1880 to restrain them from publishing a volume of Irving's works with the title "Irving's Works." They did not deny that Irving had written the works included, which were unrevised, uncorrected, in some instances incomplete, and previously unpublished. The court denied the presence of a trademark and held that "any one lawfully printing the writings of Irving may designate them 'Irving's Works.' "[36]

Belford Brothers, three "Canadian thieves," had flooded the American market with a cheap pirated edition of *Tom Sawyer* in 1876.[37] Mark Twain contemplated legal action until he discovered that an English copyright had to be entered within sixty days for Canadian protection, and that this had not been done. Twain declared, "We find our copyright law here to be nearly worthless," but several times later he attempted to use the copyright law to stop actions to which he objected.[38] In 1880, Belford, Clark & Co., the Chicago firm formed by one of the Belford brothers, published "Sketches by Mark Twain," consisting of uncopyrighted works. Three years later, Twain claimed that Belford, Clark & Co. had infringed his copyright, in a suit based on his exclusive right to the *nom de plume* or trademark, Mark Twain. The court ruled that "No pseudonym, however ingenious, novel, or quaint, can give an author any more rights than he would have under his own name. ... That is, any person who chooses to do so, can republish any uncopyrighted literary production, and give the name of the author, either upon the title-page, or otherwise as best suits the interest or taste of the person so republishing."[39] Twain also unsuccessfully sought injunctions on the grounds of piracy against retail booksellers—John Wannamaker and Estes & Lauriat—to stop them from selling his subscription books.[40]

The provisions of copyright law reflect contemporary attitudes toward authorship, printing, and publishing as trades and toward their products as intellectual and economic commodities. They also reveal the level of organized power available to each of these interest groups. Nowhere is this more apparent than in efforts to construct an international copyright agreement acceptable to authors and members of the book trades. The first international copyright bill, introduced in 1837 by Senator Henry Clay of Kentucky, attempted to reconcile conflicting interests by extending copyright to works by foreign authors if the works were manufactured in the United States.[41] Clay's measure failed because of opposition from members of the Standing Committee on Patents, to which the bill was assigned. The committee report echoed the objections of printers and publishers who feared that in the absence of a protective tariff on imported books, granting copyright to foreign works would raise prices and destroy the market for American products.[42]

The issue of international copyright, basically a question of protecting American manufacturing interests, has always been closely tied to that of a tariff on imported books. Books were first singled out for special treatment in 1842, and import duties had risen to 25 percent by 1864.[43] Although the 25 percent duty was imposed as a war revenue measure, the protective tariff on books remained at this high level for almost half a century. During that period, academic and scientific groups fought bitterly against the so-called "tax on knowledge," while members of the book trades joined together in a vigorous effort to preserve high tariffs. Some authors saw import duties as a way to discourage foreign editions of their works, and an 1883 petition signed by Thomas Bailey Aldrich, Oliver Wendell Holmes, and John Greenleaf Whittier maintained "that the prosperity of authors is closely connected with the prosperity of publishers, who are their agents in manufacturing, advertising and selling the books which they write."[44] This alliance between authors and publishers is noteworthy since at the time most American authors still saw publishers as the greatest obstacle to international copyright.

Two international copyright bills were introduced in 1885 and 1886—the first with no manufacturing clause, the second, by Senator Jonathan Chace of Rhode Island, a protectionist bill. According to Richard Watson Gilder, Chace's bill commanded "unprecedented support—that of the authors, the publishers (including the hitherto pirates who are sick of the cut-throat business) and the printers—i.e. the trades unions."[45] The Chace Act and the McKinley Tariff Act of 1890, which admitted free books in languages other than English but maintained the 25 percent duty on English-language books, succeeded where other attempts at agreement on international copyright had failed because together they harmonized previously conflicting interests.[46]

By the act of March 3, 1891, *any* "author, inventor, designer, or proprietor . . . and [their] executors, administrators, or assigns" was eligible for copyright provided that all requirements were met, including that the work deposited was "printed from type set within the limits of the United States, or from plates made therefrom. . . ."[47] With certain exceptions, the importation of foreign editions was prohibited. The Librarian of Congress was instructed to provide a list of all copyrighted books and other works to the Secretary of the Treasury, who was required to print a weekly catalog of these titles for the use of customs officials in detecting illegal imports. This is the origin of the *Catalogue of Title-Entries,* later the *Catalogue of Copyright Entries,* which constitutes a full published record of copyright registrations from that day to this.

The 1909 general revision of the copyright act broadened the manufacturing clause to cover then-new technologies, so that the text could be printed "either by hand or by the aid of any kind of typesetting machine." The printing of the illustrations and the binding of the book were also to be done within the limits of the United States. An affidavit of manufacture, attesting that these requirements had been met and identifying the place, date, and establishment where they were performed, was to accompany the deposit copies. In order to meet the objections of British authors that it was impossible to arrange for an edition printed in America before publication there, a thirty-day ad interim copyright was granted to deposits of foreign editions of books in English.

For almost one hundred years the manufacturing clause has remained a source of conflict among authors, publishers, and the printing trades, and a symbol of American economic protectionism.[48] A series of amendments has progressively narrowed the scope of the clause: in 1954 all manufacturing requirements were eliminated for foreign works protected under the Universal Copyright Convention, an exemption that has been attacked as discriminatory against American authors.[49] Despite efforts by authors, publishers, and the Library of Congress Copyright Office to have the clause struck from the 1976 law, manufacturers' arguments prevailed and an extension was granted to July 1, 1982. An exemption introduced in the 1976 revision enables American authors to arrange for foreign publication, so that the sole remaining restriction is on American publishers, who are prevented from getting their printing done abroad. Whereas in the nineteenth century publishers were aligned with printers on the subject of international copyright, today they—along with authors—condemn this restrictive policy, an indication of how far publishers have moved away from the manufacturing role.

In 1982, again amidst intense lobbying, Congress voted to extend the manufacturing clause for another four years. President Reagan vetoed the bill, but Congress overrode a Reagan veto for the first time and forced the extension into law.[50] In the present climate of debate over free trade and protectionism, pressure for the United States to join the Berne Convention, and increased efforts to protect U.S. copyrighted works from piracy, we can be sure that 1986 will bring another round in this controversy.[51]

Substantive changes in the copyright law between 1790 and 1891 affected the term and the subjects of copyright—prints and music were added in 1831, photographs in 1865. Procedural changes, principally related to the number and location of deposit copies, are of interest because they altered the nature of the records created and the likelihood that they have survived.[52] Beginning in 1802, a copy of the record had to appear on the title page or the page immediately following. A supplementary act of 1834 required that all transfers and assignments be recorded in the district court of the original registration. The most significant procedural revision came in 1870, when responsibility for copyright registration and deposit was transferred from the clerks of the district courts to the Librarian of Congress. All extant records were ordered forwarded to the Library from the state repositories, and from this date a complete and uniform record of copyrighted works has been maintained at the Library of Congress. This copyright archive, exhaustive for the post-1870 period and comprehensive for the years between 1790 and 1870, is a primary resource for the history of American authorship, printing, and publishing.[53] Approximately 23,000 deposit copies were received for the period between 1790 and 1870 by the Library in 1870, a very small number relative to the 150,000 registrations.[54] The low rate of survival is the result of several factors, including noncompliance before deposit enforcement procedures were tightened in 1865. In addition, a very high proportion of registrations represents nonbook items.

The emergence of the Library of Congress as a comprehensive national collection dates from 1870 and was the goal of Ainsworth Rand Spofford, Librarian of Congress from 1865 to 1897, when he lobbied for deposit for use and strict enforcement.[55] New technologies continue to pose substantive and procedural questions to be resolved by the legislature and the courts. For example, the 1981 decision to accept automated databases for registration has raised the problem of "dynamic databases" that are subject to regular revision and expansion. At issue are a West Publishing Company national law reporter system and the OCLC database.[56]

In the twentieth century as in the nineteenth, copyright law fosters creative, technological, and economic activity. By extending a limited monopoly to the products of intellectual and creative endeavors, the drafters of the Constitution intended to mediate between the natural rights of authors and the public interest. The agents of this uneasy partnership were the printer and publisher. Nineteenth-century copyright law was far from perfect (as is our own), but by giving authors legal title to property they could sell, by granting protection to publishers who invested money in what they had bought, and by making available to printers a body of foreign works that they could reprint cheaply, copyright law stimulated and facilitated the development of authorship, publishing, and printing in nineteenth-century America.

Notes

1. Sara J. Lippincott, *Greenwood Leaves: A Collection of Sketches and Letters*, by Grace Greenwood (Boston: Ticknor, Reed, and Fields, 1850), 283–85.

2. *Copyright Enactments: Laws Passed in the United States Since 1783 Relating to Copyright* (Washington: Library of Congress, 1973), 21. Hereafter cited as *Enactments*.

3. R. R. Bowker, quoted by W. Boyd Rayward, "Manufacture and Copyright: Past History Remaking," *Journal of Library History* 3 (1968): 8. For comments by Dickens see, for example, *The Letters of Charles Dickens. The Pilgrim Edition*, vol. 3, ed. Madeline House, Graham Storey, Kathleen Tillotson, and Noel C. Peyrouton (Oxford: Clarendon Press, 1974), 231–34.

4. See, for example, Ellen B. Ballou, *The Building of the House: Houghton Mifflin's Formative Years* . . . (Boston: Houghton Mifflin, 1970), 59–95; James J. Barnes, *Authors, Publishers, and Politicians: The Quest for an International Copyright Agreement, 1815–1854* (Columbus: Ohio University Press, 1974); William Charvat, *Literary Publishing in America 1790–1850* (Philadelphia: University of Pennsylvania Press, 1959), 17–18; Charvat, *The Profession of Authorship in America, 1800–1870,* ed. Matthew J. Bruccoli (Ohio State University Press, 1968), 30–32; Eugene Exman, *The House of Harper: One Hundred and Fifty Years of Publishing* (New York: Harper & Row, 1967), 48–68; Warren S. Tryon and William Charvat, eds. *The Cost Books of Ticknor and Fields and their Predecessors 1832–1858* (New York: Bibliographical Society of America, 1949), 52–53; David Kaser, *Messrs. Carey & Lea of Philadelphia: A Study in the History of the Booktrade* (Philadelphia: University of Pennsylvania Press, 1957), 67, 91–116; Simon Nowell-Smith, *International Copyright Law and the Publisher in the Reign of Queen Victoria* (Oxford: Clarendon Press, 1968), 64–84; Graham Pollard's introduction to I. R. Brussel, *Anglo-American First Editions 1826–1900; East to West* (London: Constable, 1935), 4–12; Luke White, Jr., *Henry William Herbert & the American Publishing Scene 1831–1858* (Newark, N.J.: The Carteret Book Club, 1943), 12.

5. *Enactments,* 1–22. For the text, legislative history and political background of the Statute of Anne, see John Feather, "The Book Trade in Politics: The Making of the Copyright Act of 1710," *Publishing History* 8 (1980): 19–44; Harry Ransom, *The First Copyright Statute* (Austin: University of Texas Press, 1959), 110–17. For a comparison between the 1790 Act and its English and American predecessors, see Lyman Ray Patterson, *Copyright in Historical Perspective* (Nashville: Vanderbilt University Press, 1968), 3–19, and his "Private Copyright and Public Communication: Free Speech Endangered," *Vanderbilt Law Review* 28 (1975): 1161–1211.

6. See Frederick R. Goff, "Almost Books," *The New Colophon* 1 (1948): 125–33. The initial impact of the copyright law was reviewed by Goff, "The First Decade of the Federal Act for Copyright, 1790–1800," in *Essays Honoring Lawrence C. Wroth* (Portland, Maine: Anthoensen Press, 1951), 101–28, and Martin A. Roberts, *Records in the Copyright Office Deposited by the United States District Courts Covering the Period 1790–1870* (Washington: Government Printing Office, 1939). A project recently completed at the Library of Congress with support from the Center for the Book transcribes and indexes the information for books and maps registered in the district court record books and on the deposited titles. There are approximately 800 entries in *Federal Copyright Records, 1790–1800,* comp. Carter Wills, ed. James Gilreath (Washington: Library of Congress, forthcoming in 1987).

7. Patterson, *Copyright in Historical Perspective,* 194.

8. Washington Irving to John Miller, 1824, the Pierpont Morgan Library, New York. Quoted by permission of The Washington Irving Society.

9. Emily Ellsworth Ford Skeel, *A Bibliography of the Writings of Noah Webster,*

ed. Edwin H. Carpenter, Jr. (New York: New York Public Library, 1958), 36–37, 46, 50.

10. Edwin and Virginia Price Barber, "A Description of Old Harper and Brothers Publishing Records Recently Come to Light," *Bulletin of Bibliography* 25 (1966–67): 1–6, 29–40; Charvat, *Profession of Authorship*, 155–67; C. Harvey Gardiner, *Prescott and his Publishers* (Carbondale: Southern Illinois University Press, 1959); John Tebbel, *A History of Book Publishing in the United States*, 4 vols. (New York: R. R. Bowker, 1972–81), 1: 212.

11. Quoted by Ballou, *Building of the House,* 149.

12. For example, see, ibid., 279. I am grateful to Michael Winship for help in clarifying the relationship between copyright and stereotype plates in trade sales.

13. For Dodge's campaign, see Ballou, *Building of the House,* 143–52. For other aspects, see Tryon and Charvat, *The Cost Books,* xlii, xlvi.

14. *Publishers' Weekly,* 24 Apr. 1886, 542.

15. *Black's Law Dictionary,* 5th ed., 1095–96.

16. Barnes, *Authors, Publishers, and Politicians,* 53–56, 84–86; Exman, *House of Harper,* 54–56; Kaser, *Messrs. Carey & Lea,* 92, 143–48.

17. Kaser, *Messrs. Carey & Lea,* 151–52.

18. Quoted in Barnes, *Authors, Publishers, and Politicians,* 54.

19. *Decisions of the United States Courts Involving Copyright and Literary Property 1789–1909, With an Analytical Index.*Copyright Office Bulletins, nos. 13–16 (Washington: Library of Congress, 1980), 15: 2373–79, hereafter cited as *C.O. Bull.*

20. Walter Sutton, *The Western Book Trade: Cincinnati as a Nineteenth-Century Publishing and Book-Trade Center . . .* (Columbus: Ohio State University Press for The Ohio Historical Society, 1961), 25–55.

21. Forrest Wilson, *Crusader in Crinoline: The Life of Harriet Beecher Stowe* (Philadelphia: J. B. Lippincott, 1941), 302.

22. The following account is based on White, *Henry William Herbert,* 60–62.

23. *C.O. Bull.* 15: 2907. The decisions are reprinted, ibid., 2901–65; for a summary and analysis of the case see Patterson, *Copyright in Historical Perspective,* 203–12.

24. *Letters of Noah Webster,* ed. Harry R. Warfel (New York: Library Publishers, 1953), 383.

25. Patterson, *Copyright in Historical Perspective,* 198. In 1909 the renewal term was extended to twenty-eight years. The 1976 revision introduced the concept of automatic copyright commencing with the fixation of a protectable work in a tangible form, published or unpublished, for a term consisting of the life of the author and fifty years after the author's death.

26. Noel Gerson, *Harriet Beecher Stowe: A Biography* (New York: Praeger, 1976), 71.

27. *Enactments,* 37.

28. The following account is based on the report in *C.O. Bull.* 15: 2482–86.

29. Patterson, "Private Copyright and Public Communication," 1166.

30. *Gray et al.. v. Russell et al.* (1839), *C.O. Bull.* 14: 1120–27.

31. *C.O. Bull.* 14: 1545–1625. The case is summarized in Charles Francis Adams, *Richard Henry Dana: A Biography,* 2 vols. (Boston: Houghton, Mifflin, 1890), 2: 282–327.

32. Ballou, *Building of the House,* 390–92.

33. *C.O. Bull.* 14: 1272–73.

34. *Enactments,* 66.

35. This account is based on Ballou, *Building of the House,* 393–94.

36. *C.O. Bull.* 14: 2128–29.

37. On the firm's history see "Alexander Belford—In Memoriam," *Publishers' Weekly* 70 (1906): 1098–99; Tebbel, *History of Book Publishing,* 2: 444–48.

38. *Mark Twain's Letters to his Publishers 1867–1894,* ed. Hamlin Hill (Berkeley: University of California Press, 1967), 106–7.

39. *C.O. Bull.* 13: 647–51.

40. *Mark Twain's Letters,* 200; *C.O. Bull.* 13: 651–53.

41. Barnes, *Authors, Publishers, and Politicians,* 61–74; Marjorie McCannon, *The Manufacturing Clause of the U.S. Copyright Law.* Study no. 35, Copyright Office, February 1963 (Washington: Library of Congress, 1972), 4.

42. Barnes, *Authors, Publishers, and Politicians,* 68–71.

43. This account is based on Donald Marquand Dozer, "The Tariff on Books," *Mississippi Valley Historical Review* 36 (1949): 73–96.

44. Reprinted in Dozer, "Tariff," 81.

45. Ibid., 92.

46. *Enactments,* 49–54.

47. *Enactments,* 49–50.

48. For a summary of issues and developments through the 1960s, see Rayward, "Manufacture and Copyright: Past History Remaking," 7–31.

49. *Enactments,* 129–31.

50. *Publishers' Weekly* 4 June 1982, 16: 23 July 1982, 62.

51. I am grateful to Lewis Flacks, Policy Planning Adviser, Copyright Office, Library of Congress, for a summary of recent developments and observations on the future of the manufacturing clause.

52. For a survey of the changes and the research potential of the records, see G. Thomas Tanselle, "Copyright Records and the Bibliographer," *Studies in Bibliography* 22 (1969): 77–124. See also Roger E. Stoddard, "United States Copyright Deposit Copies of Books and Pamphlets Printed Before 1820," *Publishing History* 13 (1983): 5–21, and his "United States Dramatic Copyrights, 1790–1830: A Provisional Catalogue," in *Essays in Honor of James Edward Walsh on his Sixty-Fifth Birthday* (Cambridge: The Goethe Institute and The Houghton Library, 1983), 231–54.

53. The copyright collections are described in my forthcoming *The History of Books: A Guide to Selected Resources in the Library of Congress* (Washington: Library of Congress, in press).

54. Roberts, *Records in the Copyright Office,* 11.

55. John Y. Cole, "Of Copyright, Men & a National Library," *Quarterly Journal of the Library of Congress* 28 (1971): 114–36.

56. *Library of Congress Information Bulletin,* 26 August 1985, 237–38.

7. Printing for the Instant City: San Francisco at Mid-Century

Robert D. Harlan

One of Gertrude Stein's more obscure pronouncements was directed at her childhood home of the 1880s, Oakland, California, of which she said: "there is no there there."[1] That description clearly would have applied some three decades earlier to San Francisco, across the bay, which was all but deserted in 1848 when its inhabitants rushed to the newly discovered gold deposits in the interior to try their luck at prospecting. Its population of 813 was decimated. The city council ceased to meet. Its two newspapers closed. And the harbor was filled with ships abandoned by their crews.

Within a year the ghost town had become an instant city of at least 25,000 people. Without adequate housing, paved streets, or reliable city services able to cope with problems of health and security, San Francisco resembled an encampment more than a city. As new waves of emigrants from increasingly distant points collided with earlier arrivals, it became the most cosmopolitan assemblage of its size at that time in the United States or its territories. The population on any two days must have been as constant as that of a major airline terminal, for either the mine fields or, in the opposite direction, home was the intended destination, not San Francisco. In spite of the long and difficult initial migration to the city, probably three-quarters of the first generation of emigrants departed within the first decade of their arrival.[2] Wanderlust was a general characteristic of the Californians. Frustrated in his attempt to fix persons and business firms at specific addresses, the compiler of an early Sacramento directory lamented that "the population of California is the most migratory, perhaps, in the world. The man who last week was a citizen of Sacramento may this week be a resident of Marysville, and next week enroll himself among the denizens of Oroville or Shasta."[3]

By the early 1850s there had passed through San Francisco, in order of their arrival but not necessarily their departure, Californians, Oregonians, Mexicans from Sonora, Canadians, Americans and Hawaiians from the Sandwich Islands, Peruvians, Equadorians, and Chileans, a large contingent of Irish by way of Australia, Americans and Europeans from the eastern United States, and, directly from Europe in large numbers, Germans, Frenchmen, and citizens of the United Kingdom. Chinese from Canton represented one-third of all new immigrants as early as 1852. Observers of this melee commented upon the "Babylonian confusion of tongues" and the "medley of races and nationalities."[4] A profound feeling of instability and rootlessness prevailed, to which devastating fires—there were six between December 1849 and May 1851—and severe earthquakes in 1851, 1856, 1865, and 1868 contributed.

Gold and goods as well as people passed in impressive amounts through San Francisco, which by the mid-1850s served as both the gateway and the emporium for the entire West Coast. With the establishment in 1867 and 1868 of steamship lines to China, Japan, and Australia, it also became the hub of the Far Eastern trade. The city's population continued to increase at an exceptional rate, from about 50,000 in the mid-1850s to 80,000 in 1860 to 150,000 in 1870. In only two decades the remote village had been transformed into one of the great port cities of the United States. With the completion in 1869 of the transcontinental railway, which significantly raised San Francisco's prospects in eastern estimations, the first phase of its development seemed to end triumphantly.

However, serious, ugly problems marred this record. Inflation and high labor costs were endemic in the 1850s and reappeared during the Civil War. There were three serious depressions. Violence, crime, and political corruption could be checked only when vigilance committees—themselves unlawful, but probably necessary—provided the impetus for better official control. The city's social fabric strained under the palpable hostility of Americans towards all foreigners and of everyone towards the Latin Americans and Chinese. Ethnic enclaves within the city—Little Chile and Chinatown, for example—had the appearance of armed camps. And most San Franciscans regarded themselves as exiles in an unfriendly land.

In his revisionist study, *The World Rushed In: The California Gold Rush Experience* (New York: Simon & Schuster, 1981), James Holliday has likened the gold rush to a national tragedy on the scale of a great war in its disruption of American families and communities. The prospector's life was often as imperiled as that of the soldier, and he was infinitely more alone. The emigrant in San Francisco felt no less alone. For both the literate soldier and emigrant, reading served as a major diversion, providing support, comfort, and amusement. Most in demand was news from home, since hardly anyone regarded San Francisco as home. Familiar newspapers were the preferred medium for the news, even when they were decidedly dated. The preference for imported newspapers persisted long after the establishment of several good local papers, a condition that Richard Henry Dana noted on his return trip to San Francisco Bay in 1859, when he observed the crush at the docks upon the arrival of the latest mail steamer, carrying "the newspapers and verbal intelligence from the great Atlantic and European world."[5] In its November 1865 issue, the periodical *Puck,* the self-proclaimed San Francisco version of *Punch,* attempted to put a better face upon this ceremony, declaring that it proved that ". . . in San Francisco we have as large a reading public as can be found in any city of the same size in the world."[6]

Further evidence of the robust reading habits of the city's population is revealed in the disproportionate number of bookshops located in San Francisco in relation to its age, size, and distance from the eastern sources of supply, a record that no doubt contributed to California's fifth-place ranking in number of bookshops in the 1860 federal census.[7] Like the city's population, these shops also appeared and disappeared at an alarming rate, but the competition of too many shops worked to the patron's advantage. Almost exceptionally, local inflation seems not to have affected book prices, which by and large were those charged in the East.

The success of eastern American and of European publishers and dealers in getting substantial shipments of newspapers, periodicals, and books to San Francisco was not only a triumph of greed over logistical problems, but also indicates the important San Francisco and California market for this material.[8] We will probably never have a detailed picture of the individual titles supplied, for although the importation records of the United States Customs House in San Francisco exist, the inventories for shipments of printed material are not itemized in detail. Booksellers' and bookdealers' advertisements in local newspapers and in their pub- lished catalogs suggest inventories of both breadth and depth. As early as 1852 the leading shops boasted stocks of 50,000 to 100,000 books. Without doubt some of the books shipped to San Francisco, particularly those consigned to San Francisco auction houses, were unsellable. Like the London dealers in the eighteenth century, those in the eastern United States in the nineteenth century were not above dumping on the American provincial market. Local San Francisco booksellers soon appreciated the advantages of establishing eastern contacts, either through hired agents or personal buying trips.

A major concern of the San Francisco bookseller was always the timely supply of eastern best-sellers. Although more expensive, shipment by way of the Isthmus of Panama could deliver goods enhanced by timeliness in weeks rather than the months required by the Cape Horn route. For example, copies of the latest works of that most popular of authors, Charles Dickens, could be supplied in record time. The final installments of *David Copperfield* were published in London in November 1850. They were available in San Francisco in late January 1851. Other examples suggest tolerable punctuality. In his 1860 catalog, San Francisco's premier bookseller Anton Roman advertised George Eliot's *The Mill on the Floss* and Nathaniel Hawthorne's *The Marble Faun,* both first published that same year.

Only one of Charles Dickens's novels was locally printed and published. It is the drab, textually corrupt, and unauthorized "California Edition" of *Hard Times* (1854) which was probably set from the earlier serial publication of this work in the London periodical *Household Words.* I know of only one other example of a San Francisco edition before 1870 of a popular English novel. This is Charles Reade's *Peg Woffington* (London, 1853, San Francisco, 1855). This record suggests an acceptable delivery time, although more piracies might have appeared but for the high local costs of labor and material.

Except for the period of the Civil War, which witnessed shipment delays and some shortages, national and international news was adequately provided by a large selection of imported newspapers, and the flow of popular periodicals and new books provided—and sometimes overprovided—for local demands. What, then, was the function of San Francisco's printing trade during the city's first two decades?

Bibliography of Nineteenth-Century San Francisco Imprints

To answer that question we need to ask another: What was printed and published? Existing bibliographies of mid-nineteenth-century San Francisco imprints do not provide a satisfactory answer, even though for that city, as for other cities and regions, bibliographical control of the earliest period has received the most attention to the best effect. Herbert Fahey's *Early Printing in California* (San Francisco: The Book Club of California, 1956) traces in detail to September 9, 1850, the date on which California was admitted to the Union, the product of the California press, which after 1848 had been preponderantly the San Francisco press. The comprehensive scope of this work is commendable. Fahey expands upon Henry R. Wagner's *California Imprints* (Berkeley, 1922) which takes as its terminal date June 1851 on the grounds that imprints before a great fire of that month, the last of a series, are uniformly rare. Both works treat the period generally accepted to be that of the California incunable. The standard source for early imprints is Robert Greenwood's *California*

Imprints, 1833–1862 (Los Gatos: Talisman Press, 1961), which, however, becomes increasingly selective as it progresses chronologically, omitting eventually all government publications, newspaper and periodical publications, special formats, and nearly all ephemera. The bibliography contains 1,748 entries of which most are San Francisco imprints.

While Greenwood consulted Wagner, Fahey, and other sources, his bibliography is based primarily upon the California slips in the massive, unfinished, and still basically unpublished American Imprints Inventory, the product of the WPA's Historical Research Survey and the creation of the indefatigable Douglas C. McMurtrie. During the life of this project, from 1937 to 1942, nearly two thousand persons throughout the country were employed to "read," card by card and back to back, the catalogs of some ten thousand American libraries, several of which had not previously been inventoried at all, making notations on slips of every American imprint they located up to 1876 (or 1890 for eight midwestern and western states where printing commenced relatively late). The resulting partially edited fifteen million slips still represent the most extensive inventory of early American imprints in American libraries. Many of the works described on these slips were not represented in the union catalog at the Library of Congress. I have been told that this is also true of the *National Union Catalog, Pre-1956 Imprints.*

A victim of World War II, the project was halted in 1942, and following the death in 1944 of its great advocate, Douglas McMurtrie, it ended. The very survival of the slips was in doubt for a time. From Chicago their odyssey took them to Madison, Wisconsin, then to Washington, D.C., and, eventually, the Library of Congress before they finally and securely came to rest a few years ago at the Kilmer campus of Rutgers University. Unfortunately, the integrity of the original collection has been compromised over the years. For example, after more than one search, the California slips for the years 1866 and 1867 cannot now be located. Sad to say, a duplicate collection of the California slips, including presumably those for the years 1866 and 1867, which George L. Harding rescued when the California State Library decided to discard them, have apparently been misplaced by an eminent library to which they were presented for safekeeping. Some of the California slips have been edited and published, for example, those representing non-documentary imprints through 1858 (Washington, D.C.: WPA, 1942). Also, a series of master's theses emanating from Catholic University of America in Washington, D.C., provides checklists based upon the California slips for the years 1856–1865, 1868–1870, 1872 and 1874, excluding for the most part official publications. Greenwood consulted all of these sources and more in compiling his bibliography.[9]

Greenwood did not have access to the *National Union Catalog, Pre-1956 Imprints,* which is still the greatest published inventory of American library holdings, but neither do we have access to this work when a chronological or geographical approach is desired. REMARC, the online publication of the Library of Congress shelflist, does provide both date and place of imprint tags, but I have found its yield of early San Francisco imprints disappointing and often inaccurate. *A Checklist of American Imprints,* the successor to Ralph R. Shaw and Richard H. Shoemaker's *American Bibliography,* has great potential as the source for California imprints to 1876 since it is based upon the American Imprint Inventory slips, but the latest volume of this work, published in 1982, has reached only the year 1834.

The ideal source to identify imprints is, of course, the printer's records, as they provide primary information. A general indifference to such material until recently has conspired in California with fire and earthquake to obliterate all but a few such records. For mid-nineteenth-century San Francisco, fragmentary records of two firms have survived— the Alta California press from January 4 through August 24, 1850, and O'Meara and Painter from January 1857 through November 1859. These are deposited in the Kemble Collections of the California Historical Society Library in San Francisco. The nearly complete records of San Francisco's premier printing house from 1858 to 1868, Towne & Bacon, and of its predecessor, Whitton, Towne & Company, are extant because the Towne of that firm took them with him when he resettled in the East. They were not returned to California until after the earthquake and fire of 1906. These records are housed in the Stanford University Libraries. None of the published California bibliographies has utilized these sources.[10]

The distance of the in-progress *Checklist of American Imprints* from the period of San Francisco printing, the debased state of the California slips in the American Imprints Inventory, the limitations of Greenwood, and the complete lack of a systematic bibliography of San Francisco imprints for the last quarter of the nineteenth century seem to me to mandate the creation of a new bibliographical record of San Francisco imprints through 1900. This enterprise would probably not be feasible but for the publication of the *Catalog of Printed Books* of the Bancroft Library at the University of California, Berkeley. Comprising a basic set and three supplements of thirty-nine volumes in all, published between 1964 and 1979, this work photographically reproduces the cards for about 200,000 titles in the library acknowledged to contain the most comprehensive collection of nineteenth-century California imprints. Its strengths are several. First, the San Francisco bookdealer Hubert Howe Bancroft created it to serve as a collection of source material for research, a policy from which he never deviated. Indeed the collection began modestly enough as an assemblage of books, pamphlets, and other materials to support the compilation in the 1860s of a West Coast almanac. This policy provided for both breadth and depth, encompassing "everything that bore on western history, whether it was prose or poetry, book or pamphlet, broadside or newspaper, authoritative or partisan. . . ."[11] "It was my custom," Bancroft explained, "when collecting to glance through any book which I thought might contain information on the territory marked out. I made it no part of my duty at this time to enquire into the nature or quality of the production; . . . in making such a collection it is impossible to determine at a glance what is of value and what is not. The most worthless trash may prove some fact wherein the best book is deficient, and this makes the trash valuable."[12] While the validity of Bancroft's policy is not now questioned, it was unusual if not exceptional for his time. Two results of Bancroft's broad sweep are his library's superlative collections of California newspapers and pamphlets, the latter often arranged by Bancroft or his associates into factitious subject volumes on such topics as San Francisco Medicine; San Francisco Harbor; San Francisco City Lots; Irrigation in California; Pamphlets by California Authors: Scientific; Poets, etc.; San Francisco Charities; San Francisco Lodges; California Sheet Music; and so on. Many of the publications in these collections are unique copies.

Another of the collection's strengths results from the acquisition by Bancroft and his agents of ephemeral material before it was used up or discarded and while it was still inexpensive or free for the asking. As a publisher and bookseller, Bancroft knew how to work effectively with the trade, which, in turn, was impressed by the financial resources at his disposal. He did not limit his buying to local or California sources but had considerable success in finding rare and unique material in the eastern United States and, in particular, in London. He also had the insight to provide for the secure storage of his collection in a well-constructed brick building in outer San Francisco, and as a result it survived the 1906 conflagration undamaged, unlike the city's other great private library assembled by Albert Sutro, which, on the advice of experts who feared the effects of fog upon the 200,000-volume collection, had been transferred from the outskirts to the downtown district where it was almost completely destroyed by the fire.

Since its purchase in 1905 for the University of California, the original Bancroft collection has been considerably augmented and strengthened by purchases and gifts. Although it was consulted for the American Imprints Inventory, the Bancroft Library catalog used for that inventory is now fifty years old. The more current published Bancroft Library *Catalog* is, therefore, the first resource to be utilized in the construction of a new bibliography of nineteenth-century San Francisco imprints.

During the past four years, several research assistants and I have been compiling such a bibliography, based upon photocopies of all of the appropriate entries in the Bancroft Library *Catalog* but enhanced with additional entries taken from the card catalog of the California Historical Society Library, REMARC, selected sections of the card catalogs of the California State Library and the Huntington Library, and the *National Union Catalog, Pre-1956 Imprints.* Also used were the second edition (1970) and its supplement (1976) of *California Local History* (Stanford University Press), the Library of Congress *Catalog of Broadsides in the Rare Book Division* (Boston: G. K. Hall, 1972), antiquarian dealers' catalogs, and, of course, Greenwood's *California Imprints.* The bibliography contains about 8,500 slips representing books, pamphlets having fewer than forty-nine pages, broadsides, periodicals, and newspapers.

San Francisco Printing, 1850–69: A Statistical Summary

A pilot project, based upon portions of this file, has examined the first two decades of San Francisco imprints, from 1850, when the city was incorporated, through 1869.[13] During this period 2,571 books, pamphlets, and broadsides, 75 periodicals, and 255 newspapers were printed and published in San Francisco. Nearly all of the citations for periodicals and newspapers are from the Bancroft Library *Catalog.* The following figures on the sources of the 2,571 books, pamphlets, and broadsides citations reveal a similar dominance (the figure for each source represents the citations it adds to the total, excluding citations it repeats): the Bancroft Library, 2,041; California Historical Society Library, 213; *California Local History,* 105; the Huntington Library, 61; REMARC, 12; *National Union Catalog, Pre-1956 Imprints,* 3; the Library of Congress *Catalog of Broadsides in the Rare Book Division,* 2; and 2 citations from antiquarian book dealers' catalogs. Greenwood yields 132 citations not found in any of these works. However, the file contains 344 citations not in Greenwood, an increase of about 27 percent.

The information contained in the citations for the 2,571 books, pamphlets, and broadsides includes author, title, printer, publisher, date, total pages, language, edition, copyright statement, printing process (letterpress or lithography), Greenwood number, and citation source. It has been fed into the Information Builders, Inc., Focus database management system on a CMS operating system. Because nearly all of the Bancroft Library holdings have been fully cataloged, a feat reflecting much in-house original cataloging, our database, unlike any of the published bibliographies of California and San Francisco imprints, records full subject designations for all of its entries. The subject designations are based upon the subject headings used by the Bancroft Library or the Library of Congress but are expanded to facilitate a fuller exploitation by the computer.

The relative power and flexibility of the Focus system allows for complex, hierarchically organized data structures, which, in turn, facilitate manipulation and analysis of multiple combinations of data fields. For the pilot project, several key data fields have been used to examine the scope of the imprints, and relationships between title count, form, pages, subject, individual printer, and date have been identified. The citations for the 75 periodicals and 255 newspapers are not represented in this Focus project, but the results of a manual title count have been utilized.

It is important to remember that the primary purpose of this pilot project has been to formulate and then to test a methodology utilizing a computerized database management system and that the project is limited chronologically. About one-third of the 2,571 books, pamphlets, and broadsides have not been examined or examined sufficiently to address questions of the *physical* item, for example, important aspects of binding, paper, format, and typography. Nor have such topics as distribution, copublishing, book buying, and book reading audiences been much exploited. We are currently inputting into Focus the information in the citations in our bibliography for the next decade, 1870–1879, and will then proceed by decades to 1900. As the chronological coverage is expanded, trends will become clearer and more reliably interpretable.

A Survey of Titles

In the following preliminary survey, first periodicals and newspapers, and then books, pamphlets, and broadsides are analyzed. Figure 1 shows the distribution by titles of these categories. But the survey begins with a few observations on the most elusive category of printing: job work.

Job work. The poor survival rate of job work, both physically and bibliographically, is well known. Frequently taking the form of dated tickets, bills, invitations, announcements, and so on, a large category of this work was meant to be used up, discarded, and forgotten. When it has survived at all it is often because of an item's provenance, its spectacular typographical display, or perhaps its use of gold ink on silk, as is the case with one San Francisco menu in the Bancroft Library. Lawrence C. Wroth's calculation of a survival rate for colonial American ephemera of about one extant item out of four printed[14] is probably too generous for nineteenth-century American job work, including that of California, which was so plentiful as to be commonplace. Rare indeed is the imprint bibliography that attempts even to include it. Yet job work formed a major, often *the* major, source of a printer's income. Evidence from the three San Francisco printers' records that I have already referred to—Alta California, O'Meara and Painter, and Towne & Bacon—indicates this fact clearly enough. Very significant, I think, is Bruce Johnson's finding, based upon his analysis of the categories of printing and their proportionate

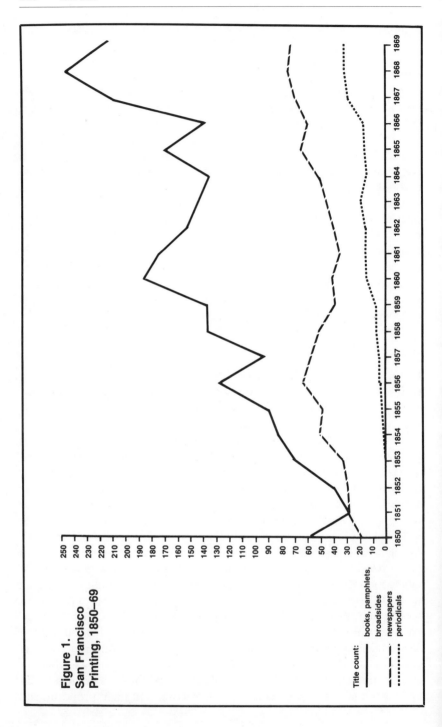

Figure 1.
San Francisco
Printing, 1850–69

Title count:
———— books, pamphlets,
        broadsides
– – – newspapers
·········· periodicals

representation, that consistently about 60 percent of Whitton, Towne & Company's and Towne & Bacon's income was derived from this kind of work.[15] Yet the reputation of both firms within the city's printing trade rests primarily upon their more enduring book printing. In format, typographical treatment, and subject matter, San Francisco job printing was remarkably varied. Although all of the city's printing firms were engaged in its production, an effort was made by some to suggest that it was a specialization which only they were qualified to perform. Advertisements make much of a printing firm's stock of fancy and ornamental foundry type, its wooden display type, and its mammoth press for the production of mammoth posters.[16]

Among the hundreds of San Francisco imprints I have examined, including several handsomely produced books and pamphlets, the most strikingly beautiful and technically flawless are job work, and among these I would single out the stock certificates printed for mining companies. Keith Maslen has proposed in his work on the William Bowyer ledgers that job printing can serve as an index to civilization.[17] The exceptional attention and care lavished on the production of mining stock certificates by San Francisco's printers speak eloquently of at least one characteristic of the city's "civilization" at mid-century. But job printing can also provide startling contradictory evidence, for example, this entry, dated July 5, 1850, in the Alta California ledgers: "$16.00 . . . 100 Posters Puppy dog lost."[18]

Periodicals. Between 1850 and 1870, at least seventy-five periodicals were printed in San Francisco. They varied considerably in length, scope, and quality. While a few caught on and survived for some time, many only lasted between one and two years. The most distinctive of the lot, I believe, was the satirical *Puck,* in which lively text and elegant lithographic illustrations were combined to produce an exceptional magazine. The largest number of periodical titles, twenty-seven, appeared in 1868. The previous year had witnessed the production of the largest number of *new* periodical titles, fifteen (fig. 2).

About one-fourth of these works were literary in their orientation, the remaining three-fourths having vocational, religious, political, or other affiliations. The literary journals did not fare well, particularly those too dependent upon the effusions of local poets and essayists. Several of the most effective articles, which can still be read with pleasure and benefit, are historical and descriptive. Some editors took the high moral path. Mrs. A. M. Schultz, the first woman magazine editor in California, promised that her *Hesperian* would "scrupulously avoid anything demoralizing in its influence."[19] That did not work too well. A popular promotional scheme attempted to establish an affiliation between San Francisco periodicals and popular eastern models. *Pioneer,* for example, labeled itself the *Knickerbocker Magazine* of the West. Since the originals were also readily

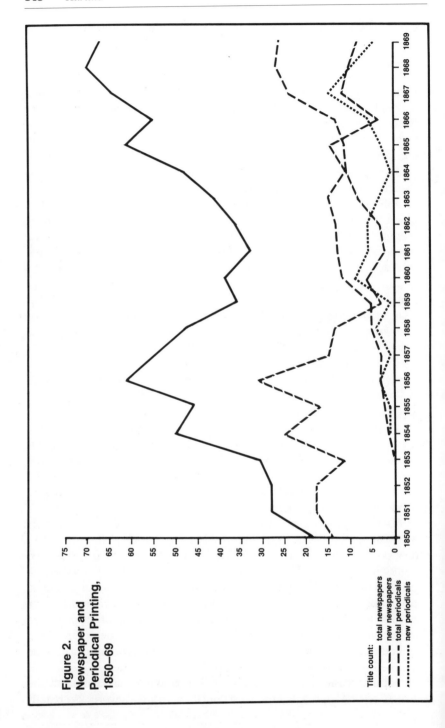

**Figure 2.
Newspaper and
Periodical Printing,
1850–69**

Title count: ———— total newspapers
              – – – new newspapers
              ·—·—· total periodicals
              ·········· new periodicals

available to western readers, that particular approach may not have been effective. California's most distinctive literary periodical, *The Overland Monthly*, established in 1868 by Anton Roman, did survive, with one interruption, until the 1930s, in large measure because its deliberate western bias was sufficiently compelling to secure eastern as well as western patronage.

Western or California emphasis worked even better in periodicals with practical application, such as the *California Culturist* and *Mining and Scientific Press*, the latter being the only journal in America devoted to the subject of mining. With its instructive articles, useful illustrations and diagrams, and editorial call for "home manufacturing," it could hardly lose. Perhaps because of its wide circulation outside of California it reminded would-be subscribers that its format, sixteen pages and sixty-four columns, was identical to that of the familiar *Harper's Weekly*.[20]

If the San Francisco periodicals of the first two decades share a distinctive feature, it is probably the quality and number of their illustrations which, with few exceptions, were executed by resident lithographers and wood engravers. Plates of California flora are particularly impressive. When such plates were used in *Hutchings' Illustrated California Magazine*, they facilitated its success in promoting the state's picturesque qualities.

Newspapers. San Francisco's newspapers before 1870 can be characterized as numerous, short-lived, and amateurish. While, exceptionally for San Francisco printing, they conform to the product of the frontier press, they are distinctive in providing the most accurate index to the city's unstable social structure and, in particular, the precarious status of its large foreign-language-speaking population.

Two hundred fifty-five separate newspapers, 13 new ones a year, on average, appeared between 1850 and 1870. In the years 1856, 1868, and 1869 the number published exceeded 60 (fig. 2), a figure comparable to that of the large eastern cities. For example, New York City had 71 papers in 1856, compared to San Francisco's 61, and in 1868, San Francisco's 68 exceeded New York City's papers by 8. Historians of California have made much of this record—too much, I think, when local circumstances are taken into account and when the test of quality is applied. An important statistic to consider is this: nearly half of the newspapers lasted for less than six months.

One historian has suggested a reason for the surfeit of San Francisco newspapers—the one thousand "professionals" available in the decade after the initial gold rush for local newspapers to call upon.[21] Money and special interests were not in short supply either. Nor did the city lack for individuals with strongly held points of view. Every man was his own journalist. "It is the inalienable right of every citizen," the editor of the San Francisco *Sunday Gossip* observed, "to keep a hotel—if he can; and to edit a paper—if he can't."[22] Conceding the "inauspicious moment of publication when the community is overburdened with newspapers of every hue and description," the editor of *Young America* persisted nevertheless in launching yet another.[23] In his *The Natural Wealth of California,* Titus F. Cronise found an explanation for this phenomenon— "the tastes and habits of the people inclining them to indulge in this style of reading more than any other."[24]

Newspapers were particularly sensitive to economic depressions, a condition that accounts for the decline in the number of titles in the mid-1850s and again in the post-Civil War years. Unpopularly held political positions could be disastrous and dangerous. Two newspaper offices were badly damaged in 1851 when their editors opposed the work of the Vigilance Committee. The news of President Lincoln's assassination incited mob action that destroyed in one hour five of the city's newspapers because of their supposed secessionist sympathies. Fires and earthquakes provided an ongoing weeding process. Certainly, some newspapers were eminently worthy of an early demise, providing as they could only an unappetizing menu of stale news and dull gossip.

The newspaper served as the primary conduit to San Francisco's large population of foreigners whose first language was not English, addressing the local issues and problems which concerned them. Many foreign language books, other than Chinese, were available in the city's bookshops, but they were almost entirely imported: of the 2,571 books, pamphlets, and broadsides in our database, only 3 percent are not in English. No foreign language periodicals were printed in San Francisco, although again, as with books and newspapers, imported titles were readily available. However, 46 of the 255 newspapers published locally were in foreign languages. Of this number, 20 (43 percent) were in French.

In the United States, probably only in Louisiana were more French-language newspapers published than in San Francisco,[25] but San Francisco's high number reflected serious publishing problems more than cultural dominance. Of the twenty French-language newspapers which appeared in San Francisco before 1870, possibly two-thirds survived for less than a year. One, *La Presse,* lasted one day. For a variety of reasons, including conflicts within the French community, lack of funds, and unrealistic expectations, the French-language press in San Francisco had little staying power. The same was said of the French by their critics. San Francisco's first chronicler, George Soulé, likened them to a light wine "sparkling, yet without strength or force of character."[26] Hubert H. Bancroft echoed that opinion: "Depth of resource, practical sense, and force of character could not be replaced by effervescing brilliancy and unsustained dash."[27] Americans, in particular, found the French complacent, aloof, and courteous to a fault. They would not learn English and seemed indifferent to the work ethos for which the sedate and plodding Germans were so admired. For their part, the French complained of the lack of the most basic trappings of civilization. What could one make of a city with an ordinance forbidding sidewalk cafes, and none of whose printing shops had French-accented type, so that the earliest French-language newspaper, *Le Californien,* had to be lithographed? The doyen of San Francisco's French-language newspapers, *L'Echo du Pacifique* (established in 1852), managed to last about a decade. In contrast, two German-language papers, *California Demokrat* and *California Staats-Zeitung,* both established in 1852, were published continuously until 1918.

Newspaper printing provided a significant but subordinate part of the income for some of the city's printers, particularly those who also acted as publishers. Newspapers were often slight works of no more than a quarto or octavo gathering, seldom printed in runs exceeding one thousand copies. Probably the easiest profit was to be made from the steamer editions, which doubled as souvenirs for persons departing the port: they could command premium prices.

Books, pamphlets, broadsides. Figure 3 displays, by year, title counts for books, pamphlets, and broadsides. The prevailing view of San Francisco's distinctive fine press movement places its origins with the better commercial printing of the 1860s and cites as its progenitors the firms of Edward Bosqui and Towne & Bacon. I find nothing typographically distinctive or original in the work of these firms. Bosqui's restraint is attractive to our eyes, although it must have appeared downright Spartan to his contemporaries, and one can only admire the consistently quiet competence of the Towne & Bacon firm. But the best that can be said of the work of these firms, and that is highly complimentary, is that it is as good as the best being produced in the East at the time.

Many commissions for book printing, including the superior work of Bosqui and Towne & Bacon, came from the city's two authentic publishing houses: Anton Roman and H. H. Bancroft. While both establishments deferred to East Coast dominance over the standard trade publishing lines, each firm did develop its own lively specialization. Roman's interests were in part imperial—American-imperial—for example, in his publishing a Russian-English phrase book for use by the Russian-speaking inhabitants of the newly acquired territory of Alaska and a Chinese grammar for the American import merchant. But one also sees in his publication list an embryonic California look, in which the contributions of local poets are mixed with trendy publications on exercise, diet, wine growing, and eastern mysticism. Bancroft, too, ploughed that field but moved more prudently into the publication of school textbooks and digests and summaries of legal cases. For the latter there was a brisk East Coast market. The only runners-up, and they are distant ones, to

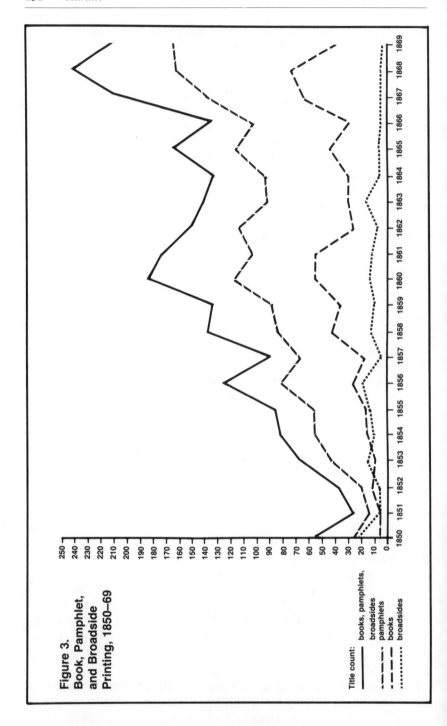

Figure 3.
Book, Pamphlet,
and Broadside
Printing, 1850–69

Title count: ———— books, pamphlets, broadsides
              – – – – pamphlets
              — - — books
              ·········· broadsides

Roman and Bancroft are Hutchings & Rosenfield, which flourished in the 1850s, D. E. Appleton & Co., and Henri Payot. Before 1870 Bancroft published 97 books; Roman, 65; Hutchings & Rosenfield, 19; and Appleton and Payot, 18 each.

Six hundred thirty-two books were printed in San Francisco between 1850 and 1870, of which about one-third were commissioned by the five firms just enumerated, the others being orders from authors, smaller publishing houses, and ad hoc publishers of one sort or another. Whatever else the term "instant city" might mean as applied to mid-century San Francisco, it cannot be inferred from it that San Francisco was a major book publishing center.

In all, 1,737 pamphlets were printed in San Francisco before 1870. The vast majority of these titles were issued not by conventional publishers but by private organizations and by individuals. The pamphlets are slight works, averaging between fifteen and twenty pages and probably seldom printed in runs of more than a thousand copies. Their chief interest relates to their subject matter.

The small number of broadsides (202) may be more indicative of their poor survival rate than of any decline in the popularity of this format. Of course many broadsides, not reflected in my listing, were also job work. The 202 broadsides are predominantly official or semi-official announcements.

Two hundred ten printers of books, pamphlets, and broadsides at work between 1850 and 1870 have been identified. They printed four-fifths (2,007) of the titles in our file, the remaining one-fifth (564) designating no printer (table 1). The distribution of the titles among these printers indicates what a minor role the business of book, pamphlet, and broadside printing assumed. Only fifteen named firms produced more than twenty-five titles, while eighty-five printed only one. Johnson's figures for Whitton, Towne & Company and Towne & Bacon indicate that for the city's leading book and pamphlet printer no more than 20 percent of their total work derived from this category of printing.[28] The distribution of the titles by form and by the three categories of printer shows some interesting trends. The top fifteen printers dominate book and pamphlet printing, producing about 50 percent of the titles. The remaining 195 known printers account for about one-quarter of book and pamphlet printing.

Another gauge of productivity and relative productivity is the total number of pages represented by all of the books and pamphlets (fig. 4). This is not the total number of copies printed, nor a conventional measure of output, such as ems for composition or tokens for presswork. But it does provide a rough guide. Table 2 presents the page counts and percentages for books, pamphlets, and broadsides for the top 15 printers,

Table 1
Printers by Titles Produced

Form	Titles Printed	% of Total Titles	% of Total Form	Titles Printed	% of Total Titles	% of Total Form
		15 Major Printers			195 Named Printers	
Books	339	13.18	53.64	155	6.03	24.52
Broadsides	34	1.32	16.83	34	1.32	16.83
Pamphlets	973	37.85	56.01	472	18.36	27.17
Total	1,346	52.35		661	25.71	
		Printer Unknown			Total Output	
Books	138	5.37	21.84	632	24.58	100.00
Broadsides	134	5.22	66.34	202	7.86	100.00
Pamphlets	292	11.35	16.82	1,737	67.56	100.00
Total	564	21.94		2,571	100.00	

Major Printers: Printed more than 25 titles between 1850 and 1870.

Table 2
Printers by Pages Produced

Form	Pages Printed	% of Total Pages	% of Total Form	Pages Printed	% of Total Pages	% of Total Form
		15 Major Printers			195 Named Printers	
Books	62,768	42.26	55.10	20,355	13.70	17.87
Broadsides	34	.02	16.83	34	.02	16.83
Pamphlets	20,120	13.54	58.45	9,610	6.48	27.92
Total	82,922	55.82		29,999	20.20	
		Printer Unknown			Total Output	
Books	30,789	20.73	27.03	113,912	76.69	100.00
Broadsides	134	.09	66.34	202	.13	100.00
Pamphlets	4,691	3.16	13.63	34,421	23.18	100.00
Total	35,614	23.98		148,535	100.00	

Major Printers: Printed more than 25 titles between 1850 and 1870.

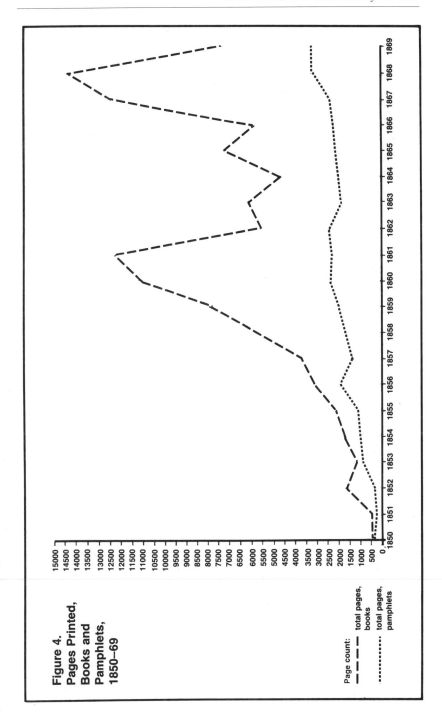

Figure 4.
Pages Printed,
Books and
Pamphlets,
1850–69

Page count:
– – – total pages, books
········· total pages, pamphlets

the other 195 known printers, and the unknown printers. The relatively high percentage of broadsides for which the printer is unknown is striking. Table 3 identifies the top fifteen printers by name and indicates their relative productivity in terms of total title production from 1850 to 1870 and in terms of average annual output during the time the publisher was in business.

The total number of books and pamphlets produced in San Francisco between 1850 and 1870 may not seem large for a city of its wealth and dynamic growth. That the highest average annual title count should be only 35.5 for any firm is significant. That one of the top fifteen firms should have produced an average of only 4.4 titles per year is equally so.

Table 3
Fifteen Major Printers by Title Production

Printer	Titles Printed	% of Total Titles	Years Active	Average Yearly Output	Rank by Yearly Average
Towne & Bacon	390	15.17	11	35.5	1
F. Eastman	138	5.37	20	6.9	8
Commercial Steam Book & Job	115	4.47	14	8.2	5
Whitton, Towne & Co.	110	4.28	7	15.7	3
Alta California	108	4.2	20	5.4	12
E. Bosqui	86	3.34	6	14.3	4
B. Sterett	79	3.07	15	5.3	13
O'Meara & Painter	53	2.06	7	7.6	7
Agnew & Deffebach	49	1.9	11	4.4	15
C. Robbins	46	1.79	10	4.6	14
J. Winterburn	39	1.52	5	7.8	6
Turnbull & Smith	38	1.48	6	6.3	11
Bacon & Co.	36	1.4	2	18.0	2
M. Carr	32	1.24	5	6.4	10
Francis & Valentine	27	1.05	4	6.7	9

Total titles: 2,571 titles printed between 1850 and 1870.

It would be very useful to be able to compare these figures with those of comparable American cities of the time, but there are no comparable figures, and there may be no comparable cities. What can be safely deduced, I think, is that no printing firm could have survived on the income from 35.5 titles per year, let alone 4.4, and that a proportion of job work to all work done at other firms would be as high as or higher than the proportion found for Towne & Bacon.

This information can indicate something of the scope of the city's book, pamphlet, and broadside production and of the dimensions and even the structure of its book trade, but it cannot reveal much about the subject matter of this material, and subject matter provides the best index of the role of the trade in the early history of San Francisco. The following comments on subject analysis pertain only to books, pamphlets, and broadsides; any attempt to describe in more than the broadest terms the subject content of the newspapers and periodicals would be pointless.

Table 4 lists the major subjects and shows their representation among the 2,571 books, pamphlets, and broadsides. The top-ranking subjects reveal the preoccupation of San Francisco and California's printing clients with the process of organizing themselves, whether for profit, civil order, personal security, or personal advancement. That one of the leading categories should be commerce is fully compatible with California's own priorities and with the sources of the state's and San Francisco's wealth.

Private organizations rank first, and chief among these are fraternal societies, primarily the Freemasons and the Odd Fellows. Familiar to many emigrants, both Americans and Europeans, these societies represented a welcome presence in traditionless San Francisco. They received generous support. By about 1860 there were within the city's boundaries twenty-two Masonic lodges and fifty I.O.O.F. districts. Second in rank among the private organizations are benevolent societies, many of which served and gave encouragement to ethnic and nationalistic groups. Others had more specialized functions, and among these should be numbered the Dashaway Society, an early version of Alcoholics Anonymous, whose initiates had to pledge to dash the bottle away for six months, and the Ladies' Seaman's Friend Society dedicated to protecting seamen from the corrupting influences of the city. Chief among the historical organizations was the Society of California Pioneers, established in 1850, which inaugurated in the instant city of San Francisco the tradition of instant history of the California experience.

The category of public organizations ranks as high as it does because of legislative action at city, county, and state levels. Surprising only to those uninformed on western American history are the relatively high rankings of land claims and actions-at-law, as legal actions are called in the Library of Congress subject headings. Land claims offer a good example

Table 4
Subject Analysis of
2,571 Books, Broadsides, and Pamphlets

Subjects	Number of Titles		% of Titles
1. Private organizations			
Societies			
Benevolent	115		
Fraternal (Freemasons, 74; Odd			
Fellows, 43; Others, 27)	144		
Political	21		
Historical	20		
Social	13		
Agricultural	11		
Miscellaneous	19		
Total, societies		343	
Religious Groups			
Churches	125		
Sunday schools	26		
Societies	5		
Total, religious groups		156	
Total, private organizations		499	19.4
2. Commercial organizations			
Mines and mining		188	
Real Estate			
Auctions	47		
Homesteads	35		
Total, real estate		82	
Banks and banking		48	
Railroads		45	
Bookselling and publishing		39	
Shipping		24	
Miscellaneous		56	
Total, commercial organizations		482	18.7

Subjects	Number of Titles		% of Titles
3. Public organizations			
Legislatures			
San Francisco (board of education, 25; fire department, 24; board of supervisors, 12; miscellaneous, 41)	102		
California (education, 12; miscellaneous, 20)	32		
United States	9		
Total, legislatures		143	
Laws			
San Francisco	35		
California	32		
United States	7		
Miscellaneous	5		
Total, laws		79	
Total, public organizations		222	8.6
4. Politics (current events)			
Elections, campaigns			
San Francisco	12		
California	33		
United States	8		
Total, elections, campaigns		53	
Civil War		43	
Vigilance committees		17	
Miscellaneous (taxation, harbor, foreign relations)		68	
Total, politics (current events)		181	7.0
5. Land claims		175	6.8
6. Actions-at-law		163	6.3

Table 4 (Continued)

Subjects	Number of Titles		% of Titles
7. Education			
San Francisco			
Public	19		
Private (college, university)	35		
Total, San Francisco		54	
California			
Public	7		
Private	95		
Total, California		102	
Total, education		156	6.1
8. Directories and almanacs			
San Francisco	51		
California	74		
Pacific States	16		
Total, directories and almanacs		141	5.5
9. Belles lettres			
Poetry	39		
Fiction	22		
Biography	11		
Ethics	11		
Drama	5		
Miscellaneous	26		
Total, belles lettres		114	4.5
10. Sermons and eulogies		67	2.6
11. Description and travel			
California	31		
Pacific states and the West	13		
Mexico	7		
Miscellaneous	12		
Total, description and travel		63	2.5

Subjects	Number of Titles		% of Titles
12. Music			
Songbooks	40		
Opera libretti	15		
Total, music		55	2.1
13. Science		38	1.5
14. Libraries			
Mercantile Library Association	29		
Others	6		
Total, libraries		35	1.4
15. Militaries		25	1.0
16. Miscellaneous		155	6.0
Total		2,571	100

of a regional activity providing a sizeable amount of work for the city's printers, and they warrant a few comments.

The unresolved condition of land titles was, perhaps, the most pervasive problem confronting California for nearly two decades. Many titles had been secured under the Mexican regime, before the American occupation of Alta California in 1847. The establishment of acceptable titles over the next several years involved a California Land Commission, the California district courts, the United States Supreme Court, and the United States attorney general. There were about eight hundred claims, which, one historian calculates, should have been settled within two or three years.[29] In reality, the average time for each claim was seventeen years. Speculators and corrupt officials have been blamed in large measure, but so have lawyers who, Hubert H. Bancroft said, "looked with much complacency on the general prospect."[30] Printers must have been equally pleased to grind out the transcripts, lawyers' briefs, summaries of court cases, and copies of wills and deeds, as well as some polemical literature on the subject. The press runs for most of these publications were short, probably averaging fifty copies, so that even the smaller printing shops could easily handle the commissions. But creative advertising could suggest the need for a fully equipped shop; witness, for example, an advertisement run by Whitton, Towne & Company stressing that only their extensive inventory of book type enabled them to print complete jobs with dispatch, the length of documents not hindering their speedy completion. The amount of printing generated by one case could be substantial. The dubious distinction of the claim requiring the most printing, some, 3,584 pages, belongs to the New Almaden Mine Claim of Andres Castillero.[31]

How was the printing of these subjects distributed among the printers? The distribution is general but still in line with the ranking of printing firms by size. In only one case is there an obvious aberration: the high percentage of printing for fraternal societies done by Frank Eastman. The explanation is close at hand: Eastman was a leading Mason in San Francisco.

If one were to attempt a profile of the San Francisco printing trade and of the product of its press from 1850 through 1869, it would include these features: Printers were generalists, seeking and perhaps finding security in diversification in format and subject matter. The printing trade was dominated by at most fifteen firms, of which Towne & Bacon, its predecessor, Whitton, Towne & Company, and its successor, Bacon & Company, were clearly in the lead. Few books, but a substantial number of pamphlets, were produced by the trade. The books complemented and did not compete with eastern importations, and a very high percentage of pamphlets treated local or regional topics and concerns. Job work, whose actual products have mostly vanished, accounted for a large proportion of work. Newspaper printing was a volatile line of business, but newspapers performed yeoman service in representing the city's large foreign population. However, few books, pamphlets, or broadsides provided this service, for in general printing for the most cosmopolitan of cities was distinctly American. The periodicals produced by the trade represent some of the best publishing and most attractive illustration and printing achieved in the city. The printing business was sensitive to fluctuations in the city's, the state's, and even the country's economy. I provisionally ascribe the sharp decline in book titles and book pages from 1861 to 1865 to the American Civil War, during which the supply of material from the East, including paper, may have been affected. Some event or trend in 1869 caused a precipitous decline in book pages and in book, periodical, and newspaper titles. Was it perhaps the completion of the transcontinental railroad which, contrary to general expectations, triggered a sharp depression in California? Certainly the statistical data invite further investigation. The dominant subject content of books, pamphlets, and broadsides reflects the preoccupations of a major but still adolescent city attempting to organize itself, and of its inhabitants trying to find for themselves a secure position.

Notes

1. Gertrude Stein, *Everybody's Biography* (New York: Random House, 1937), 289.

2. Peter K. Decker, *Fortunes and Failures: White Collar Mobility in Nineteenth Century San Francisco* (Cambridge, Mass.: Harvard University Press, 1978), 75.

3. I. N. Irwin, *Sacramento Directory and Gazeteer for the Years 1857 and 1858* (San Francisco: Valentine, 1857), [iii].

4. Hubert H. Bancroft, *History of California* (Santa Barbara: Wallace Hebberd, 1970 reprint), 6: 223.

5. Quoted by Charles Wollenberg, *Golden Gate Metropolis: Prospects on Bay Area History* (Berkeley: Institute of Governmental Studies, University of California, 1985), 105.

6. Editorial, "A Reading Public," *Puck,* 18 Nov. 1865.

7. Hugh S. C. Baker, "A History of the Book Trade in California, 1849–1859," *California Historical Society Quarterly,* 30 (1951): 367.

8. Ibid., 97–115, 249–67, 353–67.

9. It is doubtful that the "more" included or should include the two standard nineteenth-century American trade bibliographies covering the period, O. A. Roorbach's *Bibliotheca Americana* and James Kelly's *The American Catalogue of Books,* which together list American imprints from 1820 to 1871. Their generally poor "hit" rate of one in eight publications is even poorer for San Francisco imprints. Roorbach lists two. Kelly does better, especially for the works of San Francisco's two leading publishers of the 1860s, Anton Roman and Hubert H. Bancroft. The explanation for the particularly poor showing for the West lies in part in its publishers' own regional focus as much as in the eastern trade's parochialism, a predilection not discouraged by the regional structure of copyright registry until the late 1860s.

10. For an example of the value of printers' ledgers in bibliographical analysis, see Bruce L. Johnson's "James Weld Towne: Printer, Publisher, and Paper Merchant" (Ph.D. diss., University of California, Berkeley, 1984).

11. John W. Caughey, *Hubert Howe Bancroft: Historian of the West* (Berkeley: University of California Press, 1946), 83.

12. Quoted in the Bancroft Library's *Catalog of Printed Books* (Boston: G. K. Hall, 1964), 1: [4].

13. Several research assistants have contributed to this project. I would like particularly to acknowledge the major contributions of Marcella Genz, who supervised the compilation of the bibliographical files, and David A. McDaniel, who built the Focus system for this project and generated the tables and graphs.

14. Lawrence C. Wroth, *The Colonial Printer* (Charlottesville: Dominion Books reprint, 1964), 216.

15. Johnson, "James Weld Towne," 19–20.

16. See, for example, the following excerpt from John P. Bogardus, comp., *Illustrated California Almanac for 1855* (San Francisco: R. H. Vance, 1854), 33: "We have recently made large additions to our job printing office and take pleasure in informing our friends, customers, and the public in general, that we are now better than ever before, prepared to execute all kinds of Plain and Ornamental

Printing. . . . For printing Books, Pamphlets, Catalogues, blanks or small posters, we have now in operation a New Patent Adams Power Press, the only one of its kind now in California, and which for the execution of Fine Work is not surpassed by any press now manufactured. For Printing Bill heads, circulars, etc., we use one of the Ruggles' Patent Machine Presses, capable of throwing off 1,500 impressions per hour. . . . For Printing Marriage, Address, Ball tag or business cards, we have one of R. Hoe & Co's Patent Card Presses which will print, with ease, 1,200 cards per hour. . . . For printing large mammoth posters, either in black or colored Inks, we have a large sized Washington Hand press, just received from the manufacture of R. Hoe & Co., New York; also a large assortment of Cuts, suitable for Posters, such as Steamers, River Boats, Clipper Ships, Railroad, etc., etc."

17. Quoted by Wallace Kirsop, "Literary History and Book Trade History: The Lessons of *L'Apparition du livre*," *Australian Journal of French Studies* 16 (Nov.–Dec. 1979): 498.

18. Entry for 5 July 1850, *Alta California* ledgers, Kemble Collections, California Historical Society Library.

19. Editorial, *The Hesperian*, 1 May 1858.

20. *Mining and Scientific Press: A Journal of Useful Arts, Science, and Mining and Mechanical Progress*, 8 July 1865.

21. Doris Muscatine, *Old San Francisco: The Biography of a City* (New York: G. P. Putnam's Sons, 1975), 158.

22. Editorial, *The San Francisco Sunday Gossip*, 29 Nov. 1861.

23. "Salutatory," *Young America*, 12 Oct. 1856.

24. Thomas F. Cronise, *The Natural Wealth of California* (San Francisco: H. H. Bancroft, 1868), 683.

25. Clifford H. Bissell, "The French Language Press in California," *California Historical Society Quarterly* 39 (Mar. 1960): 7.

26. Bancroft, *History of California*, 6: 223.

27. Ibid.

28. Johnson, "James Weld Towne," 19–20.

29. John W. Caughey, *California* (New York: Prentice Hall, 1940), 364.

30. Bancroft, *History of California*, 6: 536.

31. Ibid., 557.

8. California on Stone, 1880–1906: A Proposed Sequel to Harry Peters's Pioneering Study

Bruce L. Johnson

Harry Peters's *California on Stone,* which was published in a limited edition of 501 copies in 1935, has been praised as "the bible of an army of collectors," but criticized for its lack of "a central thesis, serving in aggregate more as an index than as a history."[1] Peters himself realized that he was offering a suggestive rather than an exhaustive study, but he hoped the new book, which was published four years after his *America on Stone,* would "present enough material to satisfy collectors, and most others who may be interested in the subject, for a few years."[2]

It is now fifty years later, and, even with its deficiencies, Peters's *California on Stone* still holds up quite well, given its author's intention to write not a history (although there is much history in the book), but a reference guide for collectors. The bulk of *California on Stone* is an alphabetical list "of the artists, lithographers, publishers, and craftsmen who worked in California or on Californian subjects together with notes on their work."[3] The book covers the period between 1849 and 1880. Peters presents information about 248 people and firms that fall into one or more of these categories, but because several had printing offices in two or more cities, 264 cities are represented by these 248: 87 have San Francisco locations noted, 52 have "unknown" locations, and 30 other towns and cities appear, including New York with 44 offices, London with 18, Paris with 9, and Boston with 9. The geographical scope of the book, therefore, is worldwide: Berlin, Havana, Edinburgh, Budapest, Liverpool, and Amsterdam are also represented as cities in which California-related materials were produced "on stone."

Peters lists only those "artists, lithographers, publishers, and crafts-men" for which he found examples of work. The examples fall into fifty-eight subject categories that range from "Advertisements" to "Vigilance Committee" and include also "Book Illustrations," "Maps and Charts," "Music Sheets," "Certificates," "Letter Sheets," and "Views." Peters's subject index is somewhat confusing in that it mixes various uses of lithographic reproductions (such as book illustrations), with the subjects depicted in the lithographs. *A Ball in the Mines,* for example, which is one of eight lithographs produced in London by Hanhart to illustrate J. D. Borthwick's *Three Years in California,* is listed not only under the broad category of Book Illustration, but also under Dress, and Miners' Life. Another book illustration, *Bar of a Gambling Saloon,* used to illustrate the London edition of Marryat's *Mountains and Molehills,* is included under Amuse-ments—Gambling, Chinese, and Dress, as well as under Book Illustration.[4] This kind of mixed index has been useful, one might suppose, for quickly identifying those prints "suitable for framing" for, among other places, a saloon or other appropriate dive in need of visual enhancement.

Peters identifies about 750 "fairly important items," to use his phrase, in *California on Stone,* and notes that his "careful listing and study of all the more important accessible collections confirm this estimate of the volume of the surviving body of California lithographs."[5] Peters was mistaken. In beginning my survey of California lithographs from both before 1880 and after which are held by public institutions in the San Francisco Bay Area, I have succeeded in identifying more than one hundred fairly important lithographs that are "not in Peters," plus at least eight firms or individuals not represented in his alphabetical list.[6] Although my initial intent had been to begin research for a sequel to this pioneering study, it seems obvious that a checklist of additions to Peters itself would probably be in order as well.

Harry Peters spent a lifetime in studying, collecting, organizing, and publishing the results of his research. The observation, however, that one published result of this labor, *California on Stone,* is not a history is well taken. Peters's lists of people, companies, and examples does not really have a central theme or focus other than the obvious one of their California connection or context. When all is said and done, one is hard put to provide a satisfactory answer to the blunt question, "So what?"

In attempting to answer that rather obvious question one must fit nineteenth-century California lithography into its historical context, be-cause it was through this visual medium, above all others, that California was popularized and sentimentalized in the eyes of the country and the world. With only an occasional exception, pain and crime and tragedy, which were found in California as in other states of the nation, were forgotten in the sunshine. The enduring dilemmas of slavery, racial prejudice, and political corruption were, for the most part, ignored in favor of the "California dream"—an affirmative humor or optimism that took an ever-smiling nature as its too-easy correlative. It is my thesis that lithographic illustration played a central role in developing and nurturing that myth.

One almost hates to contemplate yet one more study of "myths and realities," but that does seem to be the direction my research is taking. A sequel to *California on Stone,* therefore, and indeed any reconsideration of Peters's book itself, will develop the theme of the lithographic illustration as a promotional medium for the Golden State. That promotion, much of it quite subtle, emphasizes, in the words of Walt Whitman,

> The flashing and golden pageant of California,
> The sudden and gorgeous drama, the sunny and ample lands,
> . . . .
> Populous cities, the latest inventions, the steamers on the rivers, the railroads,
>   with many a thrifty farm, with machinery,
> And wood and wheat and the grape, and diggings of yellow gold.[7]

Peters includes lithographic book illustrations, maps and charts, music sheets, certificates, letter sheets, and views in his compilation. All of them, with the exception of letter sheets, form part of the history of lithography in California after 1880. By that time, however, the letter sheet, a pictorial writing paper that declined in popularity in the late 1860s, was being replaced by the picture postcard, which was often lithographic itself. The one major category not covered by Peters, because its development and use took place after 1880, is actually of primary significance and is inextricably tied to the rise of agriculture in the state—the lithographic label. Although the other six broad categories of lithographic illustration all play a part in the history of California lithography after 1880 and will be surveyed and considered in a sequel to Peters, the evocative images preserved in an imaginative genre of commercial art, the lithographic label, reinforced in the national consciousness the images of California which have been so carefully cataloged by Harry Peters. They are memorable pictorial symbols in which gold grows on trees (citrus trees, that is), available for the planting and picking. Lithographic labels on agricultural products of all kinds encouraged the golden myth with fanciful, even audacious, symbols and brand names, epitomized perhaps in one orange-grower's claim: "Eat Me and Grow Young."[8] And even though it is upon this use of lithography that I have focused my initial efforts, the names of most of the artists, lithographers, publishers, and craftsmen in California who produced lithographic images of *all* kinds were the same.

Between 1880 and 1906, the latter year being the date when much of the state's (and practically all of San Francisco's) printing industry was laid low by the great earthquake and fire of April 18, there were at least fifty-nine lithographers working in San Francisco. The names of only fourteen appear also in Peters; the firms of A. L. Bancroft, Edward Bosqui, Britton & Rey, H. S. Crocker, Francis Korbel, Max Schmidt, and others had been joined by newcomers, most of which focused exclusively on lithography, which some of the earlier firms had not done. Dickman-Jones, Mysell-Rollins, Pacific Lithographing, Louis Roesch, Stecher Lithograph, and Union Lithograph were among the longest-lived of the post-1880 firms.

When compared with that of the rest of the country, lithographic printing in California had a raison d'être that was atypical. Historians, especially art historians (and I place Harry Peters in that class), have been concerned with lithography as art, even fine art. The reproduction of oil paintings, the rendering of city views and maps, and other similarly large pieces have always been the prime matters of interest and concern. And even though California lithographers did their share of this kind of work— *California on Stone* proves the point—lithography as advertising for commercial businesses seems always to have been of greater significance. Most fine-art reproductions sold in San Francisco were probably of eastern origin, not Californian, and the concern of lithographers in the state from the very beginning remained the support through lithographic reproduction of advertising and commercial business enterprises.[9]

A prime example is the young German immigrant, Max Schmidt, who actually cuts across both periods and clearly exemplifies the role of lithographer as promoter of California and its products. Schmidt had learned the art of "transferring" lithographic art work while employed by the San Francisco *Stock Report,* a publication specializing in mining and stock-market news. When the *Stock Report*'s lithograph department was closed, he secured a position for three months at the plant of G. T. Brown & Company. Later he worked for Francis Korbel and Brothers, a cigar box and label manufacturer, which eventually discontinued those businesses in favor of champagne bottling.

Schmidt's shop, offering design, lithography, and zincography was in 1873 a small room on Clay Street. Various partnerships and acquisitions changed the name from its original form, Schmidt & Buehler, to M. Schmidt & Company in 1875, Schmidt Label & Lithograph Company in 1883, Mutual Label & Lithograph Company in 1899, and Schmidt Lithograph Company after 1906.

The need for printed labels had been felt, of course, before Schmidt and Frederick Buehler formed their company in 1873. Francis Cutting is generally acknowledged as having been the pioneer packer of California. He arrived in San Francisco in 1858, and by the following year Cutting &

Company was not only canning pickles, but also growing the cucumbers from which the pickles were made and manufacturing the glass jars in which they were packed. For about twenty years the labels that were attached to the jars and cans were printed by companies that also produced books, newspapers, magazines, and other job work. Before 1868, for example, James Weld Towne, perhaps San Francisco's most prolific printer during the first twenty years after California became a state, regularly printed by letterpress the labels for the cigar manufacturer William Shanky, for Dr. Adams for his German Tonic Bitters, and for the oyster-canning firm of Gorman & Jackson.[10] Towne also printed by letterpress the labels or texts on lithographs printed by Kuchel & Dresel, Britton & Rey, Edward Bosqui, and other lithographic firms operating in San Francisco before 1868.[11]

Because the volume of food processing and marketing was still relatively small, to print labels in several colors, whether by letterpress or lithographically, was not practical economically. Beginning in the 1870s, as the canning industry continued to prosper and grow under the guidance of Cutting, Mark J. Fontana, E. W. Hume, and others, Max Schmidt took advantage of a ready opportunity when he began printing labels to be used on their canned goods. The label lithography and box-end imagery that was to sustain the romantic image of California throughout the nation began in earnest in 1877, when William Wolfskill shipped to St. Louis as an experiment a load of oranges in wooden crates, a month-long journey that had never before been attempted. The success of "Wolfskill's California Oranges" meant that by 1880 every new grower who packed shipments for the eastern market tried to identify his particular brand in the public eye; lithographic labels with distinctive designs had become a marketing necessity.[12]

When Schmidt began printing in San Francisco, the process of "zincography"—similar to lithography except that the illustration or design is engraved on a plate of zinc rather than a block of limestone—had only recently been developed. Schmidt's brother Richard, still in Germany, sent Max a pamphlet describing the process; Schmidt learned it and began to produce letterheads and plain labels as well as various cuts used by the San Francisco *Chronicle, Call, Bulletin,* and *Post.* Wine labels and mining company stock certificates comprised the greatest volume of his business in the early period, but the continuing growth of the fruit and fish industries on the Pacific Coast opened up several new possibilities for other kinds of clients.

As his business prospered, Schmidt added more lithographic and general printing equipment to his plant. Before he acquired his own presses, much of the actual printing had been done by Kane & Cook, printers at 422 Commercial Street. Besides purchasing equipment, Schmidt also began to acquire other firms that had as their specialty the printing of labels. A major boost to his business came in 1880 as a result of the failure of Pettit & Russ, label and theatrical show bill printer. Schmidt acquired its entire plant for $15,000. Five years later he acquired the label and job printing shop of Alfred Chaigneau & Company. The additional equipment thus acquired made it necessary to seek more space, and Schmidt moved to San Francisco's Main Street. By 1902 Schmidt's company, called Mutual Label and Lithographic Company, was at the corner of Second and Bryant streets and was advertised as the successor to Schmidt Label & Lithograph Company, and to Dickman-Jones Company, and also to the lithographic department of H. S. Crocker, the Western Lithograph Company, and the Los Angeles Lithograph Company.[13] In 1903, besides more than 300 million labels of various kinds, mainly for the burgeoning food and agriculture industry of California, Schmidt's output included 10 million commercial letterheads, 35 million cartons, and 100,000 poster sheets.[14]

The equipment Max Schmidt used during the first three decades of business changed continually in quantity and quality. His numerous acquisitions of other printing companies made it almost inevitable for him to possess more machinery than any other lithographic plant in the city, including many stop-cylinder presses, pony presses, and platen jobbers, as well as four-color lithographic presses. Box-making machinery was also part of the plant, and for many years Schmidt had the only paper-coating plant on the Pacific Coast.

In his first thirty years of business Schmidt's company was completely wiped out twice by fire. The 1906 earthquake and fire that laid the business and manufacturing district of the city in ruins destroyed for a third time everything in the possession of the Mutual Label and Lithograph Company. Like countless other businesses in the same predicament, Schmidt's was forced to relocate temporarily in the East Bay; he borrowed money to rent a box factory at Fifth and Adeline in Oakland in order to remain in business. Even before the end of the year Schmidt was planning the reconstruction of his San Francisco plant, and by 1908 he was again doing business at Second and Bryant. Schmidt's firm continued to produce labels, and today it forms part of the Stecher-Traung-Schmidt Corporation of Newark, California.

Although, naturally, much different in detail, the story of Max Schmidt and his lithographic companies is similar to that of other enterprising printers in California who "cashed in" on this important market. Examples include:

S. W. Backus, of Backus Printing Company, who, after Francis Korbel, was owner of *The Wasp,* a San Francisco journal of social commentary and vitriolic colored cartoons (printed lithographically), which in its greatest period was under the editorship of Ambrose Bierce.

George Baker, whose efforts at woodcut and lithographic illustration in Sacramento and, after 1862, in San Francisco, are documented by Peters. Baker remained a lithographer and artist in San Francisco until 1904.

Edward A. Dakin of the Dakin Publishing Company, who began his firm in 1889 on Sansome Street. Besides printing labels, Dakin became one of the foremost publishers of maritime and fire insurance maps (along with the Sanborn Map Company of New York). Almost all of these maps, like the labels, were produced lithographically in Dakin's financial district plant.

The firms, then, have been identified—at least sixty of any significance, and probably several smaller ones that have eluded my initial survey. Additions to the lithographic work done by the firms included in Peters's *California on Stone* have been made, and more examples will no doubt be discovered in the months and years ahead. And work has begun on the identification of lithographic reproductions, done on stone and by other means, for the period after 1880.

Panoramic maps and bird's-eye views of California cities form an important component of Peters's work. San Francisco publishers and lithographers offered stiff competition, at least as far as quality is concerned, to their eastern counterparts. Britton & Rey and A. L. Bancroft continued to be the most important firms producing panoramic maps and views after 1880. All the views printed by Bancroft were drawn by Eli S. Glover; most of them depicted California cities, but cities in Washington, Oregon, and Montana are represented as well.[15]

In southern California the accelerated development that came with the completion of the Santa Fe Railroad in 1885 prompted the Los Angeles Board of Trade to flood the country with all manner of promotional material, including maps and bird's-eye views lithographed not only by Bancroft, Bosqui, and Britton & Rey in San Francisco, but also by new firms in southern California, such as the Los Angeles Lithographic Company.

In the area of books, county history and atlas publishing flourished until the end of the century. Thomas H. Thompson, who came to California in the mid-1870s, published atlases of Sonoma County (1877), Fresno County (1891), and Tulare County (1892), just as he had, in partnership with Albert Augustus West in the 1870s, issued other atlases—of Santa Clara County (1876), Alameda County (1878), and Solano County (1878). All of these county histories and atlases are illustrated with lithographic views of cities and sketches of the homes of the "important" residents—those who paid to be included in the books.

In compiling *California on Stone*, Harry Peters relied heavily upon the work of Laura Retting White, a resident of California, who did most of the legwork in surveying the collections, both public and private, and in interviewing collectors, dealers, scholars, and the lithographers themselves to gather insights and examples. Besides me, several people, including Laurie Gordon, John Salkin, Gordon T. McClelland, Jay T. Last, and T. Patrick Jacobson, have been actively studying California commercial lithography and have begun the exhaustive compilation of materials and statistics that will be necessary to bring some order to a subject that is excruciatingly difficult to catalog in detail—particularly difficult because of the enormous output of California lithographers, especially label printers, after 1880.

Using lithographic product labels as the initial focus, here are several findings:

Of the four major problems faced by growers of perishable agricultural products in California—packing, shipping, identifying, and advertising—two were resolved by the paper label. The branded trademark and stenciled images found on early packing crates were gradually replaced with circular labels, averaging about six inches in diameter, which were quickly followed by large paper labels that varied little in the decades after about 1885.

The images found on the labels were designed to catch and hold the attention of a potential customer, much as advertising posters had been doing for decades, and, in a more subtle way, to promote the state of California. McClelland and Last have identified eleven themes predominantly found on labels printed after 1885 (much as Peters notes the scenes of gambling and racing, the cartoons, the mines and mining operations, and other categories important during the first thirty years of California's statehood). Besides stock labels and the obvious depiction of flowers, birds, and animals, scenes of early California that feature the state's Spanish and Mexican heritage, images of the Old West and Native Americans, and various patriotic themes, most with a California twist, were used as designs and promotional themes.[16]

Labels, like city views and book illustrations, were printed lithographically on stone, although photomechanical reproductive processes were gradually introduced in the late nineteenth century. Relying upon the technique of "keying" for the correct superimposition of the several stones, images in six and more colors were produced. By blending a few selected ink colors, sixty separate colors with "secret formulas" were created for use on painstakingly hand-stippled lithographic stones, and bronze metallic inks and varnishes added a golden glow to the labels. Most designs were ornate, delicate, and posterlike, and the images reinforced every romantic notion of California life.

A single design could be used to produce many transfer proofs, which were then assembled in position for transfer to a large press stone that was used for printing in multiple copies on large sheets to be cut later. An incredible amount of time was thus saved. Labels were produced not in the thousands or hundred thousands, but in the millions.

Other lithographic techniques were used as early as the 1870s. For example, Bosqui called the varnished and embossed chromolithographs in his *Grapes and Grape Vines* (1877) "oleographs." But it was not until the twentieth century that stone lithography was widely replaced by photocomposition and offset lithography. Even then stone lithography was used by major firms well into the century.

"California on Stone, 1880 to 1906: A Proposed Sequel to Harry Peters's Pioneering Study," is quite clearly only a work in progress, but the broad outlines are equally clear. Whether through stock certificates, bird's-eye views, illustrations for county atlases, topographic maps and charts, or the seemingly lowly lithographic label, the selling of California was the intent and the result of the work of lithographers and those engaged in ancillary trades, both before and after 1880. The lithographic labels are especially reflective of the state's social history, agriculture, and commercial enterprise; they are often more important for what they do not depict than for what they do.

Given sufficient time, energy, and cooperation, this project will continue and, like the plantings of California's Luther Burbank, bear fruit in the years ahead.

Notes

1. Harry T. Peters, *California on Stone* (Garden City, N.Y.: Doubleday, Doran & Company, 1935). The more appreciative comment is from an obituary for Peters, *Proceedings of the American Antiquarian Society*, Oct. 1948, 208. The comment about the lack of a central thesis is by Peter C. Marzio, *The Democratic Art, Chromolithography, 1840–1900: Pictures for a 19th-Century America* (Boston: David R. Godine, in association with the Amon Carter Museum of Western Art, Fort Worth, Tex., 1979), xiii.

2. Harry T. Peters, *America on Stone* (New York: Doubleday, Doran & Company, 1931). Peters's remark is from his *California on Stone, 3.*

3. Peters, *California on Stone,* [17].

4. J. D. Borthwick, *Three Years in California* (Edinburgh and London: William Blackwood and Sons, 1857); Frank Marryat, *Mountains and Molehills; or, Recollections of a Burnt Journal* (London: Longman, Brown, Green and Longmans, 1855).

5. Peters, *California on Stone,* 8.

6. The Library of the California Historical Society, San Francisco; the Oakland Museum, Oakland; and the Bancroft Library, University of California, Berkeley.

7. Walt Whitman, *Song of the Redwood Tree* (Oakland: Eucalyptus Press, 1934), [21, 23].

8. Laurie Gordon and John Salkin, " 'Eat Me and Grow Young': Orange Crate Art in the Golden State" *California Historical Quarterly* 56 (Spring 1977): 52–70.

9. Marzio, *The Democratic Art,* 189–90.

10. Towne & Bacon Journals, vol. 1, pp. 12, 19, and 144, Towne & Bacon Archives, Jackson Business Library, Stanford University.

11. See, for example, Towne & Bacon Journal entries for 1856, passim.

12. Gordon and Salkin, " 'Eat Me,' " 54.

13. *Crocker-Langley San Francisco Directory for . . . 1902* (San Francisco: H. S. Crocker Company, 1902), facing 1324.

14. *Crocker-Langley San Francisco Directory for . . . 1905* (San Francisco: H. S. Crocker Company, 1905), facing 1366.

15. Walter W. Ristow, *American Maps and Mapmakers: Commercial Cartography in the Nineteenth Century* (Detroit: Wayne State University Press, 1985), 463.

16. Gordon T. McClelland and Jay T. Last, *California Orange Box Labels: An Illustrated History* (Beverly Hills: Hillcrest Press, 1985), 8–35.

9. Institutional Book Collecting in the Old Northwest, 1876–1900

Terry Belanger

Thanks to the remarkable report published by the U.S. Bureau of Education in 1876, we have an excellent idea of the number and size of all manner of libraries in the United States at the time of our national centennial. The report, entitled *Public Libraries in the United States of America: Their History, Condition, and Management*, provides detailed library statistics on a state-by-state and town-by-town basis. By combining information from the 1876 report with statistics taken from the United States Census of 1870, we can easily derive an overview of the Old Northwest and its libraries in the 1870s.[1]

In 1870, the Old Northwest—that part of the present United States occupied by Ohio, Indiana, Illinois, Michigan, Wisconsin, and Minnesota— had a combined population of about ten million people, one-fourth the population of the country as a whole; it occupied approximately 11 percent of the land-mass of what is now the continental United States. Between 1870 and the end of the century, the population of the region increased from ten to nearly eighteen million, but it retained quite closely its percentage of the country's entire population: about a quarter of the whole. In 1870 as in 1900, Ohio and Illinois had the largest part of the Old Northwest's population, with about a quarter each, and Indiana, Michigan, Wisconsin, and Minnesota followed—pretty much in that order— both in 1870 and 1900 (though by 1900 Indiana was losing ground slightly, and Minnesota was gaining). By 1876, Chicago was already the largest city in the region, with about 300,000 inhabitants. Cincinnati was second, with slightly more than 200,000. Behind Chicago and Cincinnati in 1876 were

Cleveland, with slightly fewer than 100,000, and Detroit, with about 80,000. Milwaukee folowed with about 70,000; Indianapolis and Minneapolis both had fewer than 50,000.[2]

The 1876 report counted a total of 11.5 million books in the libraries of the United States to which the public had access. The Old Northwest, with 1.8 million books in its libraries in 1876, possessed less than 16 percent of the national total, though its population was about a quarter that of the entire United States: the biggest slice of the 1876 library pie was, as one would expect, not the Old Northwest but the northeastern part of the United States. By 1900, the number of books in American libraries had quadrupled to more than 44 million; about 19 percent of them were in Old Northwest libraries, or about 3 percent more than the 1876 total.[3]

Thus a picture of considerable stability emerges in the Old Northwest in the last quarter of the nineteenth century as regards library holdings: substantial growth, quite closely paralleling that of the nation as a whole. This stability may at first seem somewhat surprising. Minnesota, for example, achieved statehood only in 1858, less than twenty years before the start of the period; even Michigan and Wisconsin became states only in 1837 and 1848 respectively. But we must be careful not to attribute too much unreconstructed Daniel Boone-ism to the settlers of the Old Northwest. Michigan, for instance, was largely settled by persons coming from New England, New York, and Ohio.[4] The early arrivals might have lived at first in dirt-floored log cabins, but they had come to the Northwest Territory from places where a considerable standard of living prevailed; they knew what libraries were for and what they could do, and they were quick to establish them. The rate of literacy in Chicago was probably higher in 1840 than it was in 1940.[5] The Territorial Legislature of Minnesota made provision for a historical society in 1849, less than eight months after the Territory itself was established, nearly a decade before statehood was achieved. The Minnesota Historical Society was established "before there was any considerable body of history to record," as that Bostonian, Walter Muir Whitehill, once quite properly noted, for at the time there were fewer than five thousand white persons in the entire Minnesota Territory—it was as if the Massachusetts Historical Society had been established in 1620, or the Virginia Historical Society in 1607.[6]

In contemplating library statistics for the Midwest during the last quarter of the nineteenth century, we must also remember that, though the American public library movement had been born (or at least baptized) with the opening of the Boston Public Library in 1852, the growth in the number and size of municipally supported public libraries in the United States was fairly slow until the 1880s, by when the region was well-settled and eager to participate in the public library movement. As the Chicago *Tribune* stated in 1871, the principle of the free library was a discovery "more recent than that of the electric telegraph."[7] Boston Public was the largest public library in the country in 1876, but it was Cincinnati that was second, and Chicago, third.[8]

There is a considerable correlation between the number of books present in the libraries of the six states making up the Old Northwest and their populations. Ohio, the oldest state concerned, had 28 percent of the region's population and 34 percent of the books; Indiana had 18 percent of the population but only 14 percent of the books (a difference in part attributable to the absence of any large metropolitan center); Illinois had 27 percent of the population and 26 percent of the books; Michigan had 12 percent both of population and books; Wisconsin had 11 percent of the population and 10 percent of the books; and Minnesota had 5 percent of the population and 4 percent of the books. The figures show a quite even distribution of books in relation to the population of the Old Northwest.

The ratios between population and number of books in libraries were to remain fairly constant in the region throughout the entire 1876–1900 period. By 1900, Minnesota, Michigan, and Wisconsin had increased in population by comparison with the region as a whole, and the percentages of the region's books they held increased correspondingly; Indiana and Ohio dropped both in their percentage of the region's total population and in the percentage of books owned. And Illinois retained its 27 percent of the region's population and increased its percentage of the books from 26 percent to 29 percent—unsurprisingly, as we shall see, in light of late nineteenth-century library developments in Chicago.[9]

In 1900, Chicago retained its lead in population over the other cities of the Old Northwest, having nearly 1.7 million inhabitants. Cincinnati, with a population of 326,000, had been overtaken for second place by Cleveland, which now had about 380,000 inhabitants. Detroit remained in fourth place, with 286,000, now just ahead of Milwaukee, which had 285,000. Minneapolis and Indianapolis were still behind the other four principal cities of the region, with about 200,000 and 170,000 respectively—though if one adds the population of St. Paul to that of Minneapolis, the combined total of 365,000 makes the Twin Cities nearly as large as Cleveland. The Boston Public Library was still the largest public library in the country in 1900, and Chicago was now second (if one omits the newly formed New York Public Library, with its Astor and Lenox Library reference collections); then followed in order Philadelphia, Cincinnati, Cleveland, and Detroit—a respectable showing for the Old Northwest.

With this cursory overview of the books and people of the Old

Northwest in the last quarter of the nineteenth century in mind, we may now turn to an examination of the development of some of the region's library institutions during that period.

The earliest libraries in the Old Northwest were subscription libraries and other social libraries supported by membership contributions; in this, the area was similar to the East, where subscription libraries like the Library Company of Philadelphia, the New York Society Library, the Boston Athenaeum, and others had long since provided themselves with substantial collections. Municipally supported public libraries began to emerge in the Old Northwest in the 1860s, frequently established and run by local school boards, which had the power to secure tax revenues.

The Cincinnati Public Library was founded in the mid-1860s through this means, its board of managers being elected by the Cincinnati School Board. Almost immediately, the public library absorbed or received on deposit the collections of various already-existing local subscription libraries, for instance those of the Ohio Mechanics' Institute, the Historical and Philosophical Library of Ohio, the Theological and Religious Library, and the Cincinnati Hospital Library.[10] Growth was quick: in 1869, Cincinnati's was second only to the Boston Public Library among public libraries in the country.[11]

The early annual reports of the Cincinnati Public Library make clear the purpose of the institution's acquisitions policy: "The purchase of books thus far," stated the board of managers in its *1871* [Fourth] *Annual Report,* "has been guided with a view chiefly to its character as a circulating library for popular use."[12] But in that year the Library had higher ambitions, as well, the *Report* tells us: its purchases were made "not without due regard for the special wants of scholars, as well as the manufacturing and industrial interests of our people."[13] And indeed, the librarian reported a year later (*1872* [Fifth] *Annual Report*) that among the books recently purchased

> is a collection of 214 tracts in the original editions, covering the period of English history from the meeting of the Long Parliament in 1640, to the death of Cromwell in 1658.[14]

Admittedly, the bulk of the circulation of the Cincinnati Public Library in 1872 consisted of fiction and juvenile books; but there was a clear determination to have a non-circulating scholarly collection as well as circulating best-sellers.

Frequently such reference collections were justified in practical terms. In 1872, the Cincinnati Public Library opened a special room for illustrated books, a collection (the librarian's report tells us) which "can not fail to be appreciated by the architects, designers, pattern-makers, engineers, and art students of our city." The room was open fourteen hours per day

Monday through Saturday and seven hours on Sunday, and it proved very popular, "visited by a large number of citizens, and of visitors from abroad, who have uniformly expressed their surprise, as well as satisfaction, in finding in our city so fine and valuable a collection of illustrated books, and which are so freely accessible to the public."[15]

Indeed, Cincinnati Public's redoubtable librarian, William Frederick Poole, found the room *too* popular. It is not the intention of the collection to be used for idle viewing, he said in the *1873* [Sixth] *Annual Report;* but a misapprehension

> has occasionally occurred when a resident, taking a visitor from a distant city through the library, and wishing to impress on him the importance of the institutions of Cincinnati, has asked to have the most expensive books put on exhibition; it may be Piranesi, or the folio edition of Audubon's Birds. The parties profess to have no artistic habits, and no special interest in Roman antiquities or natural history; the motive is simply to see expensive picture-books. Such a use of these works would soon ruin them.[16]

Librarian Poole publicly stated his hope that private donations of money would shortly be forthcoming to augment tax revenues in buying books for the library, following the pattern established by the philanthropic citizens of Boston. "It is difficult," he wrote,

> to conceive how a resident of Cincinnati could do an act which would redound more to the credit of Cincinnati—to its literary, scientific, and social status—than by furnishing the means of filling this splendid library building with useful and standard books.[17]

(Note his use of the word *standard,* one that we shall encounter again in this connection.)

The Cincinnati Public Library's books were then housed in a brand-new building, which was, again in the words of Poole, "the largest, the best arranged, the most elegant, and the only fire-proof public library building in the country."[18]

The fear of fire was justifiably great in the 1870s, and the fireproof construction of Cincinnati's new library immediately attracted a pilgrimage from Detroit. The early history of the Detroit Public Library is remarkably similar to that of Cincinnati: founded in the mid-1860s with strong school board support, Detroit could by 1870 claim to be the fourth largest public library in the country and by far the largest in size and circulation in Michigan.[19] The cornerstone of a new library building was laid in 1875, and the completed structure was opened to the public two years later. Fostered by competent directors and by a nearly threefold increase in the population of the city between 1880 and the end of the century, the

Detroit Public Library contained more than 150,000 volumes in 1900 and remained the largest library in Michigan, though by now the university library in Ann Arbor was rapidly closing the gap.[20]

At the turn of the century, we find a tension developing in Detroit between the popular and research missions of the public library. The president of the library's board of commissioners, James E. Scripps, publicly criticized the library's failure to develop research collections, stating that the library catered too much to popular tastes and had too much insipid fiction on its shelves. The library was founded as part of the educational system of the state, Scripps pointed out, and the board of commissioners of the library were still appointed by the Detroit Board of Education. Commissioner Scripps proposed making a strong division between the Detroit Public Library's circulation and its reference functions, possibly to the point where the two would be housed in separate buildings. He suggested that genealogy, western history, and "antiquities" were among the attractive areas in which the library might develop research collections.[21]

Detroit Public's librarian, Henry M. Utley, replied that genealogy was well-covered at the Newberry Library, and western history at the Wisconsin Historical Society, and that the purpose of the Detroit Public Library was to maintain good all-around working collections of useful books; antiquarian research could best be pursued at the Astor and Lenox Libraries in New York.[22] Librarian Utley's view prevailed over that of Commissioner Scripps: no immediate attempt was made to develop research collections at the Detroit Public Library.

Indeed, by the end of the nineteenth century, we hear relatively little about the need for, or even the advisability of, scholarly collections in midwestern public libraries. Where they do occur, the cause is almost always private benevolence rather than municipal outlay. In Cleveland, for example, the lawyer and book collector John Griswold White began giving the Cleveland Public Library books in his areas of interest, especially folklore and Orientalia, when in 1899 the library's general book acquisitions funds were cut by the city. His generosity never flagged thereafter. In 1910, White became the president of the library's board of trustees, and he served in that capacity for more than fifteen years; he also bequeathed to the Cleveland Public Library his twelve-thousand-volume collection of books on chess and checkers.[23]

Other midwestern public libraries were given (or otherwise ended up with) rare book collections earlier, before the close of the nineteenth century, either through the acquisition of books owned by subscription and other social libraries or through private donation. One of the most interesting cases is that of the Minneapolis Public Library, founded in 1885 as the result of enabling state legislation and a ninety-nine-year agreement between a local library association and the Minneapolis Athenaeum. The Athenaeum, a subscription library, was rich, the beneficiary of an 1870 gift of land then worth twenty thousand dollars and soon to be worth much more. The income from the property was to be used solely for the purchase of books for the Athenaeum's library, nonfiction books of a serious but nontheological character.[24]

The combined Minneapolis library boards agreed that the Athenaeum's library would become the core collection for the new public library. Income from the Athenaeum endowment would be used to buy "rare and costly books of an enduring and scholarly nature" for the public library, while city funds would be used to buy books for circulation.[25]

Under the administration of Herbert Putnam (later to achieve national fame as Librarian of Congress), this acquisitions agreement was at first followed, and Minneapolis Athenaeum money bought art books and other scholarly materials for the Minneapolis Public Library, which with its thirty thousand books was (said Putnam in 1890) already the largest library in Minnesota and shortly to be the largest library northwest of Chicago, with the exception of the Wisconsin Historical Society in Madison. But this acquisitions policy came under almost immediate attack by T. B. Walker, the strong-minded president of the Minneapolis Public Library's board. This is what he said in the public library's first annual report, in 1890: The transferred Athenaeum books would

> form a reference and standard collection of great value, as the funds from that source have been devoted to purchasing books of this description, and it is to be hoped that it will continue,—perhaps not to purchase so many rare and costly books, but works of a standard character.[26]

Four years later, Walker's position had hardened. In his presidential report for 1894, he noted that in recent years income from the Athenaeum money had been used to buy foreign-language books, "while many books of greater use should have been obtained that would have fulfilled the requirements of probably fifty or a hundred times as many readers." It seemed plain to Walker

> that a public library should be run on the one principle of furnishing the greatest number of people with the best class of books that we can induce them to read or study, and in place of purchasing rare, scarce or expensive books of any kind, that will be used only upon rare occasions and then only to have the pages turned in an indefinite way, it is better to invest in more standard or more generally used books.[27]

By this point, Herbert Putnam had resigned his position as librarian at

Minneapolis and gone on to greener pastures in the East. His replacement, James K. Hosmer, was more complaisant; by 1897, President Walker was pleased to report that

> during the past year the book purchase lists have been more exclusively in the line of popular and standard works, than have prevailed in former years. Expensive, rare illustrated books have been purchased to a much less extent during the past year. The book committees of this library and of the Athenaeum, have each made larger book purchases to meet the demands of the public general use, rather than to continue the purchase of books that are rare and of little use to the public. And it is to be hoped that this general policy will be continued without material exceptions in the future.[28]

The conspicuous use of a public library's endowment to buy popular books represented a shift in a well-established principle of mid-nineteenth-century American public library economy that private donations of money are more appropriately used for the acquisition of scholarly books. Almost every one of the widely read and influential *Annual Reports* of the Boston Public Library throughout this period, for example, emphasized the importance of private benevolence in the growth of the library's research holdings—and with good reason: the library had benefited early and frequently from major donations of money and books, beginning even before it opened its doors in 1852 with a pledge of fifty thousand dollars from Joshua Bates.[29]

The principle may be seen very clearly in the report of the 1867 examining committee of the Boston Public Library, which was under the chairmanship of Justin Winsor:

> The donations to the Trust Funds, now accruing, in being expended for books of solid and permanent value, served to strengthen very materially the [higher departments of literature]; while Mr. Bates's last munificent gift of books developed our weight in the same direction. The time was now come when it was very properly agreed that there was no department of learning, which some portion of the community was not interested in; and that every department should be cared for to meet such requirements.[30]

In fairness to the president of the board of the Minneapolis Public Library, it must be remembered that the mid-1890s were a period of considerable economic hardship nationally, and especially so for the city of Minneapolis. For six months during this period, for example, city funds for book purchases ceased altogether.[31] The restricted Athenaeum endowment provided the bulk of the money available for all book purchases for several years, and Walker was determined that it be spent for books of a popular character.

This is not to say that the Minneapolis Athenaeum money went only to buy fiction. As the 1899 *Annual Report* of the library is at pains to point out, "our library is only in its cheaper part a circulating library"; there were substantial reference collections, including a good art library and a collection of books illustrative of the natural sciences. Nevertheless, as Jessie McMillan, the Minneapolis Public Library staff member designated Athenaeum Librarian, was forced to admit a few years later, after 1894 about two-thirds of the books bought with Athenaeum money went into the circulation, not the reference, division of the Library.[32]

The Minneapolis Public Library board's President Walker must surely have realized that the situation at Minneapolis was a highly unusual one: most nineteenth-century American public libraries had to protect funds to buy works of a standard character not from rare book purchases, but from the inroads made by demands for popular novels and children's books. In his 1873 Cincinnati Public Library *Annual Report,* William Frederick Poole noted that nearly three-quarters of the circulation of his library was owing to fiction and juvenile books. "I am not disposed to mourn over or to apologize for these facts," said Poole,

> In the personal experience of all who attain to literary culture there is a time when they read novels, and perhaps too many novels. In passing through this stage of their mental development, which usually lasts but for a short period, they acquire a habit of reading, and a facility of thought and expression which is of great benefit to them in their later studies. With many persons the alternative is not whether they will read fiction or something better, but whether they will read fiction or nothing.[33]

Other librarians did indeed mourn over the high circulation rates of their fiction collections and the relatively low use of their reference collections—and by *reference collections* of course they meant a broader class of books than those which typically decorate a late twentieth-century public library's reference room. To the nineteenth-century American librarian, *reference* seems simply to have meant *non-circulating.* Reference books routinely included nonfiction monographs and all kinds of more expensive books which—especially before the 1890s—most public libraries in the United States kept in closed stacks from which books were paged on demand; as Cleveland's librarian put it in 1880, "So far as I am informed none of the more important libraries of the country permit indiscriminate access to books and for reasons that are forcible: ... the safety of property is only assured by denying general access to the shelves."[34]

Despite reader indifference to serious nonfiction collections, public librarians throughout our period and long beyond it persisted in buying what the Minneapolis board's President Walker called "books of a standard character." Over and over in public library annual reports of the 1876–1900 period, the message is the same: fiction is to be tolerated; the use of the reference collections is to be encouraged. William Frederick Poole, when Librarian of the Chicago Public Library, stated the librarian's point of view quite bluntly: "If public libraries shall, in my day, cease to be educational institutions, and serve only to amuse the people and help them to while away an idle hour, I shall favor their abolition."[35]

Be that as it may, the tax-paying public wanted light reading, and they who pay the piper call the tune. Despite the good example of Boston, private donations of money to municipally supported public libraries for acquisitions purposes did not significantly materialize in the Old Northwest in the late nineteenth century. In the 1903 *Annual Report* of the Detroit Public Library, Librarian Utley stated rather grimly that in that year the library "enjoyed the novel sensation of a money bequest—the first in its history." The bequest was for $150—and from a resident of New York City.[36] Northeastern public libraries tended to have better luck in acquiring endowed acquisitions and other funds than did libraries in the Old Northwest. There were of course the stunning exceptions of the Newberry and Crerar Libraries in Chicago, both created with magnificent private collections—not of books, but of money. But they *were* exceptional, as was the Minneapolis Public Library with its Athenaeum endowment. Most public libraries in the late nineteenth century relied almost entirely on public funding for their operations, and they seem to have been quick in adopting the principles of library economy set forth in the 1890s by Charles Francis Adams. Adams was a trustee of the Thomas Crane Library, the public library of Quincy, Massachusetts. He emphasized the educational mission of the public library, the need to be "what might perhaps best be described as a University Annex to the Common School System" and to have "a good collection of standard English works of every description."[37] But the library, he maintained, was to be regarded as a collection of books for popular use, not one designed for the use of scholars and students—especially a public library so near Boston and its large research collections.

> Even should any books of special rarity or value find their way into a library situated as the Quincy Public Library is, it would be far better that the trustees should get such books by exchange or otherwise into the libraries of Boston or some special library, than they should retain them upon their own shelves. . . . A rare, costly or purely professional book, not of an elementary character, is merely hid away upon the shelves of a local library like that of Quincy.[38]

Adams recommended a continuous policy of weeding the collection, with rare books being removed and either discarded, sold, or sent elsewhere. A small public library was most useful with perhaps ten thousand to fifteen thousand books—with a greater number its cataloging became unnecessarily complicated and expensive.

The *Library Journal* gave Adams's arguments prominent coverage, suggesting that this—the year 1893—was the first time that the Quincy Public Library's course of action had been urged with such force and directness and predicting that the policy suggested would find many supporters. It would, *Library Journal* thought,

> encourage a more systematic establishment of centres to which scholars shall resort for the special books they need. . . . If the central libraries throw themselves into this system heartily and facilitate the researches of students by liberal lending, it will lead to their more hearty support by the public by enlisting in their favor the sympathy of a wider constituency, and, as always, to him who hath shall be given. The great libraries will grow greater, not at the expense of the others, but for the good of all others.[39]

By about a decade later, in 1902, *Library Journal* could announce that Adams's 1893 advice had since been very largely acted on, especially regarding antiquated works in the sciences.[40]

There was, to be sure, a considerable difference in the late nineteenth century between the collection development policies of libraries in small towns situated close to large cities rich in library resources and the policies of the large urban public libraries themselves. But the big-city libraries were beginning to be subject to similar pressures. Their central buildings tended to be overcrowded with books, and they needed either to weed or to find more stack space. They appealed to Andrew Carnegie for building funds with increasing enthusiasm in the last decade of the nineteenth century and first decade of the twentieth only to discover that Carnegie was unwilling to provide for a central building at the expense of its branches. Detroit, for example, was told that no more than half of the $750,000 Carnegie proposed to give that city—and preferably less than half—could be spent on a badly needed central building. The bulk of the money was to go toward putting up branch libraries. Public libraries almost everywhere tried to create space by throwing off special collections, especially in such expensive and rapidly expanding fields as medicine; by 1927, for example, the Detroit Public Library was the last major public library system in the country to be maintaining a medical library.[41] Libraries saved space by buying fewer scholarly books, especially in foreign languages. Still the collections grew. Finally, even the large public libraries began to weed their collections, taking use as the criterion for retention.

If a book was not called for over a certain period of time, it was said to have ceased being a "living" book; it had become a "dead" book. As such, it became a candidate for weeding.

The large metropolitan library systems continued to grow, but they began growing in a different way: there were continued concentration on popular fiction and children's books (though with fewer apologies for trafficking in mass-market materials); an ever-increasing number of books out in the branches; increasing duplication of titles; an increasing proportion of books in English; and fewer books of specialist interest—all this, balanced by increasingly enthusiastic weeding of slow-moving materials.

As quick-or-dead deaccession policies began to be established in public libraries, their broad research mission was diminished. The contraction is more widely a twentieth-century than a nineteenth-century one; but as one can see in the cases of Minneapolis and Detroit, twentieth-century deaccessioning policies were the culmination of pressures which began to be felt in the last quarter of the nineteenth century.

Talk of deaccessioning was not confined to public libraries at the turn of the century. Harvard outgrew its library building three times in the nineteenth century, President Eliot told the 1902 (Magnolia) conference of the American Library Association, and lack of space was usually a desperate problem in Cambridge.[42] Eliot had much to say about "living" and "dead" books. For Harvard, Eliot favored remote storage of its "dead" books in some area where land was cheaper than the million-dollar-an-acre Harvard Yard. He must certainly have been disappointed when he read the report of the faculty committee he had recently appointed to study the future needs of the Harvard College Library. The faculty report rejected in principle the development of separate, large departmental libraries at the expense of the central collections. As regards separating "living" books from the "dead" it announced "a remarkable unanimity of opinion that to attempt such a discrimination is inconsistent with the interest of learning, if it implies the destruction or removal of the so-called dead books, or even the storage of them in such a way that they are not both well classified and directly accessible to scholars." The Harvard faculty report contained an eloquent plea for the importance of these books: they

> constitute in one way or another the record of human thought, expression, action, condition, or discovery; that is to say, they are the original sources to which students of philosophy, literature, history, economics, and science turn for the material on which they work. ... All have their use and value, and often prove it in unexpected ways.[43]

The committee's strong recommendation was that Harvard must keep on with its research collections undiminished.

Academic libraries in the Old Northwest of a quarter of a century before, in contrast to the flourishing public libraries, were very weak, even by the admittedly not particularly high national standards of the period. One contemporary description of the typical academic library described it as consisting of

> from six to twenty thousand volumes. It is composed in part of the libraries of deceased clergymen which have been contributed to the institution in bulk. To these are added the encyclopaedias and books of reference of the edition before the last and a miscellaneous assortment of all the most obvious books in the ordinary branches of science, literature, and art.[44]

Occasionally, money had been available for the purchase of books for college libraries. The gift in 1854 of ten thousand dollars to Ohio Wesleyan enabled its president, Edward Thomson, to go to Europe and buy three thousand books for the college library. His acquisitions policy was to avoid the purchase of current works in favor of the rare and valuable: "if one goes to the library for Gibbon," he wrote, "he is disappointed if he do not find it; but the disappointment is not a serious one; for he may find the book, perhaps, in the first respectable house he enters."[45] Those professors who did research routinely formed their own working libraries, as did independent scholars like Bancroft and Prescott.

By the 1870s a few eastern universities were beginning to realize that German models of graduate education could be successfully imitated in this country only through the creation of substantial research library collections. By 1876, Harvard already had nearly a quarter of a million books and was growing rapidly. But after Harvard there was an enormous falloff; Yale's library, second in size to Harvard's, had only about half as many books. Dartmouth, third in size, had about 50,000 books, fewer than a fourth the number at Harvard; and Brown, Princeton, Virginia, Cornell, Amherst, Bowdoin, and Columbia, next in order, had an average of fewer than 40,000 books each. Northwestern University, with its 33,000 volumes, was the largest academic library in the Old Northwest in 1876; it ranked eleventh in the nation. Then followed Georgetown, the University of South Carolina, the University of Georgia, Dickinson, and Williams: Eighteenth in size was Marietta College, in Ohio; the University of Michigan was nineteenth, with about 28,000 volumes.

These were not, for the most part, research collections. Indeed, productive scholarship in the United States in 1876 was not particularly associated with academe.[46] Harvard's President Eliot might refer to his institution's library as "the heart of the university" in 1873, and he might be listened to by Barnard at Columbia, White at Cornell, Gilman at Hopkins, or Angell at Michigan.[47] But overwhelmingly, American college and university collections were little-used accumulations with sharply restricted rights of access, staffed by faculty, intended for faculty use rather than student use, and formed as the result of voluntary donation rather than any sort of educational plan.

But change was in the wind. During the several decades following 1876, the emphasis in academic libraries would shift from preservation to use; hours of service would lengthen enormously; and the college library would increasingly be recognized as an educational force, apart from as well as in addition to the curriculum.[48] The books would be better cataloged, and subject classification would replace fixed-location schemes. Instructors began to refer to books, rather than simply quote from them. The widespread adoption of elective courses put increased demands on library collections. The system of reserve books came into existence. There was a growing acceptance of the need for departmental libraries, as well as for new central buildings specifically designed for library purposes.[49] The library began to be commonly referred to as a laboratory for the professors and the students under their direction; stack access for students became increasingly routine.

Ambitious institutions began scrambling to get books. They continued and intensified a tradition which can be traced back to the acquisition of the Ebeling collection by Harvard in 1818 and the Van Ess collection by Union Theological Seminary in 1838: the purchase not of single books but of whole libraries, especially the working collections of European scholars. As early as 1869, Northwestern University acquired more than 11,000 volumes from the library of Johann Schultze, rich in the classics. In 1870, Michigan was given by Philo Parsons the 6,000-volume library, strong in political economy, of Professor Karl H. Rau of Heidelberg.[50] Western Reserve University acquired the 12,000-volume Germanic phil-ology collection of Wilhelm Scherer in 1887. There are many other examples.[51] These were scholarly books. University library collections grew in direct proportion to the increase of faculty research interests; there was little perceived need for particularly large undergraduate collections, even as the one-textbook-per-course approach to college teaching declined.[52]

Progress began in the eastern universities and moved west. Johns Hopkins publicized its doctoral program widely, and its graduates spread out over the country, eager to continue their researches and eager, too, to have library resources to work with. The example of Cornell University is a particularly vivid one, because it had been founded as a land-grant institution but still was able to move strongly in developing programs of graduate study. Progress was rather deliberate; librarian Lodilla Ambrose of Northwestern University reported in *Library Journal* in 1893 that only 8 percent of American college students had access to college libraries of more than fifty thousand volumes; more than 40 percent had to deal with college libraries containing fewer than five thousand books. Fewer than one-third of the educational institutions in the country in 1893 had full-time librarians at their head.[53]

In the Old Northwest, the library ambitions of university administrators were for the most part very modest. Ohio was blessed with an unusual number of small private colleges, as well as three competing state universities and a state legislature indifferent to them all; the growth of Ohio State University's libraries would be a twentieth-century rather than a nineteenth-century development.[54] The situation throughout Ohio was primitive: in 1876, Denison, Kenyon, Oberlin, and Ohio Wesleyan all had slightly fewer than 15,000 volumes in their libraries; Antioch, Heidelberg, Ohio University, and Wittenberg had fewer than 8,000. Marietta, with its 27,000 volumes, had the best academic collection in the state.

In Indiana, the situation was even worse: fewer than 15,000 books at Indiana Ashbury, Notre Dame, and Wabash; fewer than 6,000 at Indiana University. Illinois could muster substantial collections among Chicago academic institutions, especially at Northwestern; but the university at Urbana, which had no other local resources to draw on, had fewer than 11,000 books in 1876. An indication of the general quality of education prevailing at state-supported academic institutions in the Old Northwest is provided by an anecdote reported in the official history of the Ohio State University. In 1902, a graduate of OSU sought admission to the University Club in New York City, but was refused because the club did not recognize degrees conferred by OSU as a qualification for membership. Only after lengthy correspondence was recognition secured at the University Club for graduates of certain of OSU's colleges.[55]

Minnesota's collections were small, and the university's interest in the library, particularly absent-minded; it is a turn-of-the-century legend of the university that once a year President Northrop would stroll towards the desk of reading-room librarian Ina Firkins, and say,

> "Well, Miss Ina, I suppose you need some books." Miss Ina would admit that this was indeed so and the president would take from his pocket a little black notebook in which he jotted down such titles as suggested themselves to her. "And what will all that come to, Miss Ina?" the president would say. Apologetically Miss Firkins would answer that she was very much afraid it would come to such-and-such a figure. Northrop would then wander away, saying that he would see what he could do.[56]

The University of Minnesota did not get a proper library building until the mid-1920s, though by then the university had a book collection of some 300,000 volumes.

The University of Illinois maintained a middling position among midwestern universities by opening a new central library in 1897 with a capacity for 150,000 books, and it was planned that "certain rooms in the third story [of the new building], now used as offices of university administration, [could] at some future time, if needed, be used for the storage of books."[57] On this occasion, *Library Journal*'s reporter, U of I's librarian, Percy F. Bicknell, expressed himself as follows:

> That this new building may stand to its own and to neighboring universities in our still young and materialistic west as a promise and index of sound scholarship and high educational ideals, is the hope of all those who believe that a university or college should appeal to the world through its laboratories, its library, and the approved but unostentatious scholarship of its instructors, rather than through its ball-nine, its athletic field, or its boat-crew.[58]

At this time, the University of Illinois collection totaled about thirty thousand books.[59]

Michigan had the best state university library collections west of the Alleghenies.[60] By 1876 the University of Michigan was already the largest academic institution in the country, awarding 409 degrees, of which two were Ph.D.'s.[61] Students at the University of Wisconsin were also fairly fortunate in their library resources: the university library was small, with fewer than 9,000 volumes even if the student society libraries were counted in; but the Wisconsin State Historical Society had more than 33,000 volumes, and the State Law Library, also in Madison, had 25,000 more, for a combined resource in 1876 of more than 60,000 volumes (and, by the end of the century, over 200,000).

There were other signs of new library life in the academic Old Northwest. In 1898 Ohio Wesleyan opened a badly needed new library; the trustees of the university had decided that the college library "sustains much the same relation to the other college buildings that the brain sustains to the other members of the body." (Their anatomical analogy was a fresh one; by the 1890s university presidents and others had become rather overfond of referring to their libraries as the heart of their institutions.) The trustees were by now well aware of the impossibility of securing gifts either of books or of money for acquisitions so long as the physical plant remained inadequate. The donor of their new library, Charles Elihu Slocum, spoke at its opening exercises about the need for rational collection development, recommending gifts of money rather than of fixed collections of books with rigid housing requirements so that the library could be properly classified, and duplicates, eliminated.[62]

To be sure, even by 1900 the American educational apparatus was still very small by comparison with what it would become; less than 5 percent of the population attended college at all.[63] In 1900, a total of about 250 doctorates were awarded nationwide, including 43 from the University of Chicago (the only ones awarded in Illinois), 5 from Wisconsin, 4 from Michigan, 3 from Minnesota, and none from Indiana and Ohio, for an Old Northwest total of 55, or slightly less than a quarter of the national total. There were no Ph.D.'s at all awarded in Indiana or Ohio in 1900.[64] The dean of the graduate school at the University of Minnesota argued in 1912 that a library of 200,000 volumes was necessary to support a modest Ph.D. program; but by 1910, only Harvard, Yale, Berkeley, Chicago, Columbia, Cornell, Michigan, Penn, and Princeton had collections with that number of volumes.[65]

Certain kinds of research materials had not yet moved west; in 1912 it was reported that the largest collection of incunables in the United States, about 900 volumes, was at Harvard, followed by the Annmary Brown Memorial in Providence with 530, about 500 at the Free Library of Philadelphia, 430 in the Van Ess Collection at Union Theological Seminary, perhaps 400 at the Library of Congress, about 350 at New York Public Library, and smaller three-figure numbers at Cornell, Princeton, Yale, and the General Theological Seminary. No significant collections were reported west of Ithaca.[66]

By the end of the nineteenth century it was beginning to become commonplace that a first-rate research faculty could be recruited more easily if adequate library resources were provided on campus. As the young William Peterfield Trent wrote in 1890, "I would rather get a subordinate place in a large university with a *library* and the chance to make a scholar of myself than to be *full professor* at a very unfledged university."[67] The need for library resources was not only deep but also broad; Eliot of Harvard had long proclaimed the equality of all areas of scholarly endeavor, scientific and humanistic alike.

The University of Chicago shot into view like a comet in the 1890s. Starting from a miscellaneous collection of about forty thousand volumes, primarily the legacy of the old, defunct Chicago University, it purchased the so-called Berlin Collection, the enormous stock of the Berlin antiquarian bookselling firm of S. Calvary and Company, in 1891 and thereby was able to proclaim itself the second largest university library in the country.[68] The purchase of the collection was negotiated by the president of the university himself, William Rainey Harper, who knew that the transaction was one of the greatest book deals ever made, and one, moreover, which would produce a profound impression in the American literary and academic world. Indeed, the announcement of the purchase made the front page of the *New York Times,* and Harper wrote at the time that "the moral effect of the library is worth very much more than the cost of it." The collection was purchased on the understanding that it held about 400,000 items; the number of books delivered seems to have been slightly less than one-fourth that number, but it was a bargain even so. Harper was able to use his new library as a lure for faculty members, and the university at a stroke established itself as a major-league player among American institutions of higher learning.[69]

The position of the University of Chicago library was greatly strengthened by the presence of other nearby institutions. In 1876, William Frederick Poole, the new librarian of Chicago Public Library, had observed that "no one library, however large its resources, [could] meet the many sided wants of a metropolitan community with a population of half a million."[70] All at once there were three major new libraries in town: besides that of the University of Chicago, there were the Newberry and the John Crerar Libraries, with the Newberry specializing in history and the humanities, and the Crerar in the sciences. Both of these centrally located libraries were extremely well funded, and both set out at once to become reference libraries intended to encourage scholarly research. "With a purely reference library," Norman Williams, the Crerar's first president, explained, "fewer individuals would use it, but those who sought it, would find books which create a taste for substantial reading and accurate knowledge."[71] With an endowment of more than $2 million, the Crerar Library grew quickly: by the end of the century, it already had more than sixty thousand books.

Meanwhile, William Frederick Poole had left the Chicago Public Library to become the first librarian of the Newberry, where he set about his business in a grand style. In 1887, for example, he went to Boston to bid at the Charles H. Guild sale and bought three thousand of the five thousand lots offered; in seven years he bought more than 150,000 books.[72]

An agreement was almost immediately worked out among the central Chicago institutions to prevent unnecessary duplication on the model of a similar accord already reached by the larger Boston area libraries; adjustments as needed were amicably made in the agreement in the following years, and a pattern of coherent research library growth in Chicago was assured.

In the last quarter of the nineteenth century, then, we see several opposite forces in action in the libraries of the Old Northwest. The public library movement was a strong one in this part of the country, and large city collections grew rapidly. Holdings originally tended to contain a fair amount of what we would now call research materials, often inherited from predecessor libraries, and public library acquisitions staff in general attempted to purchase standard fare. But patrons underused such collections; they consistently preferred to use the public library for lighter material to read at home, rather than for scholarly or reference purposes. By the end of the century, the principle was well established in small public libraries and gaining force in large ones that books were for current use; reference collections were maintained, but large collections of scholarly materials tended not to accumulate; dead books were weeded out.

Opposite tendencies were at work in academic libraries. Consisting first of collections of older, frequently outmoded scholarly books (many of them of dubious immediate pedagogical value), academic libraries slowly moved toward the more comprehensive collecting of current research materials as they increasingly found themselves under reader pressure to provide precisely the sort of traditionally standard work that public library patrons tended to neglect. Their weeding patterns were conservative. After the end of the nineteenth century they never looked back. Growth became a cause for pride, and academic institutions began to celebrate their library's acquisition of their millionth volume, and their second millionth, and their third.

In 1913, Librarian of Congress Herbert Putnam could cheerfully say in a Charter Day address at the University of California at Berkeley,

> We can congratulate you heartily upon [your new library building] which recognizes its functions and provides for its present service. And when that building shall prove insufficient, as we trust it will, we are confident that you will provide ungrudgingly for an expansion of it. ... Nor need the considerations of space and expense be prohibitory; for a hundred million books could be housed, with full facilities of access, on an ordinary city square, and no present library has over a twenty-fifth of that number. Nor would the cost of housing them exceed the cost of two battleships.[73]

In the late twentieth century, all six of the libraries of the Old Northwest's state universities are among the twenty largest in the country, as is that of the University of Chicago. These libraries do very well against national standards: there are two top-twenty academic libraries in New England, four in the Middle Atlantic states, one in the South, one in the Southwest, four in the West, one in Canada—and seven in the Old Northwest.[74]

Raw numbers are of limited use in assessing the quality of a library; more than a century ago, the librarian of the Astor Library, Joseph Green Cogswell, was reported to have maintained that he would as soon say how many tons his library weighed as say how many books it contained.[75] Still, we all suspect that larger libraries are more likely to have what we want than smaller ones; the university and research libraries of the Old Northwest are, and seem likely to continue to be, among the greatest jewels in the American library crown.

Notes

1. United States Bureau of Education, *Public Libraries in the United States of America: Their History, Condition and Management* (Washington, D.C.: Government Printing Office, 1876). The "public libraries" in the report are those to which the public could gain relatively easy access and include circulating libraries, other social libraries, academic libraries, and other institutional libraries, as well as municipally supported public libraries. In this paper, unless otherwise noted, all 1876 library statistics (representing data gathered for the most part in 1875) are drawn from the alphabetical tables set forth in this report, and they will not be given separate notes. Population information is drawn from the ninth (1870) and twelfth (1900) census reports.

2. These figures are somewhat misleading, because of the habit of cities during this period of annexing their suburbs. Minneapolis, for instance, increased its geographical area (and thus its population) in 1872.

3. For library statistics for the year 1900 (i.e., 1899) given here and throughout this paper, see United States Bureau of Education, *Public, Society, and School Libraries in the United States* (Washington, D.C.: Government Printing Office, 1903).

4. Frank B. Woodford, *Parnassus on Main Street: A History of the Detroit Public Library* (Detroit: Wayne State University Press, 1965), 34–35.

5. Gwladys Spencer, *The Chicago Public Library: Origins and Backgrounds* (Chicago: University of Chicago Press, 1943), 21–33, 39–40. On the general question of literacy in the early Old Northwest, see R. Carlyle Buley, *The Old Northwest: Pioneer Period: 1815–1840*, 2 vols. (Bloomington: Indiana University Press, 1951), 2: 328.

6. Walter Muir Whitehill, *Independent Historical Societies* (Boston: Boston Athenaeum, distributed by Harvard University Press, 1962), 243.

7. Spencer, *Chicago Public Library*, 95–96.

8. There were many larger libraries freely open to the public, for example the Astor Library in New York, but they were not municipally supported and thus not truly "free."

9. Ohio's percentage of books held dropped from 34 percent to 24, in contrast to a population drop from 28 percent to 23. I have no easy explanation for the disparity, though it is perhaps significant that Ohio State University in 1900 had the smallest flagship state university collection in the region, with about 35,000 books, or only 9 percent of the region's state university total.

10. Cincinnati Public Library, *1867 Annual Report*, 20–21; *1873* [Sixth] *Annual Report*, 14; see also the *1869–70 Annual Report*, which contains (42–43) a section entitled "Basis Offered By the Board of Managers for the Consolidation of Libraries with the Public Library."

11. Cincinnati Public Library, *1869 Annual Report*, 15. Admittedly, the difference between first and all others was substantial: the Boston Public Library had some 145,000 books at this time, and Cincinnati fewer than 22,000.

12. Cincinnati Public Library, *1871* [Fourth] *Annual Report*, 6.

13. Ibid.

14. Cincinnati Public Library, *1872* [Fifth] *Annual Report,* 14.

15. Ibid., 26–27; *1873* [Sixth] *Annual Report,* 24.

16. Cincinnati Public Library, *1873* [Sixth] *Annual Report,* 29.

17. Ibid., 33.

18. Ibid., 32.

19. Woodford, *Parnassus on Main Street,* 78.

20. Ibid., 154.

21. Ibid., 140–41.

22. Ibid., 141–42.

23. C. H. Cramer, *Open Shelves and Open Minds: A History of the Cleveland Public Library* (Cleveland: The Press of Case Western Reserve University, 1972), 105–37.

24. Bruce Weir Benidt, *The Library Book: Centennial History of the Minneapolis Public Library* (Minneapolis: Minneapolis Public Library and Information Center, 1984), 25.

25. Minneapolis Public Library, *1899 Annual Report,* 26.

26. Minneapolis Public Library, *1890 Annual Report,* 6.

27. Minneapolis Public Library, *1894 Annual Report,* 8.

28. Minneapolis Public Library, *1896 Annual Report,* 9.

29. Walter Muir Whitehill, *Boston Public Library: A Centennial History* (Cambridge: Harvard University Press, 1956), 34–35.

30. Ibid., 70, quoting the Boston Public Library's 1867 *Annual Report,* 35.

31. Minneapolis Public Library, *1899 Annual Report,* 26–27.

32. Ibid., 13, 15, 27.

33. Cincinnati Public Library, *1873* [Sixth] *Annual Report,* 20.

34. Cramer, *Open Shelves and Open Minds,* 37–38.

35. Dayton (Ohio) Public Library, *1894–95 Annual Report,* 25.

36. Detroit Public Library, *39th Annual Report,* 1903, 23.

37. Thomas Crane Public Library, Quincy, Massachusetts, *1893 Annual Report,* 6.

38. Charles Francis Adams, in *Library Journal* 18 (1893): 118.

39. Ibid., 107.

40. *Library Journal* 27 (1902): 258.

41. Woodford, *Parnassus on Main Street,* 181–83, 296.

42. *Library Journal* 27 (1902): 56.

43. Ibid., 261

44. Quoted by Lodilla Ambrose in "A Study of College Libraries," *Library Journal* 18 (1893): 114.

45. E. Thomson, *Letters from Europe* (Cincinnati: Hitchcock & Walden, 1856), 12–13; quoted by Orvin Lee Shiflett, *Origins of American Academic Librarianship* (Norwood, N.J.: Ablex Publishing, 1981), 29.

46. For a discussion of this point, see Hendrik Edelman and G. Marvin Tatum, Jr., "The Development of Collections in American University Libraries," *College & Research Libraries* 37 (1976): 222 with notes.

47. Arthur T. Hamlin, *The University Library in the United States: Its Origins and Development* (Philadelphia: University of Pennsylvania Press, 1981), 50, 22.

48. Ibid., 48.

49. William I. Fletcher, *Public Libraries in America* (Boston: Roberts Brothers, 1894), 267.

50. William Warner Bishop, "The University Library to 1941," in *The University of Michigan: An Encyclopedic Survey,* ed. Walter A. Donnelly, Part 8, *The Libraries* ... (Ann Arbor: University of Michigan Press, 1956), 1373.

51. For a list of European scholars' libraries acquired by American academic institutions, see W. Dawson Johnston and Isadore G. Mudge, *Special Collections in Libraries in the United States,* U.S. Bureau of Education Bulletin no. 23 (whole no. 495; Washington, D.C.: the Bureau, 1912), 124–25.

52. Kenneth J. Brough, *Scholar's Workshop: Evolving Conceptions of Library Service* (Urbana: University of Illinois Press, 1953), chap. 3, 37–77.

53. Ambrose, "Study of College Libraries," 113, 115.

54. William A. Kinnison, *Building Sullivant's Pyramid: An Administrative History of the Ohio State University, 1870–1907* (Columbus: Ohio State University Press, 1970), 190–91; 194.

55. Alexis Cope, in *History of The Ohio State University,* ed. Thomas C. Mendenhall, vol. 1, *1870–1910* (Columbus: Ohio State University Press, 1920), 342.

56. James Gray, *The University of Minnesota, 1851–1951* (Minneapolis: University of Minnesota Press, 1951), 529–30.

57. Percy F. Bicknell, "The New Library Building of the University of Illinois," *Library Journal* 22 (1897): 304.

58. Ibid.

59. Winton U. Solberg, *The University of Illinois, 1867–1894: An Intellectual and Cultural History* (Urbana: University of Illinois Press, 1968), 372–73.

60. Bishop, "The University Library to 1941," 1372.

61. Edward G. Holley, "Academic Libraries in 1876," *College & Research Libraries* 37 (1976): 19.

62. Ohio Wesleyan University, *Inception, Dedication, Addresses, and Description, of the Charles Elihu Slocum Library for The Ohio Wesleyan University* ... *June 20, 1898,* 5–6, 10–11.

63. Hamlin, *University Library in the United States,* 102.

64. Edelman and Tatum, "Development of Collections," 238–43.

65. Ibid., 222.

66. Johnston and Mudge, *Special Collections,* 10.

67. Shiflett, *Origins of American Academic Librarianship,* 97.

68. Robert Rosenthal, "The Berlin Collection: A History," in *The Berlin Collection: Being a History and Exhibition of the Books and Manuscripts Purchased in Berlin in 1891 for the University of Chicago* (Chicago: Joseph Regenstein Library, 1979), 4, 21. See also Brough, *Scholar's Workshop,* 88.

69. Ibid., 13–20.

70. U.S. Bureau of Education, *Public Libraries in the United States* (1876), 2: 897.

71. J. Christian Bay, ed., *The John Crerar Library, 1895–1944: An Historical Report* (Chicago: the John Crerar Library, 1945), 52.

72. William Landram Williamson, *William Frederick Poole and the Modern Library Movement* (New York: Columbia University Press, 1963), 141, 150.

73. Herbert Putnam, "The Quick in the 'Dead,' " *Bulletin of the New Hampshire Public Libraries,* n.s. 9 (1913): 195.

74. Association of Research Libraries, *1983–84 Statistics,* compiled by Nicola Duval and Alexander Lichtenstein (Washington, D.C.: Association of Research Libraries, 1985).

75. U.S. Bureau of Education, *Public Libraries in the United States* (1876), 1: 60.

☆ GPO : 1987 O – 187-355 : QL 3